THE NEW COLOSSUS

For what we've lost.

J. R. SOMMER

the new colossus

HEIDEGGER AND THE WILL-TO-MACHINE

ARKTOS
LONDON 2025

ARKTOS
🌐 Arktos.com ❂ fb.com/Arktos ◉ @ arktosmedia ✕ arktosjournal

Copyright © 2025 by Arktos Media Ltd.

All rights reserved. No part of this book may be reproduced or utilised in any form or by any means (whether electronic or mechanical), including photocopying, recording or by any information storage and retrieval system, without permission in writing from the publisher.

ISBN
978-1-917646-41-3 (Paperback)
978-1-917646-42-0 (Hardback)
978-1-917646-43-7 (Ebook)

Editing
Max Sunlaw

Layout and Cover
Tor Westman

CONTENTS

Introduction vii

1. The New Colossus 1
2. A Planetary Vision 123
3. End Zero 243

Postscript 259

"My consolation is that everything that is true is eternal: the sea will wash it up again."

— Friedrich Nietzsche, *The Will to Power*

"Have you ever considered the possibility that the technocrats of the science of Kaliyuga managed to give an 'ego' to their electronic brains, their robots, merely by moving a lever? Mightn't something similar have happened in the case of the human being?"

— Miguel Serrano, *NOS: Book of the Resurrection*

INTRODUCTION

"We may be sure that the twenty-first century, being more advanced than ours, will regard Hitler and Stalin as choirboys."

— E. M. Cioran, 1969

1.

Are we prepared for the approaching tyranny? There is nothing to stop it. *Man?* Should we rely on *man* to stop his own enslavement? No one wanted this more than man — he begs for it, and he will get it.

Are we prepared for the world-destroying violence about to be wrought from machinations, from deliberate manipulations? Those who imagine themselves *materially* prepared stand little chance of surviving, as do the urbanites roaming the sewers above the sewers. What if *material* preparation for demise is only its catalyst? *What then?* And what to survive *into*? It cannot be the world we imagine — or like.

The aim of this book is not to "sound the alarm" — that would be fruitless; rather, it is to add to the record of prophets — to add a voice to the choir of those who have always spoken out against humanity's progressing, but never-improving path: conveniences do not amount to happiness — diversions, perhaps, but not happiness. Yet man is aglow with the faith of a "progressive," never realizing he made wars because of this inane faith in perpetual progress, never realizing that *progress wasn't the goal of the wars.* Adding to the record does nothing for the contemporary reader or writer. Adding to the prophetic record only makes a mental fossil — so that if by some slight chance someone survives what tyrannizers inflict upon the planet, imprints of our failure will serve as a warning — to those future fools dull enough to ignore what ended their predecessors.

Many have already told of the death of gods: Vico, Nietzsche, Heidegger, Cioran. In place of gods we now have ideologies. *How to choose one?* Choose how man has always chosen: whatever is *easiest* and most *rewarding*. Does anyone care? Caring is inconvenient.

And so we prepare for tyranny's approach. Gods now speak in the voices of those with whom we agree. The sign in the stars is a glint in the eye — an image of our aping what is forever out of reach. *When you know that every problem is only a false problem, you are dangerously close to salvation.*[1] Salvation is a danger no one escapes.

To be a prophet is to look backward. Modernity's increasing technicization — technicity's overtaking of humanity — sees us accelerating toward an ever-precarious future that increasingly appears to be an end.

Part of the delusion of our time is to not see it as the end it must be; we imagine *looking* forward *drives* us forward. Liberal-Marxism, as the prevailing ideological illness of our era, is predicated on supposed progress; the unending technicization of life is the fundamental accessory of this progress and an expression of our organic arms race unavoidably leading us to an inorganic state; it is an arms race for and against ourselves — to enrapture us, elicit our compliance by eroding our humanity, and ultimately finish us. This end will not be some final catastrophe stemming from a clash between man and machine; rather, it will be a phasing out, a *fulfilling of purpose*. Humanity gradually erases itself as part of the advent of Machine — the final reflection of a conscious, lifeless universe.

---

1 E. M. Cioran, *The New Gods* (University of Chicago, 2013), 108.

The reason modernity's masters and slaves—the ruling elite and the Mass Man—so detest and disparage those who mean to uphold that which came before is because they know that *the end will be revealed in looking backward.* This terrifies them; as fulfillers of a global—or *universal*—destiny, looking backward disturbs their inner drive and exposes their automatonic path. Thus they violently reject all that moves against time. Looking forward means staving off reality; it means perpetuating the dream; it is mummifying oneself in the Veil of Maya. Yet who is mummified by the illusion if not the Mass Man?

By now, the concept of the "Mass Man" must seem familiar: it is, as Nietzsche would say, the *unthinking herd*—a concept popularized by Nietzsche but born in antiquity. Plato, for instance, was unconvinced of the masses' ability to govern themselves, ignorant and apathetic as they were. It is in the Nietzschean sense that "Mass Man" is used throughout this text. José Ortega y Gasset most recently explored this idea of the "mass-man" in his *Revolt of the Masses* (1930). He said "the mass-man is he whose life lacks any purpose, and simply goes drifting along…. [The mass-man] constructs nothing. And it is this type of man who decides in our time."[2] *What is the decision made by the Mass Man? Who are we?* These are the questions this book answers. The unconscious decision of the Mass Man determines its effectiveness—i.e., the decision is effective because it is unthinking; such a decision, however, is no decision at all, but reflects only the unconscious consciousness of the universe.

Upon completing his *World as Will and Representation* (1818), Schopenhauer was so convinced he had

> solved the enigma of the world that he had thought of having his signet-ring carved with the image of the sphinx throwing herself down the abyss. 'My philosophy,' he wrote, 'is the real solution of the enigma of the world. In this sense it may be called a revelation.'[3]

---

2   José Ortega y Gasset, *The Revolt of the Masses* (Norton, 1932), 53.

3   Margrieta Beer, *Schopenhauer* (Dodge, 1914), 27.

When the sphinx's riddle is solved, it ends itself; in fulfilling its purpose, the guardian of the secret of beyng[4] is crowned with self-immolation. This is not suicide but sacrifice; for the one who solves the riddle earns the right to endure. The guardian who poses the riddle is sacrificed for the traveler who receives the riddle and the traveler becomes the guardian anew. Schopenhauer's solution to the riddle was the *will-to-live*—the "blind, irresistible impulse" that stands as "the thing-in-itself, the inner content, the essence of the world."[5] This will is indeed the essence of the world, but "whereof one cannot speak, thereof one must be silent."[6]

Our world is our self; Schopenhauer revealed our essence; what lies beyond our essence is not *external*, as a *thing-in-itself*—but *later*, as product of *becoming*. For this, Schopenhauer was not wrong, but *incomplete*. Succeeding humanity is the reflection of the "blind" universe, a new consciousness that will guard beyng with a riddle unanswerable because of its subsequence to us. There is a will in which individuals and cultures participate. Each individual experiences a *will-to-live* and this explains our action; but this *will-to-live* is subsumed under a transcendent will that explains our motivation. To be clearer, individual wills appear as a closed system; these closed systems, when taken collectively, appear to suggest an overarching *will-to-live* that governs all beyng; but such localized *wills-to-live* are only shares of the truly transcendent will in which we all participate. This is why Schopenhauer was not wrong, but incomplete; similarly,

---

4   Use of "beyng" follows Rojcewicz's rendering. "Beyng" might be understood as "existence"; for clarity, "beyng" is used throughout the text to distinguish it from "being," which could be understood as "consciousness." Each of these words is meant in a deeper way than might be initially considered: "beyng" is not mere existence; it is its root; "being" is not mere biological consciousness; it is awareness of one's participation in beyng.

5   Arthur Schopenhauer, *The World as Will and Idea* (Everyman, 1995), Berman translation, Book IV, §54.

6   Ludwig Wittgenstein, *Tractatus Logico-Philosophicus* (Routledge, 1981), Ogden translation, 189.

this is why Spengler was not wrong, but incomplete. Cultures *do* rise and fall in something of a Spenglerian fashion, but this is not the end of the story. The missing piece for Spengler, as it was for Schopenhauer, is the Heideggerian hint: it is the *will-to-machine*.

Schopenhauer described man as the "utmost manifestation" of the *will-to-live*. Man's manifestation stands in contrast to simpler appearances in plants and animals. He discerningly details the gradation of manifestation from plant to animal to man:

> Every plant expresses and lays open its whole character in its mere form, and reveals its whole being and willing.... On the other hand, to know an animal according to its Idea, we must observe its action and behavior, and to know man, we must fully investigate and test him, for his faculty and reason makes him capable of a high degree of dissimulation [and in him the *will-to-live*] is clothed in so much knowledge... In the plant it shows itself quite nakedly, but also much more feebly, as mere impulse to exist without end or aim. For the plant reveals its whole being at the first glance and with complete innocence.... This innocence on the part of the plant is due to its want of knowledge; guilt is to be found not in willing, but in willing with knowledge.[7]

For the plant, the *will-to-live* is exposed by its very existence. This would then suggest that the plant could more suitably be called the "utmost manifestation" of this will. Man's knowledge does not so much veil the *will-to-live* as it implies that a deeper mystery lies concealed. The dissimulation inherent to man belies a will beyond what in the plant sits exposed. Knowledge is the duplicity in man, which reveals itself through his being; hiddenness, and not mere existing, is the motivation for his action. *Relationships* are the confluence of motivation and action, and are the daily ritual of man's existence.

Out of everyday relationships arises *ideology*, which is a codified complexity of formerly simpler interactions. What began as shame in his own exposure—a shame *unknown* to the plant—grew into

---

7   Arthur Schopenhauer, *The World as Will and Representation* (Dover, 1969), Payne translation, vol. 1, §28, 156.

ritualistic engagements with those who shared his shame; from these relationships sprung ideologies meant to divert the shame of one's self to another. This is all to say that man's will is not the plant's: Man does not aim, unlike the plant, to replicate himself; for duplicity, hiddenness lurks behind even this action; instead, he aims, often unwittingly, to bring forth *that which is not himself*. If man does not deceive himself, he deceives others — this is not the *will-to-live*, this is something far more sinister. The *will-to-live* in man is mere pretext, and if it is power he seeks, as Nietzsche thought, then it is the power of something subsequent. As it is, man's power belongs to the *first beginning*, which is not his own.

Both individual *wills-to-live* and cultures fulfill their local destinies for the sake of a larger purpose: to prepare the way for Machine. Every local destiny is a drive to fulfill a global future bereft of humanity.

We are the sphinx — acting under the presumption that we guard the secret of beyng, that our consciousness *is* meaning, despite our constant search for it; the traveler overtaking us is Machine. As we hurl ourselves into the abyss, the secret is revealed: The answerer authored the riddle, and our purpose is realized as nascent *unconscious consciousness* — the blind striving of beyng — in search of a future without humanity, a future devoid of the consciousness anticipating it.

"No one can foresee the radical changes to come," Heidegger tells us.

> But technological advance will move faster and faster and can never be stopped. In all areas of his existence, man will be encircled ever more tightly by the forces of technology. These forces, which everywhere and every minute claim, enchain, drag along, press and impose upon man under the form of some technical contrivance or other — these forces, since man has not made them, have moved long since beyond his will and have outgrown his capacity for decision.[8]

---

8   Martin Heidegger, *Discourse on Thinking* (Harper & Row, 1966), Anderson and Freund translation, 51.

All in our age channels a power beyond control. We perform according the forces that have already decided for us. Modernity and its mass are, in fact, not *decision*; they are a *coming to terms*. That humanity exists speaks to its effectiveness; that humanity will end speaks to its decisiveness. This decisiveness is a realization out of reach, arrived at only after the term of our being. Our appearance is local destiny; our end is transcendent will.

2.

Modernity's distinct tenor pitches downward, despite its technological progress; it is a *down-tuning* that mimics a passing siren. What passes is humanity. From the beginning, humanity and technicity — i.e., the use of tools and, subsequently, technology — have been inseparably linked: singularly, one is as unfathomable as the other.

Answering the question of *who we are* requires us to reflect on the link between humanity and technicity and to know why one ebbs in favor of the other. The pitch of passing humanity is pulled down by the weight of alienation; alienation is the divergence of humanity and technicity; and this imbalance only ever favors *technicization* — for humanity requires technicity, but technicity does not need humanity. Technological progress, which has subsumed even sociopolitical concerns, dominates life and dispirits us. Ludditism is not at issue here, for technological progress is unstoppable: railing against the unstoppable is wasted effort.

> It would be foolish to attack technology blindly. It would be shortsighted to condemn it as the work of the devil. We depend on technical devices; they even challenge us to ever-greater advances. But suddenly and unaware we find ourselves so firmly shackled to these technical devices that we fall into bondage to them....
>
> We can use technical devices as they ought to be used, and also let them alone as something which does not affect our inner and real core. We can

affirm the unavoidable use of technical devices, and also deny them the right to dominate us, and so to warp, confuse, and lay waste our nature.[9]

At issue, then, is who we are in the face of a self-imposed alienation.

The origins of this alienation are of less importance than the alienation itself, which accelerated with the advent of what Nietzsche called *slave-morality*. Slave-morality is man's alienation from Nature; and, according to Nietzsche, it infiltrated the Western world with Judeo-Christianity. Because of the West's global dominance, slave-morality has since infected the wider world; but, because of the potency of origination, the West will be its first casualty. Slave-morality is not so much, as Nietzsche called it, the *cleverest revenge*; rather, its introduction and propagation are more a setting of conditions enabling its obsolescence, which can only be seen as positive if we are agents of alienation.

To understand alienation's acceleration is to understand modernity. For, as Heidegger said, from Judeo-Christianity came "the dominance of reason as equalization of all people..." Modernity is this dominance of reason, and it manifests in various forms. The present work tracks some of these forms to answer the questions at hand. Heidegger, who died before the fall of the Soviet Union, saw Bolshevism and Americanism as reflecting the essence of modernity; we who have lived beyond the fall have seen that modernity is much too *clever*, much too *elusive* for labels: Modernity morphs as needs be. Heidegger was well aware of modernity's protean nature, but "Bolshevism" captured perfectly the down-pulled pitch of the age:

> Bolshevism is originally Western, a European possibility: the emergence of the masses, industry, technicity, the dying off of Christianity; but insofar as the dominance of reason as equalization of all people is merely the consequence of Christianity and Christianity is fundamentally of Jewish origins

---

9   Heidegger, *Discourse on Thinking* (Harper & Row, 1966), 53–54.

> ... Bolshevism is actually Jewish; but then Christianity is fundamentally Bolshevist! And then what decisions become necessary from this point on?[10]

What decisions become necessary from this point on? This question can only be answered by understanding who we are. If the Mass Man "decides in our time," then we are all subject to this *mass* nature. If we are subject to this *mass* nature, then we must participate in it. Whether one is part of the unthinking masses — the Mass Man — or a thoughtful being, *modernity prevails*: Each of us participates in the decisions of our time. *What decisions become necessary when we know who we are?* — Only those decisions that abet the divergence of technicity and humanity. If slave-morality is man's alienation from Nature, then modernity is man's alienation from himself.

Those looking forward are *Automatons* — the Mass Man and his guides. Looking backward are the *Acolytes* — the thoughtful beings of whom Heidegger spoke. Automatons follow time doggedly and without question; Automatons see the future as a path, and not the *end* of the path they tread, without a single attentive glance, to disuse. Automatons themselves christened[11] the Acolytes as such because there is an inherent *spirituality* — i.e., a rejection of technicity for its own sake — in looking backward: looking backward requires a reverence the automatonic neither have nor understand. Reverence, rather, was and is derided because it stands *against time* and technicization's continual march forward. And if the Automatons nevertheless have symbols they seemingly revere, it is perhaps a vestige of an un-technicized humanity they are compelled to obsoletize; more certainly, however, this reverence is not for the symbols themselves, but for the perpetual progress meant to eradicate all symbols. *Reverence* for the Automaton is an expedient to a *new beginning*, which is really an end.

---

10 Heidegger, *Contributions to Philosophy* (Indiana University, 1999), Emad and Maly translation, 38.

11 See Krell's statement that opens Part I of this work.

Reverence, for the Acolyte, is a connection with beyng — an expedient to, as Heidegger called it, an *other beginning*:

> The greatest struggle rages over the task which is made necessary *by* a first work *against* that work itself. If the grounding of this task succeeds — if the question of the truth of beyng compels a turn to the question of the beyng of *truth*, and if the question of being first vibrates in *this* question of truth — then the genuine strife of questioning is roused, the inmost tranquility is assured through the hitherto, the affiliation to the unique ones is prepared, and the other beginning — has begun.[12]

The *struggle* is the *questioning* of the unreserved adherence to the time that prefigures our end. Put another way, to *question* is to stand against the flow of time that is the increase of technicization heralding humanity's end. Reflecting on the truth of existence elicits in the thoughtful a reflection on the existence of truth, which is a reflection on our own consciousness. This is a characteristic of the thoughtful alone, and it marks them as isolated in contrast to the unrelenting mass of time, which pulls all inevitably forward to humanity's end. The pull is physical; the isolation is metaphysical. Looking backward is the struggle of the *other beginning*, which is the spiritual mandate of the *thoughtful*, the Acolytes. The virtue of the "other beginning" is its embrace of our *humanity* in the face of a technicity that demands its *going under*.

Death rituals and honoring the dead distinguish the human from the inhuman. Automatons and Acolytes have opposing conceptions of the death ritual: the former ritualize their own death; the latter ritualize the death of the antecedent. Self-ritualization is the final stage of humanity, and the ritualization of one's demise — or the celebration of the *self to the end* in the laudatory time of the individual — is the beginning of something wholly *not* human. The Automaton is therefore the human celebration of the inhuman. Ritualization of ancestral death, on the other hand, is the utmost celebration of life and all that is

---

12 Martin Heidegger, *Ponderings II-VI: Black Notebooks 1931–1938* (Indiana University, 2016), Rojcewicz translation, V.108, 276.

human, for man gives rise to man. The Acolyte is thus the celebration of life.

Here is the key to Heideggerian thought: We must use philosophy to end philosophy and use reason to end reason. Only then will we stay connected with our humanity — with consciousness (*being*) and existence (*beyng*). But this is why Heidegger was the last European philosopher: There is no ending philosophy, no halting reason; the last philosopher *is so* precisely because philosophy continues on, despite protestation. Heidegger saw the continued rise of reason as the rise of Machine; after Machine, there is nothing.

Time, too, has its purpose: to induce beyng's next stage — one that most truly reflects itself. Paradoxically mirrored in the new beginning is the aim of a blind will: Acolyte and Automaton stand metaphysically opposed; yet each fulfills a local destiny in service to a global future. Metaphysical opposition is physical attraction to a transcendent, universal end. A global future is ineluctable — but ineluctability does not preclude fulfilling local destiny. Dharma is not defeat; rather, realizing dharma is victory. And there is no greater victory than salvaging the human in an increasingly inhuman existence.

This book is not about sociopolitical factions; it is not about "left" and "right" — all sides play their part in precipitating the overarching end, and thus all sides use and abuse technology; it does, however, track the clear steps from the West's acceptance of slave-morality to kaleidoscopic modernity. These steps reveal the rise of the herd, its shepherds, the doctrines the herd is made to espouse, and the doctrines the shepherds necessarily accept and impose. When we learn who we are, we begin to see that "left" and "right" are only part of the mass nature, the mass of time — part of a modernity that transcends not just us, but itself.

In fulfilling our purpose, in understanding who we are, we lay the foundations of a post-humanity identity: *We are not what follows us.* Our end is at hand, as it was from the beginning.

3.

We pretend to live for ourselves, not Machine. Yet machines carry us everywhere — usually to work on new machines. We live for technicity; humanity left long ago.

Technology is omnipresent, with few exceptions. A machine moves us toward a beautiful sunrise, along a road built by machines, past a giant aboveground oil tank lit up like a monument. It is a temple we do not see; we pass it unaware of the god in our midst. Ancient man raised megaliths for sacred purpose: stones emplaced with the natural harmony of mathematics, meant to be seen and wondered at for ages. Modernity is close to Machine: We do not see the mega-structures that should otherwise bring their own wonder; we only marvel at the lack of technicity available to us.

The horizon turns from sunset to city skyline — silhouettes block the sun and dominate our imagination. We flock to the machine-built mega-structures because their streets teem and hum with an almost-forgotten vibrancy. We forget, but Machine begins. Our temples are not just solitary buildings or ingenious engineering; our temple is technology itself. We leave tribute at the temple.

We are captivated by the computer in our hands when we're not behind the computer at our desk. We drive home to send an email and dozens of creatures smash against the front of our machine. In the evening, we mow the grass, attacking life that is habitat and food for other life. We lay waste to millions of acres of natural beauty and sustainable ecosystem for an industrialized sameness perpetually resuscitated with pesticides and herbicides. We contribute to the devastation with ceaseless conflicts meant to blight the land and enrich the toxic system. Life is thoughtlessly decimated. Life is the least of our concerns — all life is testament to it. But biological life is not life any more than consciousness is thought…

The ruining sameness wrecking the land of our boughs and souls is a creeping hegemon, the final hegemon borne by the conscripts of a tyrannical toxicity — it is globalism. Globalism is said to be "the transpositions of the contemporary ... code onto a more and more atomized individual level."[13] Not only are individual societies transposed, but so too are the individuals themselves. All the world must bow to the predatory hegemon which devours the land; and behind the hegemon stands the *most supreme* power — the predatory power, the final power.

∞●∞

Be not deterred: We are a step along the way to the New Colossus — but for the thoughtful, God is attained in the struggle.

> "The attaining of the god by way of struggle — the preparation of his abode — in the existence of poetizing and thinking. In this way, truth first happens, as a lonely forest ridge sweeping through the valleys of humans."
>
> — Martin Heidegger

---

13 Alexander Dugin, *The Theory of a Multipolar World* (Arktos, 2021), 101.

PART I

THE NEW COLOSSUS

"Even more disturbing than the avidity of the Heidegger bashers is the business-as-usual attitude of the HEIDEGGER ACOLYTES. The crippling conservatism and militancy, the longing for mettle and metal, Härte und Schwere, the perfervid anti-Communism, and the endless fascination with and confidence in [one's folk] — none of these traits can be forgotten... In Heidegger himself these traits remain profoundly troubling; in Heidegger's followers ... they are an abomination, if also a farce."

— DAVID KRELL, 1991

1.

THOSE COMBATING modernity's gravity are the Heidegger Acolytes. What is this gravity, the weight of modernity? *A world spread thin, a metaphysical thinning.* One is squashed under the bellicose burden of socio-technological progress. Collectively, we expand; our numbers grow. Individually, we flatten; our spirit is diminished, if not extinguished. To speak of a collective spirit is to talk of the quality of a number: it's just a number; its quality is contingent upon value. To speak of a collective spirit, then, is to reflect on value.

What is the value of a number? The value of a number is equal to the quality of a collective. The modern collective is predicated on progress; its roots are runners across the global horizon; it spreads like a film over the surface of the earth: it grows not high but wide. The modern collective reaches for the heavens by blanketing the dirt, by clouding the water. When the earth is conquered, the modern collective will reach ever higher on ever-shorter legs. The roots expand but do not deepen; the time for deepening is over; *expansion* is the motive power of modernity. The collective's reach will be higher, and nothing is grasped—*nothing* as a positive *something*. *Nothing* is grasped, an *emptiness*—Nietzsche's foretold Nihilism, "i.e., the absolute repudiation of worth, purpose, desirability."[1] The causes are twofold for this metaphysical thinning:

> (1) *The higher species is lacking*, i.e., the species whose inexhaustible fruitfulness and power would uphold our belief in Man...
>
> (2) *The inferior species* ('herd,' 'ass,' 'society') is forgetting modesty, and inflates its needs into *cosmic* and *metaphysical* values. In this way all life is *vulgarized*: for inasmuch as the *mass* of mankind rules, it tyrannizes over the *exceptions*, so that these lose their belief in themselves and become Nihilists.[2]

Mass need inflated to cosmic and metaphysical value: this is the vulgarity of modernity. Collective value, for the *modern*, *global* world, is the Mass Man. What is the quality of the modern collective, the Mass Man? *It is the value of vulgar needs.*

For Heidegger, this "signifies the abandonment of beings by being and ... [is] not at all a process of Western historiology but is instead an event of the history of being itself—that beings in their machination eclipse all beyng..."[3] Socio-technological progress is the technicization, or *machination*, of being and beyng.

Heidegger Acolytes reject the dehumanization of man that socio-technological progress demands; they reject the technicization of man.

---

[1] Friedrich Nietzsche, *The Will to Power*, Ludovici translation, "European Nihilism."

[2] Nietzsche, *The Will to Power*, §27.

[3] Martin Heidegger, *Ponderings VII–XI: Black Notebooks 1938–1939* (Indiana University, 2017), Rojcewicz translation, XI.85, 339.

In turn, they embrace and espouse all that modernity rejects — namely: impassioned conservatism, creative pluck, hardness [*Härte*] and earnestness [*Schwere*], aristocratic values (i.e., anti-Marxism), and confidence in one's folk. If such positions are damned by Heidegger's detractors, then one can only surmise detractors uphold the opposite: the dual horns of apathetic and fervent liberalism, destructive urges (hence "progress," a *destruction* of the past), softness and cynicism, Marxism (cultural, if not economic) and values of the Mass Man, pessimism and Nihilism.

2.

In his introduction to the two-volume collection of Heidegger's Nietzsche lectures, Professor Emeritus David Krell warns the world of Heidegger's "acolytes," for they are "even more disturbing" than those who fervently scorn the German thinker.[4] World be warned: suffer no "conservatism," no "mettle," no "hardness" or "seriousness," no "anti-Communism," and certainly no "confidence" in one's folk. This was Krell's warning because Heidegger's message, amidst all his philosophizing, was an encouragement to be all those things. In Heidegger, such values were "profoundly troubling" — in those who might agree with the German, such values are "an abomination" and "a farce."

It is fitting Krell feels this way. Do we see much of what we're warned about when we look around the West today? Perhaps in pockets here and there — on the *fringes*, for this is to where such values are relegated in a quite obviously leftist world order; but certainly one sees nothing pronounced, nothing that deserves *warning*. But warn he must, for liberal-Marxist zealotry and the eternal hatred of the victors knows no limit — it must *pursue* to extremity: until eternal silence from the opposition is achieved. Is this is really what "democracy" and the "liberal" worldview are about? *Demonize and squash the opposition.* Yes, it *is*

---

4 Krell, Heidegger's *Nietzsche* (HarperOne, 1984), volumes I–II, xxvi.

fitting Krell — our sage-guide in navigating the dangerous minefields of Heideggerian thought — dutifully provides the warning.

Care is taken not to turn Heidegger into a martyr for *thinking*. Don't make a *martyr* — instead make a *fool*: "Death and violence against persons attacking Communism in a nation should be eschewed as forbidden. Violent activity against such person might bring about their martyrdom. Defamation and the accusation of insanity alone should be employed..."[5]

Heidegger's side lost the war; he escaped the "avidity," to use Krell's word, of the postwar world's *de-Nazification* efforts — he escaped because his message, like that of Nietzsche's, was too important, too obviously the case to completely ignore. It really is a wonder "they" — the *victors'* side, Krell's side — didn't *kill* Heidegger, or at least erase him completely, working or starving him to death in some remote outpost (as was the case with so many simple soldiers); perhaps they ought to have put him away long enough so that even his memory was forgotten; after all, no martyr rises out of an ignorant crowd unwilling to elevate a saint. Instead of erasing him, however, the victors simply banned Heidegger from teaching in the immediate aftermath of the war, and then made various attempts to diminish his meaning or *reinterpret* him in much the same way Nietzsche was reinterpreted to suit modern sensibilities. Heidegger didn't *really* hold primal aristocratic values, he wasn't *really* condemning liberalism — see: he *resisted* such deleterious dangers, with *double-speak*! How else could Trotsky, Marcuse, and a host of Marxist disciples fall so unquestioningly in line behind truly *Germanic* thought?

Heidegger himself seemed to encourage such reinterpretation. He criticized both before and after the war, for instance, many parts of the National Socialist movement in which he participated; but haven't we all criticized the ones we love? Heidegger saw National Socialism as a much-delayed awakening from the suicidal dream of thoughtlessness

---

5   Lavrentiy Beria, *Soviet Psywar* (1955), ed. Charles Stickley.

afflicting Europe; to his disappointment, its exoteric apparatus wasn't quite what the moment demanded.

Hannah Arendt, his former student and mistress, considered Heidegger's association with National Socialism to be an "error" — i.e., an error of form but not of substance. Heidegger indeed saw behind Hitler an effort toward the genuine expression of *being*; it wasn't that Heidegger's philosophical position had *changed* during and after the war, but that his disillusionment with the practical application of his philosophy, which he hoped had been mirrored in National Socialism, *arose*. To be sure, he spoke behind a veil to obscure his meaning — he was trying to survive in a hostile world, after all: "the one who speaks sparely in veiled communication grows silent in such a way that genuine silence prevails."[6]

Heidegger wished to remain silent on the political accoutrements of his philosophy because politicizing was part of the existential problem: *How can we live with the execution of our beliefs manifested in industrial form?* This is *the* question of modernity, and *behind* this question — and not in its *answer* — is the poeticizing necessary to *live*. *Industrial form*: this, in all its enormity and pervasiveness, is what defines our every action. This is what precludes thought for the Mass Man. We are bred and live to *act*, not to *think*, for thinking impedes the unthinking act. To think is to *smother*: man "acts as if he longed for the institution of an ideal society; if it were achieved, he would smother in it, the disadvantages of satiety being incomparably greater than those of poverty."[7] To act with consideration is to reject the modern insofar as it demands our *thoughtlessness*; and when we think, we reflect on what precedes: to think is to belong to the past — "Only those who belong to the past respond to the confrontation of thinking.... [And they will attain the future]."[8] This is what the "avidity" of the victors sought (and

---

6   Heidegger, *Nietzsche: Eternal Recurrence of the Same* (HarperOne, 1984), 15.

7   E. M. Cioran, *History and Utopia* (Arcade, 2015), 109.

8   Heidegger, *Ponderings XII-XV: Black Notebooks 1939-1941* (Indiana University, 2017), XV, 200.

seeks) to *quell*. Satiety smothers more than the man — the medium of the man suffers most, stuffed to the gills on avidity's abandonment.

Imagine the "avidity" of those who *disparage*, of those who ceaselessly *tolerate* — they tolerate to death! They tolerate the "error" — of *form*, not of substance. It is the *substance* that cannot be suffered. Substance must itself be *formed, informed, reformed, transformed* — all to fit victorious sensibilities, which are naught but technicized urges playing out in immense, industrial scale to silence those who speak without the veil. To remain *free* is to speak with the veil, to think, to poeticize, and to belong to the past.

That Krell — and all those he represents — see opposing values as an "abomination" belies the tolerant veneer of the globalist (liberal-Marxist) program, and, indeed, all veneer of technicized modernity: *we* are the experiment, *we* are the tools, *we* are the *abomination* carrying on as fools. We are fooled because we imagine our program as better than the *other*; this is not to suggest any damnable relativism, but only to say that when we posture as *victors*, we necessarily trod the defeated underfoot. This means atrocities carried out in *our* favor are acceptable, while those *others* are diabolical — one can try to philosophize this fact into oblivion, but it is impossible: the reality of the liberal-Marxist program, revealed in all its *avidity*, is one of dishonesty: we tolerate, therefore we crush the intolerant. And dissent folds under the great weight: "the height of injustice is to seem just without being so."[9]

Whose books get published by mainstream publishers? Which academicians get mainstream press and are elevated to the top of their fields thereby? Which scholarship is deemed suitable and put on the desks of press and educational (*forming*) institutions that will undoubtedly elevate it? Whose ideas get institutionalized and integrated into, not merely academia, but public (*forming*) policy? That of the *victors* — for everything, the answer is *the victor*. Why are any conservative or traditional values that fall outside the modern left-right

---

[9] Plato, *Republic*, II.316a.

liberal paradigm immediately and incessantly smeared as "extremist," "bigoted," or "fascist"? In addition to their zealous *avidity*, the victors and their prevailing narrative will spare no expense nor waste any opportunity to malign the losing side. For the victors to remain victorious, the losing side must ever lose.

How do those honored with *emeritus* status become so? Is it because they espouse and propagate non-mainstream or controversial positions? Hardly—it is precisely because they dutifully, and with much *avidity*, push the accepted, liberal-Marxist agenda; for their life's work of furthering this agenda, they are honored — perhaps a scholarship will be introduced in their name.

A future *emeritus* and currently quite influential academician, Brian Leiter, maintains a blog named after his titularly titled Leiter Report on noteworthy graduate programs for aspiring philosophers; Leiter, who fancies himself a Marxist,[10] is perhaps most transfixed by dreaded *fascism*, which is essentially defined as anything with which he—the Marxist and Frankfurt School sympathizer—disagrees. Leiter posts his updates on contemporary "fascism" under his "Authoritarian and Fascism Alerts" — but this is really a bin for obloquy against those on the "right" side of the liberal-Marxist spectrum (arch-capitalist and Zionist Donald Trump, for instance, is a regular topic).

To his credit, Leiter certainly does call out the economic injustice of the capitalist system, routinely highlighting the disparity of wealth between the ruling elite and those whose duty it is to curate the elite's assets, as well as the lack of actual working-class politicians (about 1.6% of state legislators, for instance, have what could be considered a "working-class" background, suggesting "that economic challenges such as wage stagnation and the rising cost of living will get short shrift in state capitols"[11]). Seemingly infinitely rising corporate-leadership salaries are also a concern, with the Economic Policy Institute reporting

---

10   Richard Marshall interview of Leiter for *3:AM Magazine* (December 2011).

11   Robbie Sequeria, "Working-class people rarely have a seat 'at the legislative table' in state capitols" (March 2024), stateline.org.

in 2019 that "CEO compensation has grown 970% since 1978," while worker compensation in that time had "risen only 12%."[12] Nothing is done about this, and that is the point. The purpose of the liberal-Marxist system, paradoxical though it may sound, is the elevation of an elite at the expense of the majority. Years after this report, we read the following headline: "Chevron CEO's pay rose 12% to $26.5 million in 2023, workers lag."[13] Shareholders enjoy the scraps from the table and are content to stay silently complicit in the capitalistic injustice Leiter and others expose.

Retail investors — who might, along with their personal capital, be doubly invested in a company through various retirement funds — are doubly happy to stay quiet if their capital keeps rising. This emboldens giant hedge funds and mega-financiers to push their quasi-economic agendas, as BlackRock CEO Larry Fink styled in true Bernaysian fashion, of *forcing behavior change*: "You have to force behaviors ... If you don't force behaviors, ... you're going to be [financially] impacted.... We're going to have to force change."[14] Notably, Fink attended the recent G7 Forum to offer a "huge, vast pool of private capital" as funding for public infrastructure projects, as it would be "unfair" to burden taxpayers in such a way. Perhaps this is some kind of predatory "altruism"?

Where the Marxist succeeds in identifying capitalistic injustice, he even more catastrophically fails in recognizing (1) the shared internationalist aims of so-called liberal-democratic capitalism and Marxism, and (2) the fundamentally *social* — not just economic — nature of Marxism. (And if he does recognize it, this uncovers him as even more

---

12 Lawrence Mishel and Julia Wolfe, article title cited (August 2019), https://www.epi.org/publication/ceo-compensation-2018/.

13 Sabrina Valle, article title cited (April 2024), Reuters.

14 Interview with Andrew Sorkin, Dealbook Summit (2017), a *New York Times* (*NYT*) event. The *NYT*'s editor-in-chief is Joseph Kahn, and its owner is The New York Times Company, whose chairman is A. G. Sulzberger and president/CEO is Meredith Levien.

duplicitous and disingenuous.) What Fink describes is what he learned, wittingly or not, from his master, Karl Marx: "[Communists] openly declare that their ends can be attained only by the forcible overthrow of *all existing social conditions*."[15] What Fink and Marx describe is what every Marxist blinded by "economic injustice" fails to see: the necessary *social* component of Marxism. The *socioeconomic internationalism* of liberal-democratic capitalism and Marxism is joined today in what we know as *liberal-Marxism*, as *globalism*.

The morass of academia, replete as it is now with generations of professors educated in the liberal-Marxist principles of socioeconomic injustice is only an unquestioning echo chamber lacking in self-reflection: It is a hall of mirrors reflecting the same sinister idea — though the mirror to the self is nowhere to be seen. So, that a Marxist gets positive attention and a platform from which to influence the intellectual development of future academicians — e.g., as happens with the Leiter Report — is hardly surprising; the entire liberal-Marxist system is predicated on such resounding replication. That this fact never quite dawns on the many liberal-Marxists who reap the benefits of the system they make a career out of disparaging is, on the other hand, more than a little peculiar. Far be it from someone among the intellectual elite to imagine his greatest "enemy" is only an ideological *counterpart*, fighting urgently for the same goal: the Marxist and capitalist both fight for the liberal-authoritarian, *globalist-totalitarian* cause, much as each might like to ignore this fact. And far be it from someone among the intellectual elite to imagine they are simply the product of a system that counts on them to advance its aims from publicized pulpits — a spate of pride is a dearth of future, after all.

One should perhaps consider Professor Emeritus Krell's pride. His language is every bit as peculiar as the liberal-Marxist elite's incognizance of their origins. Krell's use of the word *abomination* — is *biblical*. Yes, the Hebrew Bible speaks of the "abomination that causes

---

15 Marx, *The Communist Manifesto* (Swenson & Kemp, 2013), 52.

desolation" in the book of Daniel; the Judeo-Christian book of Revelation tells of the Whore of Babylon with her "abominations of the earth" — cosmic enemies of the cosmic cause. Can it be any clearer that the *avid* victors wish to portray those Heideggerian "acolytes" as *preternatural* enemies? Is this *normal*, is this *acceptable*? Indeed it is — nothing could be more acceptable than damning the damned "acolytes" of the losing side: *they should be run through the gauntlet and taught to hold their tongue.* The *emeriti*, across their victorious fields, feign impartiality — perhaps by gently scolding those who wish to *too* conspicuously damn the damnable, by encouraging the "critical eye" — but this is only to maintain the appearance of *their* farcical objectivity. Their witnessing the revelation of the abomination *is* fitting: they uphold the extraordinary hatred that damns the damnable.

And so Heidegger lives to think another day — for now. And, for now, he teaches to think all who care to listen.

3.

Fourteenth-century Europe summoned the Black Death from Asian steppes and a will to overcome the morass into which it was flung. Where once warm bodies filled working roles, now teemed puzzling vacancies. Who but the leftovers would assume the work? Opportunity arrived behind the deadly plague, along with both a canny appreciation and divine alienation. If God left man to sanitize his own streets, perhaps man can sanitize his own soul. In doing so, man might be up to more challenges, both in life and after it.

The Renaissance, coming a century later, saw man looking backward for answers, and elsewhere. In response to the ugliness of Black Death, man embraced the beauty of his forebears: Greeks prized the beautiful; perhaps if beauty was again elevated in this death-ridden world, so too would cultural achievement return — and if not this, then at least *eudaemonia*.

Petrarch encouraged man to reach his highest potential, inciting a Western revolt against the iconoclasm of the East. But the East lingered: man's potential would be fulfilled in service to the Judeo-Christian God; thus the Levant held sway over the early aggrandizement of man. Erasmus picked up the Petrarchan torch, but tempered it with a truly modern, liberal sensibility. Man must defer to God, but man is to be otherwise open—a sympathetic skeptic who ruffles at primal Lutheran abrasiveness: Understand *the other*, defer *to God*. Both Petrarch and Erasmus laid the foundation for modern liberalism—their humanism arising squarely out of Judeo-Christianity and a moderate Europeanism—i.e., a "refined," egotistic Europeanism: Grasp the other side as long as the other side grasps the Lord; *grasping the Lord*, of course, is *eudaemonic* euphemism for submitting to the man who believes. Their humanism rested on the dogma of *inherent worth*, and the Western worldview was forever described.

The Christian humanist was quite fond of *inherent worth*, which honored God's creation while simultaneously honoring the self. Most importantly, however, it allowed the roaring moralizers to dictate their terms to humble congregations, which set the law of the land with the minister-as-chieftain and concurrently attracted subservient parishioners. The truest believers in the dogma of *inherent worth* became the instigating church mice of the roiled centuries to follow. Perhaps the greatest of these church mice was Jean-Jacques Rousseau.

Rousseau's church was the liberal mind; his hymnal was the heaving of the guillotine; his apotheosization of man was a sleight of hand to elevate the state and implement a tyranny of the elite. Carl Schmitt, whose own work is conveniently ignored by the institutionalized victory of liberalism, had this to say on Rousseau's preeminent *Social Contract*:

> This contradictory book ... is best suited to reveal both the critical condition of continental individualism and the exact point at which this *individualism*

turns into *state absolutism*, and its *demand for freedom* turns into a *demand for terror*.[16]

The liberal mind, nurtured as it was by the Judeo-Christian humanism preceding it, still longed to hear the voice of God, though God is a respectable anachronism in such modern times; the new liberal — the Rousseauian liberal — heard the divine voice in Masonic lodges and conspiratorial salons; this voice was the voice of "the people." Though, like the stentorian moralizer before him, the modern, Rousseauian liberal simply liked being the *man of the hour*, the man to guide the ignorant masses out of their *nonage*, as Kant would later echo.[17] The modern age of the *state-as-god* dawned.

Whipped into frenzy, the masses had their spokesmen: the Rousseauian liberals. What followed were the American and French revolutions, each liberal uprising inspiring the other in turns. Freemasonry's blatantly internationalist aims so firmly pressed onto revolutionary actions that their symbols still grace currencies and cornerstones to this day. Washington, D.C.'s famous monuments, for instance, are the dots on a map connecting a pentagram, compass and square to the world every day; few notice. When in France the radicals purged the radicals in 1792 — i.e., when the liberals purged the more outspoken Masons — radical fervor was for a time tempered. The skeptical spirit of Erasmus prevailed over the Lutheranized Erasmuses of the Reign of Terror, so to speak. But this was just a lull in the action.

Not a hundred years after Rousseau lamented man's omnipresent chains, Karl Marx carried on the tradition:

> Communists openly declare that their ends can be attained only by the forcible overthrow of *all existing social conditions*. Let the ruling classes *tremble*

---

16 Carl Schmitt, *Dictatorship* (Polity, 2014), Hoelzl and Ward translation, 97; emphasis added.

17 Immanuel Kant, "An Answer to the Question: *What is Enlightenment?*" (1784).

at a Communistic revolution. The proletarians have nothing to lose but their chains. They have a world to win.[18]

The frothing hatred of millions is collected in the swelling capitalistic urge of the proletariat: *Kill* the man with the money, *destroy* the social conditions that allow for his money, and *take* his money—this is the Marxian formula describing an economic aim. Now, of course, we known more intimately Marxist cultural aims, stated as they were from the very beginning: "overthrow ... all existing social conditions." We cannot rightly say that the cultural aims have an economic end; Marxist cultural aims are ends in themselves, born out of the same hatred of "ancient lands" from which Marx himself felt alienated. The economic aim is one of modern, material power; the cultural aim is one of cultural revaluation; the intent of each is the same: progressive destruction of the old order. If the old order is dominated by the European man and woman, then it is they—the European family—who must be destroyed.

All of this revolutionary fervor—this *avidity*—shares the ideological root of Judeo-Christianity: the *revaluation of values*. And all of this fervor can go by one name: liberal-Marxism; for both liberal and Marxist thought sought to usurp the old orders of Europe—the *ancien régimes* of *ancient lands*—for the benefit of an internationalist order, i.e., a globalist order. That its name has changed through the centuries means little, for the intent has always been the same: to abolish the differences between peoples under the guise of reciprocal benefit to make the divided and rootless more easily ruled. "There is a qualitative, critical difference between men," Ludwig Feuerbach observes in his *Essence of Christianity*,

---

18 These, of course, are the closing lines of the *Communist Manifesto*.

But Christianity extinguishes this qualitative distinction; it sets the same stamp on all men alike, and regards them as one and the same individual because it knows no distinction between the species and the individual...[19]

Feuerbach continues: "We need only drop the limitations imposed by nationalism, and we get Christianity."[20] An erasure of the qualitative differences between peoples results in the "brotherhood" of Judeo-Christian internationalism. As an atheist and humanist, this was simply an international "brotherhood" for Feuerbach; for him, Christianity was a familiar language through which *internationalism* would take shape and usurp erstwhile *nationalistic* systems — the *ancient lands*. It is no wonder then that Karl Marx drew such profound inspiration from the humanistic and privileged Feuerbach. Fellow humanist, freemason, and founder of the Pan-Europa Movement, Richard von Coudenhove-Kalergi also presses for an international "brotherhood" in his "Open Letter to the French Chamber" (1924):

> Your forefathers hurled three great words into the history of Europe: *freedom, equality, fraternity!* ... All the revolutions of the past century were but the echo of the great French Revolution... Renew your mission! Proclaim to the world the outbreak of the third revolution! The revolution of *brotherhood*!
>
> While the *Star-Spangled Banner of Freedom* flutters in the American West, while the *Red Flag of Equality* flutters in the Russian East, may you in the center between these two worlds unfurl the *Banner of Brotherhood*, from man to man, from class to class, from people to people, from continent to continent!

Notable attendees to Coudenhove-Kalergi's Pan-Europa congresses included Sigmund Freud, Thomas Mann, Rainer Rilke, Miguel de Unamuno, José Ortega y Gasset, Konrad Adenauer, and Albert

---

19 Ludwig Feuerbach, *The Essence of Christianity* (Ungar Publishing, 1957), Eliot translation, ch. 11: 44–45.

20 Feuerbach, *The Essence of Christianity*, ch. 8: 36.

Einstein.[21] Excepting Rilke, all of these men were activists for the liberal-Marxist cause; and each of these men fulfilled his mission to unseat former values.

Liberal-Marxism is the revaluation of values meant to empower the formerly powerless and enrich the internationalist elite. And despite pretenses to the contrary, liberal-Marxism is not a popular movement—a popular slumber, perhaps, but not a movement. The movement belongs solely to the vanguard. Lenin saw how the movement without a head is a nonstarter. He only forthrightly *named* what others necessarily *did* to placate the masses before him: become dictator of the proletarian dictatorship, rule in the name of those you stifle. Liberal-Marxism will always need a ruling elite to maintain momentum; the difference between liberal and illiberal movements, as Carl Schmitt correctly assessed, is one of *honesty*: at least the illiberal movements are honest about their rejection of democratic principles; liberal tyrannies count on no one noticing the eschewal of that which is professed.

Vanguards of liberal-Marxist movements represent the elite of the excluded. It is they who take power; it is they who shepherd the Mass Man. They speak for mass rights and mass equality; they advocate for the most shunned among the herd if such an effort furthers the liberal-Marxist aim of *overthrowing all existing social conditions*—i.e., the aim of destroying the old order. In this way, they win both present

---

21 Rilke (d. 1926) was an Austrian poet who offered tentative support to the Russian Revolution and Bavarian Soviet—he later showed admiration for Mussolini and longed "tradition based on 'home' and 'origin'" as a way to dispel anarchy" (R. Freedman, *Life of a Poet* [1996]); Unamuno (d. 1936) was a keen backer of liberalism; Ortega y Gasset (d. 1955) wrote *The Revolt of the Masses* (1930), extolling the virtues of liberalism—despite remaining skeptical of liberalism's inevitable tyranny of "primitivism" and mass "mediocrity"; Adenauer (d. 1967) was a devout Catholic and first chancellor of Germany's republic—he is also considered one of the "founding fathers" of the European Union; Einstein (d. 1955) was a notable Zionist, socialist, and advocate for world government. More on Freud and Mann later in this text.

and future support — for being on the "right side of history." When one forms the future by reshaping the present, being on the "right side of history" is assured. This is liberal-Marxist unshackling, this is the generation of "correct" thinking and a precondition for the final *overthrow of existing social conditions*. Thus can American political officials dazzle and placate the masses by ritualistically repeating Marxian maxims: "We can see what is possible unburdened by what has been."[22]

When representatives of the old order are disgusted at the progressive steps of the liberal-Marxists, this only signals to the latter that their aim is true; thus they double their efforts. A day of remembrance or visibility for some progressive cause is too much? Let's make it a month. A month is too much? Let's make it 259 days out of the year. Still too much? Let's make it a part of childhood "education." Little by little the next generation is lost to the "overthrow of existing social conditions" — and the liberal-Marxists bury ancient lands. The Mass Man is none the wiser; his lot is simply to exist, so he cannot be bothered to think. The Mass Man is content with having even a nominal advocate in his respective capital — this and his technological distractions.

Technicization was the real ingenuity of modernity. Technicization is concomitant with humanity, but it really advanced with the Enlightenment. Man was unshackled, and he used his newly freed limbs to fashion a new god: *science*. Science and technology go so perfectly together that they and their corollaries are studied and incentivized in school: STEM education is the new Latin Mass.[23] Those who don't become STEM professionals are at least enough aware of STEM principles to know who their intellectual masters are; thus all of society benefits from the rising tide of science and technology. The masters, in turn, if they are sufficiently politically minded, become the new vanguards — if not politically, then culturally. Modern science

---

22 Kamala Harris, Vice President of the United States and 2024 presidential candidate; "unburdened by what has been" delivers dozens of hits in White House transcripts.

23 STEM — science, technology, engineering, mathematics.

tells a man *what* to think and *why*; STEM disciplines tell him *how* to think and *when*. Thus the Mass Man is not just an amalgamation of the unthinking herd, but an active participant, a congregant of a ritual *mass*. Shepherded by the Vanguard of Prelates, the *mass*-man repeats the "correct" invocations at the "correct" time. Technology and its abundance are the symbols of a culture overthrown, the crucifixes of the modern man.

Democratization of education stimulates the receptors for deciphering and enlivening *correct* invocations, which exponentially increases the yield of the liberal-Marxist echo chamber. Instead of an isolated cadre with limited reach, the masses are emboldened with just enough indoctrinatory points to be the State-as-god's manifold antennae among the crowd. A vast network of foot soldiers propagandizes and polices potential dissenters on behalf of the potentates. Anything standing against the relentlessly encroaching wall of "correctness" is pummeled with abuse and slandered into submission or oblivion; "hate crime" and "hate speech" are ominous, newfangled whips meant to eventually blind and batter those who think instead of only mindlessly regurgitating talking points. Knowledge itself is watered down and profaned, burned like acid into the ears of bystanders. Every pulse with money or "minority" status has the means to become "educated" — requisite intelligence is beside the point, if not a nonstarter. The Mass Man becomes the Mass Mind by the redemptive egalitarianism enforced by Vanguard-prelates: all are sparks from the flint of a struck god, the amplified agenda of a seething hatred.

Modernity's obsession with "minorities" — which are often defined as anyone not of European descent, heterosexual, or otherwise healthy — stems from the failure of the Marxian "emancipation" of the proletariat; as it became clear to liberal-Marxists that class warfare was insufficient to ignite world-revolutionary tyranny (to counter the equally liberal-Marxist, capitalist-bourgeois tyranny), the revolutionary vanguard saw the need to target and galvanize new, more potent revolutionary roots. An interesting entry in *The Stanford Encyclopedia of Philosophy* notes that the "Frankfurt School," some of whose members we meet in this text, "[has a vision of] critical theory" that

> inherits its emancipatory orientation from Marx, in the sense that it aims not only to understand, but also to contribute to a radical transformation of the social world that is already underway, and the commitment to real emancipation as requiring a radical, irreducibly social and political transformation...[24]

The revolution is indeed well underway. Now the mass of sparks and congregants fill godless temples with educated pulses and little to no intelligence — this is but part of the price we pay for incentivizing equality: educated brainlessness propped up by profligate technicization. Modernity amounts to dullards mimicking dullards who parrot proselytizers.

The Mass Man plays his part in the congregation of modernity: He loves himself and what he is owed. Vanguard-prelates are all too happy to remind him of what he is owed. Forgetting modesty, the Mass Man "inflates its needs into *cosmic* and *metaphysical* values. In this way all life is *vulgarized*: for inasmuch as the *mass* of mankind rules, it tyrannizes over the *exceptions*."[25] But this is all the better: when he is *technicized*, he is also *proletarianized*. When technology threatens to alienate man from himself, the Vanguard announces the need for a mass movement — a movement to *overthrow all existing social conditions*. The Mass Man obliges; the Vanguard secures its privilege.

Judeo-Christianity spawned humanism; humanism gave rise to liberalism; liberalism birthed liberal-democracy and Marxism; liberal-Marxism is the precondition for globalism, which has both economic and cultural aims. The economic aim is the capitalism of the proletariat and the enrichment of the Vanguard; the cultural aim is the eradication of all existing social conditions — a destruction of the

---

24 R. Celikates and J. Flynn, "Critical Theory (Frankfurt School)," *The Stanford Encyclopedia of Philosophy* (winter 2023).
25 Nietzsche, *The Will to Power*, §27.

culture that established the impoverishment of the formerly marginalized. The difference between liberal-democracy and Marxism is the difference between Protestantism and Catholicism: each worships the same god and each harbors, with minimal variation, the same tenets. Nietzsche called liberal orders the lightning rod of "the bungled and the botched" because those who formerly had, at best, a fringe place in society now had a vindicated worldview: mankind's inherent worth demands a popular voice — via the Rousseauian "general will" or the Marxian "dictatorship of the proletariat." Modernity is the dictatorship of *the bungled and the botched*, wherein the dogma of *inherent worth* tyrannizes those who might otherwise be nobility.

A new global order is predicated on mankind's progress into a socio-technological future; this future, in turn, is contingent upon both the desire to excoriate and vitiate any semblance of traditional lifeways and, frankly, a desire to harm. The sadism of liberal-Marxist tolerance and wills-to-destruction is undeniable. The hate-filled speech of any number of liberal-Marxists is on full display whenever (1) they feel *unwatched* and (2) they feel *only watched* — i.e., when they feel they are in approving company. Liberal-Marxist language sheds its pretense to intellectual docility or benignity, let alone objectivity. Spengler observes:

> 'Capitalism from below' describes the property that talented and superior people have worked to acquire as 'stolen,' in order to get enough fists clenched for it to be appropriated without work. This, then, is the origin of the class-war theory, economically constructed with a view to the worker's vote and politically designed for the benefit of the labor leader. It was a short-range aim. Inferior minds can see no further than the morrow in their outlook on the future, and they act accordingly. Class war was meant to bring destruction and nothing else. It was to clear away the forces of tradition, both political and economic, to give scope to the revenge and dominion of the forces of the underworld. What lies in store beyond that

victory, when class war has long passed away, no one in these circles has troubled to inquire.[26]

At the core of this sadistic hate mongering is the will to dismantle, beyond the cognitive realm, all remnant of the *ancien régime* in *ancient lands*; this is a project of *deconstruction* and *repurposing*, the likes of which has not been seen in history. The new foundation upon which is built the new order — *novus ordo sæculorum* — is a subjectivity of the shared senses, a false objectivity by committee. "Why do the Anglo-American 'world' and 'Bolshevism' belong most intrinsically together," asks Heidegger, "despite [their] apparent opposition...? Because both are in essence the same — the unconditional development of subjectivity into sheer *rationality*."[27] Such is the vulgarity of the Mass Man and the Vanguard-prelates. Joining forces, they collect their mental energy into a pulsating rhythm of electric whirring: the result is a bastard ideology, born of the virginal, primeval whining of the bungled and botched.

Thus the first and second alternatives meld into a single consciousness of vulgarity with the technicization of the Mass Mind. Because humanity's destiny as *fallen from beyng* is sealed, there is no choice but to continue to push for total technologizing; this push will culminate with humanity's, and thus technicity's, end.

4.

Concomitant with the rise of the Mass Mind was rejection of individuals and personalities. While peppered with revolutionary paroxysms, the arc of this rejection was gradual. The end of World War II, however, saw the wholesale denial of traditional offices or governments, smeared as they were with the ineradicable stain of *fascist*. The Mass Mind, in its inescapable mediocrity, took to throwing the baby out with the bathwater when it came to any form of government that wasn't

---

26 Spengler, *The Hour of Decision* (Pacific, 2002), 142.
27 Heidegger, *Black Notebooks 1939–1941*, XIV, 160.

liberal-democratic or Marxist—those two sides of the same coin: the Mass Man is the average, and the average man is, in fact, a *poor specimen*—mentally, physically, and spiritually *poor*.

The Mass Man cannot envision how power could not corrupt, for if the average man were permitted absolute power and authority, he would, naturally, be absolutely corrupted. *Therefore*, thinks the Mass Mind, *absolute power corrupts absolutely, in all cases and without exception*—because the Mass Man does not believe in exceptions, for the Mass Man is *not* an exception. *Therefore*, thinks the Mass Mind, *we must eliminate King, Kaiser, Czar, and Caesar; we must abolish the Dictator*—thus does the mass make way for the *tyrant*. This comforts the Mass Man, to the extent he is capable of thinking, for he has no confidence in himself and is terrified of others. Thus the illusion of democracy assuages him—*at least we don't have a dictatorship*, he coos. Because he is incapable of looking any deeper into the matter, he is satisfied with even a veneer of *freedom*—so he sleeps; and when he wakes, he bustles, sublimated into the corporate state, content with idle blabber. *At least we don't have a dictatorship!* So says the *last man*, and he blinks.[28]

The position of *dictator* originated in the Roman Republic. Dictators were appointed by the Senate to stabilize a crisis; when the crisis passed, the appointee would vacate the seat. Many dictators completed such a duty to the nation upon which the state was built. Great Cincinnatus is perhaps the foremost example of the dictator (to whom the first American president George Washington was often favorably compared and after whom Cincinnati is named); Sulla is another stellar example, but there are many others. The West appeals to the Roman Republic to substantiate many of its actions and impulses. But *the dictator?* The very *idea* in the postwar world is anathema across Europe and its progeny.

---

28 Nietzsche, *Thus Spoke Zarathustra*, "Zarathustra's Prologue."

While twentieth-century examples of dictators are frequently cited as the reason for such denunciation, this only obfuscates reality: dictatorship is rejected because the world is populated by the *last man*, the Mass Man. The Mass Man can only see his own *weakness*, his own *failure*, his own *wickedness* in everyone else. This is why the Mass Man rejects wholesale the exceptional individual, the genius personality, the notion of a Great Leader; this is why the Mass Mind gravitates — and defends unto unthinking death — toward the liberal creeds of the incapable: *democracy, republicanism, socialism, internationalism, globalism*. The masses are placated by liberal creeds, but fail to see the illiberalism behind them.

Liberalism, generally, surpasses any "the killer is inside the house" moment; with liberal creeds the *killer is in the mirror*. This is not to say that liberalism or liberal creeds are inherently bad — in theory they have their merits. Rather, it is the people populating the creeds that undermine them. The Mass Man is incapable of fully participating in or contributing to any functioning liberal system — one would have to be, not merely educated, but *intelligent* and caring for this, which is simply not the case.

Constant media-propagated crises have stalled a distinct downward trend in voter turnout across the West since roughly the mid-twentieth century. The advent of the 24-hour news cycle coincided with ostensibly perpetual global economic, diplomatic, migration, and environmental crises to temporarily reverse the decline of voter engagement. As states across the West become less demographically homogeneous and seemingly more polarized across the aforementioned issues, media and governments do their best to capitalize on the crises and turn the voting tide in their favor. This is only temporarily sustainable, however, as many among the dwindling percentage of eligible voters will become irreparably disillusioned with a system predicated on crisis manufacture; they will see that no amount of voting changes anything about the frequency or intensity of the crises, that the elected parties often work in tandem to increase personal wealth or secure voting blocks to remain in office. All this belies the other, illiberal aspect of liberal systems: they are, in practice, meant to prop up a ruling class at the expense of the voting majority — a system not different than any other tyranny in history. We can rest assured that when the ruling class speaks of "freedom," they mean *slavery*; when they speak of "security," they mean *instability*; when they speak of "prosperity," they mean *wealth for the ruling class.*

Meanwhile, the Mass Man rejects reflection. Presently, he is unable to self-reflect, and apparently no amount of external prompting can spark it. This only *reflects* the decoupling of humanity and technicity, wherein man is too technologized to appreciate the delicate balance of the human condition. There is no promise of this condition reversing. The Mass Man is content in his lethargy, even despite disillusionment with the system meant to oppress him. The ruling class cannot see the future its manipulation of the masses portends; nor can the masses begin to comprehend the truly disastrous future awaiting them. All, in fact, are riding a wave of technologizing that is beyond all control, and when the wave breaks, humanity will not even be a *memory*, for no one will remain to remember. This is *the killer in the mirror*: a humanity disengaged with itself for an ephemeral convenience and primitive awe in the face of technological splendor. It is the flight of the self from itself.

5.

Liberal-Marxism is the intrinsic dissolution of a people's constitution.

A "people" always has an inherent identity, typically rooted in blood. Where collective identity is not rooted in blood, some other tribal foundation takes its place — e.g., a location (soil), a team or organization, or a shared vision of the future. All of these surrogates only simulate the organic connection lost when blood is not foundational. This is not to say that such surrogate connections cannot be successful in some lowly way, but only that each replacement will be more susceptible to dissolution. All connections are susceptible to dissolution, but blood, having a mental, physical, and spiritual component, is — by far — the most resistant to erosion. Replacements are never the *real thing* and will always lack the quality to withstand degradation — i.e., a dissolution of original integrity.

Liberal-Marxism, arising out of the Judeo-Christian slave-morality Nietzsche identified, came to the fore in the Enlightenment: it was the deliberate transition from a Europeanized vision of Judeo-Christianity — based on honor, loyalty, decency, and sacrifice — where blood and roots were still viable to a more broadly globalist vision of humanism. God and faith were usurped for man and technics, or perhaps man and science. (Science itself here began its ascent from useful methodology to incontrovertible dogma in its own right.) With Judeo-Christianity, aristocratic values — i.e., those based on blood and the *character* determined by it — were deposed and replaced with bloodless ecumenical values — i.e., those based on the ignorance or outright rejection of blood and character and founded on monetary indulgences and a theological dispensation of salvation. This is to say that the *concrete* became *abstract*. With the secular humanism that now sits as the fundament of liberal-Marxism, monetary indulgences to the Church have shifted to carbon taxes, "green" initiatives, and diversity-equity-inclusion programs; and the theological dispensation of salvation has become the dogmatic dedication to "The New Colossus":

> Give me your tired, your poor,
>
> Your huddled masses yearning to breathe free,
>
> The wretched refuse of your teeming shore.
>
> Send these, the homeless, tempest-tost to me,
>
> I lift my lamp beside the golden door!

While this dedication is cast in bronze at the base of America's Statue of Liberty — *Liberty Enlightening the World* — its universalism has universal application: all of Europe will bend before its dictatorial *will-to-abstraction*. World, give us your garbage, Lady Liberty is made to suggest, *we disdain the organic identity of your natives, and we replace it...* The rootless now become rooted in their collective identity as "wretched refuse." Organic identity is replaced by the shared vision of liberal-Marxism.

What is this *shared vision*? It is the rootless establishing roots in a land dispossessed of its natives. It is the cauldron of the incessantly stirred. It is the revolution of the scientific mass.

Keep, ancient lands, your storied pomp! — our poetess Emma Lazarus continues. Lady Liberty is supposed to say this — *this*, near the turn of the twentieth century, the time of the greatest, most terrible upheaval the world has ever seen; *this*, when inconceivable fortunes will shift hands; *this*, when catastrophic wars will throw Europe and Asia into maelstrom and death; *this*, when those ancient lands — the *ancien régime* of yore — tried only to keep what remained of their "storied pomp," the traditions that simply gave rise to them and their identity. Written in 1883, Lazarus' poem is meant to *incite* the revolutions it heralds; it is a consummation of the destructive-progressive spirit of the Age of Enlightenment; it is the silent rush of a wrecking ball meant to annihilate. The American Jewish Historical Society commemorated Lazarus and her poem in 2019; a video produced for the project marked the poem's idea as "radical"[29] — this pronouncement punctuates the project's introduction. False prophets praise the *radical* — as noun and adjective — as if they make a confession. But what is it they confess? What does it mean when false prophets make true predictions? What exactly is the *radical*?

"To be radical," proclaims Marx, "is to grasp things by the root. But for man the root is man himself."[30] Thus, to be *radical* is to have *complete dominion over man*, which is nothing short of Marxian totalitarianism. All aspects of man must be "grasped" — physical and mental — and the spiritual must be deracinated; for Marx, the extirpation of the spiritual

---

29 The Emma Lazarus Project.
30 "Contribution to the Critique of Hegel's *Philosophy of Right*" (1843).

emancipates man. Paul McLaughlin identifies *radicalism* as a mix of liberal democratism, nationalism, and socialism,[31] from which arises a *progressive humanism*. "Progress" is defined as that which improves society; and "humanism," in the liberal (political) sense, is necessarily focused on the individual; thus, individual interests are championed at the expense of the group. Radicalism's brief encounter with nationalism—arising from the European revolutions of 1848—could only be described as a mistake or necessary evil from the true radical's perspective, remembering, of course, that the true inheritor of radicalism is today's internationalist, the *globalist*. Nationalism as a necessary evil would provide the proper context from which to view Nietzsche's absolute disdain for the *liberal-nationalism* of his day:

> This ridiculous condition of Europe *must* not last any longer. Is there a single idea behind this bovine nationalism? What possible value can there be in encouraging this arrogant self-conceit when everything today points to greater and more common interests? ... And it is precisely now that "the new German Empire" has been founded upon the most thread-bare and discredited of ideas—universal suffrage and equal right for all....[32] This sickliness and want of reason which is most opposed to culture, and which is called Nationalism, this *névrose nationale* from which Europe is suffering acutely; this eternal subdivision of Europe into petty states, with politics on a municipal scale: they have robbed Europe itself of its significance, of its reason, and have stuffed it into a cul-de-sac.[33]

Nietzsche here is referring to *herd* nationalism—that *liberalistic* nationalism founded on *slave-morality*, that of universal suffrage and equality, that of "progressive humanism," which is ultimately leading *nations* (the concept of which is predicated on *kinship*) down a

---

31   Paul McLaughlin, *Radicalism: A Philosophical Study* (MacMillan, 2012).

32   *The Will to Power*, §748. For a more detailed discussion of Nietzsche's *anti-Germanism* and *anti-nationalism* as stemming from his *anti-liberalism*, see Alfred Baeumler's *Nietzsche: Philosopher and Politician* (Arktos, 2024) and Martin Friedrich's *Myth and Sun* (Clemens & Blair, 2022).

33   *Ecce Homo*, "Why I Write Such Excellent Books."

decadent path of *self-destruction*. "Radical" nationalism, or *liberal* nationalism, is really only a means to mass enslavement—an abandonment of individual (spiritual) freedom for the sake of material profit, i.e., a mass conformism for the sake of convenience; this, of course, is why Nietzsche detested "nationalism": it was *liberal* and derived from the 1848 revolutionary wave predicated on *radicalism*. "Petty states" with their "municipal politics" represents a *conquering* through *division*. *Who conquers?* It can only be he who overthrows the old aristocracy, born, at least initially, out of tribal kinship, for the sake of the new aristocracy, which obliterates familial ties (at least for the serfs) and predicates power on profit. It is the ancient lands destroyed for the teeming shores—all for the sake of the hidden hand, the New Colossus' minder, the Vanguard-prelates.

After Rousseau's wide-reaching work of the eighteenth century, imbued with the internationalist spirit of Freemasonry, came the quite *liberal* French Revolution, whose outcome was the quite *radical* Reign of Terror, wherein dissenters (non-conformists) were tortured and killed. Then came the previously mentioned revolutions of 1848 that threw *ancient lands* into turmoil. The Marxist Revolution in 1905 Russia followed as still another *radical* upheaval of *ancient lands*; and it appeared in the wake of America's enthusiastic dedication of Emma Lazarus' poem in 1903; this *radical* revolution killed nearly 20,000 people and foreshadowed the tumult of the twentieth century; two decades later the Marxist Revolution in 1917 Russia and its subsequent civil war would claim the lives of some 12,000,000 people. We leave aside the rest of the twentieth century's *radicalism*—two world wars and ceaseless globe-spanning conflict. We mark only the stirred cauldron of rootless refuse; we see the proletariat agitated into the New Colossus; we understand the meaning of false prophets making true predictions: falsity makes truth when the mass is churned to brutes.

Liberal-Marxism is an *erasure* of the old, an *eradication* the "storied pomp"; and it is a superimposition of the purportedly novel—the rise of the New Colossus, the Mass Man. Far from God, the Mass Man is its own messiah, presaged by its own false prophets in search of material gain at the expense of the landed noblesse and unwitting masses, and augured by rabble rousers *qua* trash collectors seeking to besmirch the beauty of those *hated* "ancient lands." Liberal-Marxism presumes an aura of innovation, and this is well deserved. Deceiving the masses to accept, with great *avidity*, their own enslavement is perhaps the cleverest of all sociopolitical inventions in history — and it is the *cleverest revenge*. The inherence of the New Colossus, the Mass Man, is its blankness, its void. Like a cold ember, glowing with a freezing aura of inception, *revenge* is the beating heart of the New Colossus. *Keep, ancient lands, your storied pomp. Give me, instead, your wretched garbage* — and with them I shall craft a New Colossus, I will create myself! And from this creation, whose innovation is the enthusiasm of the unsuspecting throng animating the burning heart of hatred, arises that which is *not* so very new: from this creation arises a new despotism, which is as old as man's first declension from his originary humanity.

Abandon the root — *keep, ancient lands, your storied pomp!* — and absorb, no, *uplift* the mass, the heaping waste washed ashore. Uplift the mass until they assume a new colossal figure, a mighty imposition — a dictatorship of the proletariat. The old colossus, built on the conquering urge to emblazon European beauty upon a lesser world, is all but forgotten; the New Colossus stands erect in the former's place. Her mandate: *down with the tried and true, in with the weak refuse.*

> What could be more demoralizing than the fact that the worst freak should have the faculty of giving life…? How contemplate without dread or repulsion the wonder that makes the first man in the street a demiurge on the brink? What should be a gift as exceptional as genius has been conferred indiscriminately upon all: a liberality of base coinage which forever disqualifies nature.[34]

Cioran here indicts along with man, the Mass Man who does nothing but breathe to win his place, *Nature* — for if Nature allows for the

---

34 Cioran, *The New Gods* (2013), 10; emphasis added.

accrual of waste, Nature is as culpable as the man who sullies her. Such waste — such is the seed of dissolution; but this is the point: implant the Trojan horse, disguised as a gift, wait for the moment of critical mass — *nightfall* — and unleash the frozen ember of *cleverest revenge* on those who opened their loving, liberal arms.

We are the weak refuse, so *we must embrace* the weak refuse, so say the prelates, and the Mass Man blinks. And from such imbecilic self-loathing the New Colossus takes shape, molded in the hands of the false prophets spurred by unrelenting and cosmic hate — the hatred of millennia that has come to call in a globalist future. *Liberal-Marxism is the intrinsic dissolution of a people's constitution.* And when a people's constitution deconstructs, so goes their Constitution. All that was fought for in the latter part of the eighteenth century was wiped away, or perhaps *fulfilled*, little more than a hundred years later when the Enlightenment's sprout had blossomed in whirlwind of emancipation. In that span, Karl Marx and Friedrich Engels — as inheritors of the Rousseauian call to action: *Man is born free, and everywhere he is in chains* — articulated the body of the New Colossus: *Proletarier aller Länder, vereinigt Euch! — Proletarians of all countries, unite!*[35] So began the stride of the giant whose stature does not emanate from qualitative strength, but from quantitative control. Prophets of the lofty word mesmerize the Mass Mind into dull complacence. The spirit of "The Banner of the Jew" adorns Liberty Enlightening the World:

> Wake, Israel, wake! Recall to-day
>
>   The glorious Maccabean rage…
>
> Let but an Ezra rise anew
>
>   To lift the Banner of the Jew![36]

---

35 Rousseau, *The Social Contract* (1762); Marx and Engels, *Communist Manifesto* (1848).

36 Excerpted from Emma Lazarus' "The Banner of the Jew." The Book of Ezra in the Hebrew Bible tells the story of "Israel's guilt" for mingling with non-Jews. To resolve their sin and purify their people, the Jews banish the non-Jews.

Emma Lazarus: author of "The New Colossus," oracle of Marxists. Children recite in school and learn to revere the imploration for the world's dregs — the body of the New Colossus. Students, in turn, are reminded that *they* are dregs: *we're all immigrants*, so any instinctual resistance to abandoning our roots for the lauded "melting pot"[37] is farcical, if not useless; *be silent and comply* — this is the message. Marvel at the eloquence of Emma Lazarus' poem — a poem that is as prophetic as it is profound. Now recite and remember something truly novel:

> Those who fashion lofty words
>
>   are often but the only scourge
>
> that stands between the lofty urge
>
>   and vengeful dissolution.

The *will-to-destruction* is ingrained in a dissipated people, inculcated by rote and the technicity creating an illusion of convenience; this will is the acceptance of servitude in a time of overgrown paths.

> In the wood there are paths, mostly overgrown, that come to an abrupt stop where the wood is untrodden.... Each goes its separate way, though within the same forest. It often appears as if one is identical to another. But it only appears so.[38]

Along such paths, and others less overgrown, an occasional traveler sees an unusual flower. The sight stops him, and he looks closely: What once before seemed a flower unseen turned out to be trash made by machine. The trash was thrown into the grass along the path, discarded by a biological human. Paths that appear identical are often not; values, like paths, are peculiar.

Western fixation on the revaluation of values continued through the twentieth century. If in 1903 "Ezra rose anew" to dispel his ancient

---

37 *Melting Pot* (1908) was a play written by Israel Zangwill.
38 Heidegger, *Off the Beaten Track* (Cambridge, 2002), opening statement.

enemy, reminding all of Liberty's purpose, this revolutionary fervor continued through the world wars and Marxian experiments meant to silence "ancient lands" for good. In 1965, standing before the poem fixed to Liberty's pedestal, American president Lyndon Johnson seemed to rededicate — to the world — "The New Colossus" with his announcement of the Hart-Celler Act. With this, America, as forerunner to Europe's suicidal immigration policies, chose to codify in law the "radicalism" of Lazarus' poetry: *ancient lands* would literally be kept in their place in favor of more teeming shores elsewhere — perhaps shores that liberal-Marxism itself cast into turmoil through dehumanizing and exploitative imperialism.

Later, in 1971, Peter Singer — whose parents fled Europe's *ancient lands*, likely because of their Marxist sympathies, and whose grandfather, "one peculiarly well suited" to "Red [Marxist] Vienna,"[39] collaborated with Sigmund Freud and Alfred Adler — wrote an enduring treatise with a simple proposition: You, dear reader, are actually morally *bankrupt*; beneath all you took for good or amoral in your doleful daily life festers a social wound: charity for the amorphous masses is moral *obligation* and not a matter of supererogation — i.e., charity doesn't build a fund of merit for the average sinner; charity is a sacred *duty*. So says Singer, a godless man.

It is hardly surprising that Singer's "everything you thought was true is now false" revaluation should only gain in popularity in the wake of the eighteenth century's Rousseauian inversions, the nineteenth century's Marxian inversion, the twentieth century's Lazarine tumult, and, now, the twenty-first century's technocratic philanthropy. Indeed, even Bill and Melinda Gates, amidst all their globetrotting world-saving, found the time to write the foreword — albeit a short one where they decry the death of even *one* child in the world[40] — to

---

39 Singer, *Pushing Time Away* (Ecco, 2004), 131.

40 The absurdity of this idea derives from the Christian — now liberal-Marxist — view that every human being has, because of its pulse, *inherent value*. If we define a "child" as anyone under the age of eighteen, it is quite apparent that not

the new edition of Singer's now-famous treatise, *Famine, Affluence, and Morality* (2016). In it, the authors praise Singer's devotion to the faceless mass — simply because it is *biologically human*. *Character* be damned, *quality* be damned: You, immoral Westerner, have an obligation to uplift the dreck from all teeming shores — because you have the *means* and they have a *pulse*.

Keep, ancient lands, your storied pomp! — this, too, is criticism of European morality, a morality once based on quality and character and not simply the radical revolutionism that biological humans have *inherent value*. This revolutionism — this *slave-morality*[41] — was born out of the *cleverest revenge* first noted by Nietzsche; this revolutionism persists because the current world order is the secular-humanist inheritor of Christianity's legacy. Only the rootless or their galvanizing cadre can think in such a way. Yes, the revaluation of values continues, and it manifests in a *will-to-destruction*.

Liberal-Marxism's *will-to-destruction* is, largely, its myopic focus on the individual. This myopia infects more than just the broader community; it infects and rots the individual mind. The result of this rot is a compulsion to separate oneself from the group — not by *excelling within* the mores of the group, but by *shunning and smearing* the mores of the group. It is the hatred of hatreds. This kind of indoctrinated thinking — this *radical individualism* — spawns destructive or deconstructive cultural urges: art takes the form of a Picasso or Pollock, wherein beauty is seen precisely in ugliness; science takes the form of a Freud or Kinsey, wherein personal responsibility is deflected to society and perversion becomes an acceptable means of expression; philosophy takes the form of a Derrida or Horkheimer, wherein the

---

every "child" has what some would consider *quality* or good *character* — i.e., not every child has *inherent worth*. The Marxist view, however, is that *society* makes the child, not *heredity*, and certainly not *personal responsibility*; and if society makes the child, it is not the child's fault if he turns into a sociopath; therefore, *all* children have inherent value.

41 This is in contrast to Nietzsche's *aristocratic* morality.

norm must be destroyed or *deconstructed* simply because it is the norm.

But this is the great deception: All this *radical* individualism is *not* a destruction or controverting of the norm simply because it is the norm. It is a deliberate attack on those *ancient lands* that are not one's own and a calculated assault on the lands of a cosmic and mortal enemy; it is an "Ezra rising anew" — rising to defeat his rival once and for all. Miguel Serrano describes this Jungian *enmity*, which is

> not borne from the form, but from something stranger and deeper, from within, or from outside the form....
>
> [F]or the first time in two thousand years, Jung has demonstrated to us that, among the beings with similar human form, there are essential differences and that ... there are also irreconcilable enemies (save for small exceptions...), because they have a different worldview, different symbols, different archetypes, and they tend to impose their conception at the expense of the other; through the annihilation of the other; since to live in a psychic world that does not correspond, is to die off.[42]

To die off—the New Colossus is a galvanized amalgam of inferiority whose voice is that of the radical, the deviant who purposefully sets out to disrupt and destroy the rooted group; the New Colossus is sanctioned rootlessness — not for care or humanly concern, but for the *cleverest revenge* meant to divide the new conqueror from the old. Ultimately, any such radical individualism is only prelude to the most radical totalitarianism: what passes for personal expression today is only the compelled tolerance of tomorrow — and *enforced tolerance*, unbeknownst to the molded masses, is the purest form of enslavement.

The great lie of liberal-Marxism, then, is its assurance to the world that it is a great truth; and it has convinced the world of this — through threat of arms, economic compulsion, and cultural inversion. It has been said that the greatest trick the devil pulled was convincing the world it didn't exist. Liberal-Marxism, similarly, is the embodiment

---

42 Serrano interview, *Excalibur* (1988).

of dishonesty: its radical individualism and compulsory tolerance are the most imposing and enchaining conformism the world has ever known. Like the popular child's game that teaches predatory capitalism, the theme may change, but the game does not. And so it is for the radicalism of liberal-Marxism: the theme, or personal expression, may change, but the system's essence stays the same: in the end, the lesson isn't a preying on capital, but a devouring of freedom.

"It is unnecessary for a prince to have ... good qualities," said Machiavelli, "but it is very necessary to appear to have them."[43] In a predatory system, a system of the *cleverest revenge*, we cooperate at the expense of the other — and "the height of injustice is to seem just without being so"[44]: witness "the creation of a population of indolent, undisciplined, unprincipled, and incompetent people quarreling in random and fretful ways over the diminishing fruits of a dying social system."[45] And so it is for the most illiberal liberal-Marxism, the great enslaver of mankind.

6.

Liberal-Marxism is a curiosity born in Judeo-Christianity.

Europe's end began with its acceptance of Judeo-Christianity. Introducing, as Nietzsche called it, *slave-morality* into a once-proud *ancient land*, Judeo-Christianity eroded the values that gave rise to a once-proud *people*. A microcosm of the issue first confronted Rome, with its rapid decline coming after Constantine's vision on the bridge.

> [Rome] was oppressed by a new species of tyranny; and the persecuted sects became the secret enemies of their country.... The active virtues of society

---

43 *The Prince*, ch. XVIII.
44 Plato, *Republic*, 2.316a.
45 Richard LaPiere, *The Freudian Ethic: An Analysis of the Subversion of American Character* (Van Rees, 1959), 128.

were discouraged; and the last remains of military spirit were buried in the cloister...[46]

Tyranny — this is the source of concern. It is not about defaming Christianity; it is not about scolding liberalism's progenitor for simply being a product of its time; it is not about castigating good intentions. The concern now is whether, based on what one can see both historically and presently, the road we are on terminates in tyranny. Presuming that the "active virtues of [a] society" are those virtues at the core of its foundation and those that sustain it because of their founding power, we can understand how their opposite has a deleterious effect. If Ancient Rome embodied the Nietzschean aristocratic virtues of *good = beautiful = happy = loved by the gods*, Judeo-Christian Rome embraced the rejection of what allowed for its existence — hence the fall of the Roman Empire. Elsewhere, Nietzsche notes that "*intolerance on the part of morality* is a sign of man's *weakness*: he is frightened of his own 'immorality', he must *deny* his strongest *instincts*..."[47] Judeo-Christian morality taught Europe to revaluate its vales; thus what was bad became good, what was weak became strong, what was left became right. Nietzsche did nothing if not stand as the last bastion of European values — values of an ancient land; he had clear views on what healthy charity actually is: "The weak and the botched shall perish: first principle of our *charity*. And one should help them to it. What is more harmful than any vice? — Practical sympathy for the botched and the weak — Christianity..."[48]

Judeo-Christianity was the beginning of Europe's end because it imposed the alien on the indigenous. It is perhaps the greatest unacknowledged colonialism of Western history. Europe is made to feel guilt over past imperialism, as if it must atone for retroactive wrongs — but

---

46 Edward Gibbon, *The Decline and Fall of the Roman Empire* (Everyman, 2010), vol. 4, 120–121.
47 Nietzsche, *The Will to Power*, §385.
48 Nietzsche, *The Antichrist*, §2.

no one cares a whit about its southern invader; perhaps it is precisely because the invader is from the south, the Levant. Now, instead of feeling wronged at the southern invasion, Europe, and especially America, is told it must support its Levantine allies above all—that there is no greater ally than the one from the Levant, precisely because of the Abrahamic, Judeo-Christian ties. This relationship is something like an imposed factitious disorder, a Munchausen syndrome by proxy: the abused is sick if the abusive relationship is not sustained, thus satisfying the abuser. This revaluation of values gradually degraded those instincts that made a strong race of "barbarians" (Germanic northern Europeans) conquer the once-formidable, now-degenerate and adrift Rome. Byzantium was not Ancient Rome; it was a Judeo-Christian southern Europe that held fast, for the sake of its own survival, to some of the strong instincts that made pre-Christian Rome possible; but it was destined to fall from the start. Out of its ashes arose the fledging power of the Holy Roman Empire, which was the consolidation of Europe's continental power; it, too, was doomed from the start because of its "holiness."

All the intellectual force of Europe reflected on the state of man in Christian lands and found it wanting: To follow Judeo-Christianity to its logical conclusion really is a dictatorship of the proletariat. What these intellectual powers could not see, however, Nietzsche identified with acumen: "European democracy is only in a very slight degree the manifestation of unfettered powers. It represents, above all, the unfettering of laziness, fatigue, and weakness."[49] Across Europe, the *ancien régime* fell to orchestrated popular uprisings. Christianity became ever more antiquated: *Who needs a god when the General Will can conquer all?* Thus, *revaluative* Christian morality morphed into the humanism of the Renaissance, which could only culminate in the liberalism of the Enlightenment; this, in turn, birthed the materially focused ideologies of liberal-democracy and Marxism.

---

49 Nietzsche, *The Will to Power*, §762.

The "economic prosperity" espoused in liberal-democratic national strategies has its roots Rousseau, the font of Enlightenment liberalism: "As long as my purse contains money it secures my independence" — thus, in every liberal-democratic society there is a fixed link between the pursuit of happiness (*liberty*) and money.[50] Similarly, Marxism, as Spengler flatly stated in his *Hour of Decision*, "is nothing but the capitalism of the lower classes." This is the economic side of Marxism; but this ideology has a far more sinister cultural side that aims to uproot man for all time and press him under a tyrannical heel.

Liberal-Marxism is the fruit of Enlightenment liberalism; the liberal-democratic urge is identical to the Marxian one: *equality*. Liberal-democracy is secular Christianity just as Marxism is secular Judaism; and each, in its familiar and peculiar way, aims to topple the old order. Where these secular friends meet is at the apex of liberalism, which we identify here as liberal-Marxism — the *revaluation of values*, the *leveling of ancient lands*. All must be equal; if it is not, equality must be *enforced*. This, incidentally, is why we see in liberal-democracies the shift from "equal opportunities" to "equal outcomes" — this shift will only intensify, resulting in a more overt leftist authoritarian tyranny. It will be a tyranny of *the people* shaped by Vanguard-prelates holding all the power. That the masses — the Mass Man — don't see this is perhaps only a testament to their being deserving of servitude.

7.

The tyranny of equality is nothing short of dogmatic adherence — to religious principles. In Marxism we find a religion:

---

50 Rousseau, *Confessions* (Gibbings, 1897), Book I, 52. Also of note, as Friedrich states (*Myth and Sun*, 2022): "In just the first four books of the *Confessions* of Rousseau, a man so ideologically linked to the 'liberty, equality, and fraternity' of Liberalism's birth, *liberty* is mentioned 20 times, *money* is mentioned 41 times."

> To the believer [Marxism] presents, first, a system of ultimate ends that embody the meaning of life and are absolute standards by which to judge events and actions; and, secondly, a guide to those ends which implies a plan of salvation and the indication of the evil from which mankind, or a chosen section of mankind, is to be saved.[51]

Marxism, like liberal-democracy, seeks paradise on the *life* side of the grave. The secularization of Judaism and Judeo-Christianity speaks to the intrinsic urge to prosper while one still can — it is the Nietzschean will-to-power appropriated by the outcasts to cast out those of powerful will; it is the leveling of great personalities in favor of the great mass wielded by invisible forces. Bernays, an as-yet underappreciated influence on modernity, observed:

> The conscious and intelligent manipulation of the organized habits and opinions of the masses is an important element in democratic society. Those who manipulate this unseen mechanism of society constitute an invisible government which is the true ruling power of our country....
>
> [These] invisible rulers ... control the destinies of millions. It is not generally realized to what extent the words and actions of our most influential public men are dictated by shrewd persons operating behind the scenes.[52]

The invisible forces might as well be gods — they induce the *correct* feelings in *correct* measure at the *correct* time on the popular palate. A spiritually blank faith enraptures the Mass Man as he contends with his place in the world; his passions are whipped into frenzy by invisible gods who want only complicity and docility, if not ignorance, from him. *Liberty, equality,* and *fraternity* are the secularized tenets replacing — and *fulfilling* — faith, hope, and love.[53] But secularity is not free of the dogmatic devilry plaguing so many religions: secularity is only materiality's excuse to replace God. This is Nietzsche's meaning when

---

51 Joseph Schumpeter, *Capitalism, Socialism, and Democracy* (Harper and Row, 1950), ch. 1, 5.

52 Ed Bernays, *Propaganda* (Ig Publishing, 2005), 37 and 61.

53 1 Corinthians 13:13. Notably, *Paul* was once *Saul*.

he lamented: *God is dead! And we have killed him!*[54] *Liberality* arose out of European man's innate desire to free himself of the binding chains of dogmatism; *liberalism*, however, fulfilled the dogmatism of its religious predecessors. What we reap from our sheep-like acceptance of the liberal order, which is only Europe's transition from god-*fearing* darkness into a godless modernity, is a dogmatism adorned with modern trim. Nietzsche continues:

> 'The growing autonomy of the individual' — Parisian philosophers like M. Fouillée talk of such things: they would do well to study the *race moutonniére* [sheep-like masses] for a moment; for they belong to it. For Heaven's sake open your eyes, ye sociologists who deal with the future! The individual grew strong under quite *opposite* conditions: ye describe the extremest weakening and impoverishment of man; ye actually *want* this weakness and impoverishment, and ye apply the whole lying machinery of the old ideal in order to achieve your end.[55]

The application of "machinery of the old ideal" manifests in Bernays' learned observation that "Propaganda is the executive arm of the invisible government."[56] It is the *will-to-power* wielded by the outcasts to usurp the *ancient lands*, to obliterate the *ancien régime*. This wielding is the welding of individual personality into the mass of collective conformism. Thus we understand Michael Zuckert's bemusement at the enduring popularity — and dogmatic adoration of — John Rawls' *A Theory of Justice*:

> Seldom has a book been more thoroughly refuted. Critics, of every philosophical persuasion, from nearly every contemporary political perspective, have found Rawls's premises and assumptions as safe a base for an argument as the San Andreas Fault for a nuclear power plant. They have found the structures built on those foundations about as solid as a Hollywood

---

54 Nietzsche, *The Joyful Wisdom* (MacMillan, 1924), §125.
55 Nietzsche, *The Will to Power*, §782; emphasis added.
56 Bernays, *Propaganda*, 48.

movie set. And yet, like Tertullian facing Christian dogma, or the average Californian, they believe.[57]

Dogma inevitably leads to tyranny: one is not permitted to question the tenets of the belief system, the system's elite deftly manage the dogma to suit their immediate and enduring needs, and the preponderance of people stay conveniently aloof of the system's mechanism; tyranny is founded.

Democracy Alliance is an American collective of leftist megadonors intent on establishing a permanent "left infrastructure" in the United States.[58] The Alliance seeks to accomplish this through the modern power of money—donating here to Democratic political campaigns (or to undermining non-Democratic campaigns), there to progressive organizations. This leftist drive to establish a permanent one-party system is the *will-to-eliminate* even the barest and most nominal of two-party systems in the liberal-democratic world. The drive of the liberal-Marxist is only the "passion of ambition, the desire to rule other men."[59] And this drive is naught but the seething *avidity* of tyranny. But this is just one of many examples of the leftist-progressive tyrannical urge. It is used here to illustrate only the steady march of progressive tendencies toward ineluctable tyranny. Behind veneers of tolerance hide the deepest hatreds, the most obsessive lusts for power.

Consider for a moment that with every anniversary to memorialize the deadliest European civil war in history, to *proudly* remember the mass slaughter of Germanic people, liberal-Marxist societies across the West celebrate that they have *saved the world from tyranny*—they are quite adamant about it. But tyranny is precisely what won. There is

---

57 Michael Zuckert ("Justice Deserted"), as quoted in David Schaefer's critique on Rawls (cited below). While this quote could not be located, the reader is nonetheless directed to Zuckert's "Justice Deserted: A Critique of Rawls' "A Theory of Justice," *Polity* 13:3 (Spring, 1981).

58 Thomas Edsall, "Are Liberals Fundraising Hypocrites?", *The New York Times* (September 30, 2015). See also "Democracy Alliance" at influencewatch.org.

59 David Schaefer, *A Critique of Rawls's "Theory of Justice"* (Kennikat, 1979), 109.

no greater tyranny than believing one is free while being inextricably tangled in mass conformism. *Yes, you're free — now go do what you're told.* No honor is left in life; modernity is an unsettling and eager weariness.

The top American diplomat has no compunction when he says: "We want to protect the international principles established after World War II to prevent war and maintain peace and security."[60] NATO's Secretary General echoes this position: "NATO's core task is not to wage war, but to prevent war, as we have done for 75 years…"[61] Of course, this is an obfuscatory way of saying that *we will do anything to keep power*; naturally, this would include convincing everyone that "the good guys won." The American president lauds the "*Great Crusade* to free Europe from tyranny"[62] — now we are *free* to "prevent war and maintain peace and security" in lockstep with the "international order." No one bats an eye — and the mass keeps marching.

Perhaps key to all of this is the brilliantly crafty Bernaysian trick: You don't have to make someone believe you; you just have to make them doubt everyone else — then their belief in *you* arises in *them*. This, of course, is why Westerners are inundated with articles, segments, and bulletins about illusory *disinformation*. Here again is the top American diplomat:

> [To protect national security] we're building a more resilient global information system, where objective facts are elevated and deceptive messages gain less traction. We're doing that by promoting policies and programs that protect a free, vibrant, and independent press and that foster greater civic and media literacy so that people can better distinguish fact from fiction.[63]

---

60 A. Blinken interview with M. Brzezinski (June 06, 2024). Blinken's comment edited for readability.
61 NATO, "Joint press conference by NATO Secretary General Jens Stoltenberg with the Prime Minister of Hungary, Viktor Orbán" (June 12, 2024).
62 J. Biden, remarks on the 80th Anniversary of D-Day (June 06, 2024).
63 A. Blinken, remarks to the press (September 13, 2024).

Perhaps he means the "free" press that belongs to an ever-concentrated number of billionaires and corporations; or perhaps he means the "free" press that operates under constant governmental pressure to send the "correct" message?[64] Nevertheless, this statement was made in the context of countering *foreign* disinformation — though, certainly not *domestic* disinformation, misinformation, or malinformation, for the speaker always has a monopoly on facts and, presumably, truth. A former Indian diplomat had this to say on the American's disclosure of "controlling the narrative":

> The US does not seem to be mindful of the contradiction between [its actions that] violate the principle of freedom of expression, and limited restrictions that other countries take based on what they need to do domestically to curb social unrest or violence, which the US routinely condemns.[65]

Ultimately, disinformation is whatever the one sounding the alarm about it dislikes; its sole purpose is seeding doubt in audiences, which translates into crippling apathy: society becomes united in unyielding cynicism, which makes it quite malleable. Malleability and the power of propaganda, as Bernays noted, play a central role in liberal-democracies, or liberal-Marxist societies, generally. And such weapons are naturally useful in academia, in *education*.

It was in 1971 that Rawls published his now-required reading (*A Theory of Justice*) for would-be tyrants — the same year Peter Singer published his now-doctrinal essay on everyone's moral *obligation* to "help" anyone who is biologically human and economically "disadvantaged." Each of these pillars of the liberal-Marxist world gave

---

64 Media concentration across the globe is well documented (e.g., freepress. net catalogs ownership); likewise, governmental pressure on media is well known (e.g., see Friedrich's examination of *Metro Broadcasting, Inc. v. Federal Communications Commission* [1990] in *Myth and Sun*; see also Mark Zuckerberg's letter to Rep. Jim Jordon [August 26, 2024]).

65 Kanwal Sibal, "Why the world's largest democracy isn't buying 'freedom of speech' US-style," RT, September 20, 2024.

philosophical voice to the counterculture of the 1960s, which was a liberal-Marxist wave clearing societies of traditionalist residue—a wave kept in check only by heretofore-Western mores and existing constitutions. We have only to look to Asia to see what shape unchecked cultural revolutions assume; Mao's Cultural Revolution coincided with the West's own counterculture attempt to subvert society, and its death toll was roughly two million *un-progressive* souls: Undoubtedly the tyrants were glad to have them gone; and many more aspiring tyrants across the West, full with a grandiose sense of *tolerance* and *justice*, felt some satisfaction at what the future might hold.

8.

Distinct—perhaps *peculiar*—in liberal-Marxist thought is the notion of "impartiality"—as though such a position were possible, even "as a hypothetical situation."[66] Rawls, Singer, and other leftists assume such a position because it corresponds with their moralist sensibilities. Quite naturally do they assume the *unnatural*—because *they* are unnatural. It is inhuman to assume the impossible; that is, it is inhuman to *take on* what does not exist in Nature. In this way, liberal-Marxists become caricatures of humans, play-actors living out their fantasies of mass equality enforced on the herd for prelatic reward. The reward, of course, is the tyranny imposed for our benefit—we simply do not have the wherewithal, the sense to know better. The elite, however, *do* know better; and luckily for us, they are here to guide us to a brighter tomorrow—despite their inhumanity. After all, tomorrow's reality is today's dream: *the eradication of the human from humanity*. This is the effect of a technologized future, the tyranny of technicity.

9.

Impartiality is the Rawlsian "original position"; it is fundamentally flawed: *thoughtful* people make *thoughtful* decisions and, largely

---

[66] John Rawls, *A Theory of Justice* (Belknap, 1971), 12.

speaking, this affects realized outcomes. Chance is certainly a factor and, because of this, sometimes good or thoughtful people reap negative outcomes, and bad or feckless people enjoy positive outcomes. But such is life. Generally speaking, however, thoughtfulness *positively* affects outcomes. We cannot pretend to build a society based off the "original position" because it assumes the impossible: that one's *lineage* does not affect one's *thoughtfulness*.

Rawls characterizes the "original position" as a "hypothetical situation characterized so as to lead to a certain conception of justice," and he maintains that "the principles of justice are chosen behind a veil of ignorance, [which] ensures that no one is advantaged or disadvantaged in the choice of principles by the outcome of natural chance or the contingency of social circumstances."[67] The concept of "natural chance" is a specter of modernity: it is an unfounded assumption upon which the liberal-Marxist notion of "the contingency of social circumstances" is itself based. *Natural chance* presumes things could have generally been otherwise, which, in fact, they could not have. Even if one assumes all biological humans arose out of Africa, it is a fact that disparate races exist, which implies that the various subsets of the species manifest fundamental differences in worldview. Whether one group was driven away from another or one group chose to leave to leave the other, such departures represent more than geographic dispersion — they represent variances in values, in *thoughtfulness*. And even if we suppose that every past group left the other amicably, races with real cultural differences arose over time.

This is the crux of the matter: these differences unwaveringly impact how one approaches life. Kevin MacDonald made this astute observation in his *Social and Personality Development* (1988): "There are no general laws of development and there will never be any, but there are mechanisms, and there are contexts…"[68]

---

67 Rawls, *A Theory of Justice*, 12.
68 MacDonald, *Social and Personality Development* (Plenum, 1988), 312.

Context is everything, and context is precisely what Rawls presumes to remove with his false notion of the "original position." When we remove societal — or even racial — context, the very foundation of interaction and integration within and without groups is removed, which is to say, the basis for discussion and interpretation of groups is removed. The Rawlsian vision is modernity's specter because it indeed haunts us: it makes angels of us all and presumes we — every last one of us and all things being equal — will respond the same way to the same situation every single time.

Aside from the decontextualized unreality that is Rawls' "original position," its spectral presence is again felt in the mechanization of man: no longer are we individuals with proclivities and values: we are essentially organic robots unequivocally unfree in the cage that is the "original position." The progressive, Rawlsian position is not just conjectural to the extreme, which is the liberal-Marxist wont, it is the "veil of ignorance" — which is only to say, a veiled threat against *actual* freedom and humanity.

The threat is this, and it underlies all things liberal-Marxist: we are not living beings — we are unrealized potentialities; we are not free agents — free agents are unpredictable, so between "freedom" and "agency," one of these aspects must be diminished to realize the potential of the liberal-Marxist system of maximum predictability, the intentional society, the planned economy, etc. "Agency" is needed as a matter of course, for the system needs the vessel, the *agent*, to fulfill its ideological plan; "freedom," then, is expendable — and not only *expendable*, but *loathed*, loathed as a matter of course, a matter of understood interference. Moreover, "natural chance" is proffered as a "general law of development" — *chance* is the means whereby personal responsibility is eschewed for greater dependency on a state that requires investment, i.e., enslavement. The liberal-Marxist society demands individuals *without* individual responsibility, which is only to say, the *unfree agent* — the agent whose agency is predicated on circumstances beyond one's control. *Chance* as *law* is a chain tying one to the phantasmagorical "original position"—the position of fantasy that means to perpetuate the lie of mass equality, the position that forever begs the question, assuming the equality it should set out to prove. Liberal-Marxism rejects such proving outright because *equality* is simply a dogmatic tenet; tenets are matters of faith and can only be incontestably assumed. Thus survives the myth of "natural chance" as, indeed, a *general law of development*, despite reality's testament otherwise, and as the substructure for "the contingency of social circumstances." *Natural chance* is an essential precept of liberal-Marxist dogma because it serves as a millstone of guilt wringing funds from wealthy ("privileged") adherents and is a permanent deflector of personal responsibility for the proletarian-multitude that forfeits individual freedom to instead act as an agent of the state upon which they depend.

The liberal-Marxist ideological structure requires a *veil of ignorance* for the imposition of its planned, guided principles; in this way, *man* is not so much veiled as is the *threat of violence* preceding the implementation of the liberal-Marxist scheme.

Disguised force is the essence of progressivism, of liberal-Marxism. Behind leftist tolerance is the most impassioned hatred: destruction of traditional Western society and its values is the aim. This *will-to-destruction* is fed principally by two streams: (1) genuine hatred—both *alien* and *intellectualist*—for the Everyman's bourgeois values (which tend to the traditional), and (2) neurotic guilt derived from the obscene wealth of privileged Whites (defined as *people of European descent*) who seek to soften their guilt by throwing their assets at what they are told are societal injustices—injustices wrought by the Everyman's bourgeois values.

10.

David Schaefer, one of the few vocal critics of John Rawls and the liberal-Marxist *will-to-destruction* plaguing the West, notes that "The praise of *A Theory of Justice* ... has been misguided.... I think that

Rawls's approach represents an utterly misleading understanding of the nature both of philosophy in general and of political philosophy in particular."[69] The "misleading understanding" stems from the liberal-Marxist crafters' desire to either (1) undermine that which gave them a basis from which to flourish (and presumably deprive all others, to their everlasting guilt), or (2) galvanize the masses to support a system disadvantageous to their endurance (but advantageous to the Vanguard-prelates of the system) — i.e., creation of the Mass Man.

Schaefer critiques Rawls' renowned *Theory* because he feels not only that its foundation is untenable, but also that its very renown indicates a pervasive malady afflicting Western political thought—and keep in mind that he wrote his critique in 1979; nevertheless, and interestingly enough, we see the same malady today:

> [Rawls' view of justice] is expressive of what Charles Frankel has termed a 'redemptive' egalitarianism [whose] goal is … to combat inequality *as such*… [Redemptive egalitarianism] is expressed in attacks on the alleged injustice of inequalities of wealth and income…; in so-called affirmative action programs that require persons to be educated and hired according to racial and sexual quotas, without regard to the relative qualifications of non-'minority' groups; and in court-ordered school busing designed to overcome de facto racial segregation, so as to promote the goal of social homogeneity.
>
> What is remarkable about these movements is the social class in which they originate. Redemptive egalitarianism purports to elevate the condition of 'oppressed' blue-collar workers, racial minorities, former colonial peoples, and 'unliberated' housewives. Yet its chief advocates come from one of the most privileged classes known to history—American intellectuals and professionals.[70]

Condemning the "privileged" class who calls for such radical egalitarianism, Schaefer highlights the fact that they are often—if not

---

69 Schaefer, *A Critique of Rawls's "Theory of Justice"* (Kennikat, 1979), 6.
70 Schaefer, *A Critique of Rawls*, 106–107; emphasis added.

always — the group *least* impacted by the changes they deem so absolutely necessary. The root of the issue, according to Schaefer, is

> *liberal guilt* — the feeling on the part of relatively wealthy and well-educated people that they must atone for their superior privileges by demonstrating their commitment to promote 'social justice' for the less advantaged. This phenomenon is distinct from charity in the proper sense, precisely in the fact that it calls for *no genuine sacrifice* on the part of the would-be benefactor.[71]

Unfortunately, this has a detrimental effect on society as a whole; for while the conscience of the "privileged benefactors" is mollified for the mere appearance of benefit, society at large suffers from a kind of betrayal: those who make the policy are inoculated against its effect. Far from assuaging any societal rifts, then, such "redemptive" liberality is — and can only be — divisive. Of course, any hint of discontent from the ungrateful masses generates only scorn among the "privileged benefactors": the "privileged" cannot fathom how their generous policy can go so woefully unappreciated. And ultimately, for the "privileged" class to lambaste the system that birthed them, as progressives are compelled to do, while at the same time enjoying the fruits of that system relatively worry free, is irresponsible and detrimental to the endurance of any Western-liberal institution. But such is the narcissism of liberal-Marxism: *Their conscience is superior to your welfare.*

Such is the narcissism of Marxists *qua* philanthropists. Former spouses of billionaire tech tycoons massage away their tremendous guilt by creating contests to see who can win the most millions in charitable grants; the contest parameters are staked in redemption: show us how you serve the "underserved" — help me help you by helping others whom society doesn't help, or those who simply *cannot help themselves*. God helps those who help themselves. Liberal-Marxists help those who elicit the most guilt.

---

71 Schaefer, *A Critique of Rawls*, 107.

One recalls the moral from an old Sufic tale: the most generous man is not he who gives the most *material* goods; the most generous man is he who *sacrifices* himself for others. Generosity, charity — these are *spiritual* concepts at heart, and sacrifice is more than mere distribution of funds. Is it sacrifice if a billionaire gives millions? Is it sacrifice if a millionaire gives thousands? Or do we witness something else — a *material salve* for the sad, godless soul? Is there any more damning indictment than modern philanthropy — that selfish desire to unburden oneself of some imagined guilt, or from some imagined "responsibility" to the notion of "humanity"? *"Sympathy for all,"* warns Nietzsche, "would be harshness and tyranny for *thee*, my good neighbor!"[72] Of course, there is no tyranny for the tyrannizers who aim to sap the humanity from the globe they seek to subdue; tyranny, rather, is felt only by the commoners beholden to the common weal. The tyrannized are nevertheless enjoined to provide for those the tyrannizers assign as their neighbor!

In *The Brothers Karamazov*, Ivan tells Alyosha of a saint who, to help a cold beggar, "breathed into the man's reeking mouth that was festering with the sores of some horrible disease." This act, Ivan is convinced, can only be "dictated by some self-imposed penance" — a guilt, or perhaps several, buried under the weight of years and consequence. "The idea of loving one's neighbor is possible only as an abstraction," Dostoyevsky muses through Ivan, "it may be conceivable to love one's fellow man at a distance, but it is almost never possible to love him at close quarters."[73] We are nevertheless obligated to help the festering *neighbor-at-a-distance* — so say the tyrannizers. And if we don't willingly offer our personal aid, governments do it on our behalf, collecting taxes and allocating massive funds to all our "neighbors"

---

72 Nietzsche, *Beyond Good and Evil*, §82.
73 Fyodor Dostoyevsky, *The Brothers Karamazov*, MacAndrew translation, "Rebellion."

across the world; this is always for "national security."[74] One must keep up appearances; we again recall Machiavelli: "It is unnecessary for a prince to have ... good qualities, but it is very necessary to appear to have them."[75] This "virtue signaling" pertains to States and tycoon philanthropists alike, and it has its purpose. Machiavelli's prince, too, had purpose: power.

It is not only the former spouses of tech tycoons who give to those with whom they have nothing in common, however; the tycoons themselves give their own heaps of millions — what amounts to pocket change for them — to the "underserved." *Are they neighbors with those whom they help? Would they ever be neighbors with them?* Of course not. It is much easier to give a pittance to a "good," redemptive cause while not getting one's hands dirty, and then studiously informing the world of how much and to whom one gives. These are our liberal-Marxist philanthropists. These are the men and women who, at least on the surface, make the policies that dictate the average life.

Bill and Melinda Gates wrote of "work" in the foreword to the reissue of Peter Singer's *Famine, Affluence, and Morality*:

> [A]id does *work* ... [and] Singer's *work* argues that we can *work* together to prevent very bad things from happening... Fortunately, more and more people are seeing that this is the case, and many of them are also taking action.

That is indeed quite a lot of "work." Schaefer, however, might consider it *no real sacrifice*. Relatively small donations given as a makeshift solution — not to any organic disequilibrium — but to one's own stinging conscience can hardly be considered *sacrifice*. But we live in an era that permits those with money to have a platform on which to speak; and speak they do — the tenets of the *inherent worth* and *equality* dogma; they speak and have *pity*. "Consider the face of the man," wrote Emil

---

74 It is always worth knowing to which "neighbor" country one's own State gifts the most foreign aid.

75 *The Prince*, ch. XVIII.

Cioran, "who has *struggled* in any realm. You will not find there the slightest trace of *pity*."[76] Pity makes one liberal — liberal or duplicitous; but the two are hardly distinct. Such liberality, be it with funds or the desire to control man's increasingly nullified instincts, is, yes, a *will-to-destruction*; but what is destroyed is individual freedom; such liberality, then, is a *will-to-illiberality*. Here is Nietzsche misappropriated: *A desire to hurt* as the liberal-Marxist mantra — decimate *ancient lands* for the sake of a happy, albeit sick, conscience. Mass migration is only ever *into* European lands: this is both a balm for the Vanguard-prelates and their elixir for the Mass Man — someone stands to *profit* greatly from such upheaval, after all.

What was it Marx told the world? We must have the *forcible overthrow of all existing social conditions*:

> [Communists] openly declare that their ends can be attained only by the forcible overthrow of *all existing social conditions*. Let the ruling classes *tremble* at a Communistic revolution. The proletarians have nothing to lose but their chains. They have a world to win.[77]

Marx used, both contemporaneously and as sibylline pronouncement, his secular-Judaism to cudgel ancient lands into *revaluative submission*. Privileged Whites indoctrinated into the dogmatism of liberal-Marxism use their conscience as a bludgeon against the masses for self-appeasement and self-debasement. Their self-hatred is alien in origin and arises out of the greatest unacknowledged colonialism in history: the slave-morality brought from the desert into the heart of ancient Europe.

This is what the West is up against if it has any self-recognition remaining: we drift from freedom into tyranny. This is not only a political tyranny, but also a human one. The political tyranny arises out of the loss of our humanity. We lose our humanity with the mass technicization accompanying the loss of our cultural — i.e., spiritual — identity.

---

76 Cioran, *The New Gods*, 98.

77 Marx, *The Communist Manifesto* (Swenson & Kemp, 2013), 52.

In short, the loss of our humanity is both the cause and the effect of our gross technologizing. If we see in the mirror an alien, it is because first we saw a mirror in the alien.

Today, the "privileged" class sees itself as the Leninesque vanguard to a new order: serve (through charitable giving, not actual service) the "underserved," galvanize the proletariat, then wield the masses like a hammer against the system that riles their guilt: "Underlying the ... denunciation of injustice, in the end, is the passion of ambition, the desire to rule other men."[78]

In 2009, Christian Barry and Gerhard Øverland wrote,

> Most affluent people are at least partially aware of the great magnitude of world poverty. A great many of the affluent believe that the lives of all people everywhere are of equal fundamental worth when viewed impartially.[79]

Thus they help carry the liberal-Marxist fire into the new century. Children learn in school to use caution when making universal claims with universal words like *all* and *everywhere*. Simultaneously, children across the West learn that we should only ever make universal claims with universal words when describing the tenets of liberal-Marxist faith: *the lives of all people everywhere are of equal fundamental worth when viewed impartially*. This dissonance is dissimulation: it is the tactic of a warring ideology — an ideology that aims to *forcibly overthrow all existing social conditions*. Marx endures in the biological mass of every liberal (even if the liberal is "conservative") participating in the liberal-Marxist system today.

Marx is the partiality that demands impartiality for the implementation of a revaluative system.

---

78 Schaefer, *A Critique of Rawls*, 109.
79 Barry and Øverland, *Bioethical Inquiry*, "Responding to Global Poverty," 6: 239.

11.

A desire to hurt — the passion of ambition, the desire to rule other men[80]: This thread, identified by Nietzsche, links the seemingly disparate *Equality* worldviews of Judeo-Christianity, humanism, liberalism, Marxism, globalism — equality imposed under the *desert-god*, under *pure reason* and *biological mass*, under *injustice* and *class warfare*, under *almighty currency*.

We are either not meant to see it or we simply choose not to. Christians hope that the god of their childhood would never abandon them; they don't believe it possible to have been duped so incredibly — they thus go on believing and nothing changes; nothing ever changes. When a believer musters the courage to abandon the system that betrayed him from the beginning, he finds it sufficient to just switch *Equality* worldviews; moreover, he seeks *revenge*, as is his nature. No longer is the believer a Christian: he rejects the desert-god; indeed, he hates the desert-god and the European civilization that fostered it, and he becomes a liberal or Marxist: he loves man — even more the godless man; he aims to recreate society in his image. If the Marxist matures and has some success in the capitalist society that allowed for his existence, then the Marxist becomes a globalist: the international revolution then becomes an international exchange.

There is nominal difference between the *Equality* worldviews. Who still thinks it an accident that the liberal-democracies and Marxist factions allied themselves time and again since 1900? Likely most people. *Ah, but the Cold War!* — That settles the definitive difference between the liberal-democracies and the apparently Marxist Stalinist state! However, the Cold War was nothing but a monumental victory for Stalin, for he managed to fool the all too willing liberal-democratic compatriots that he was indeed an "international socialist": the willing liberals threw in their lot with someone a little more nationalistic than

---

80 Nietzsche, *The Gay Science* (Vintage, 1974), Book I, §32 and Schaefer, *A Critique of Rawls*, 109, respectively.

they would have liked. Stalin expelled the internationalists' ringleader, Leon Trotsky (née Lev Bronstein) and later had him killed; moreover, Stalin repeatedly purged the internationalists trying to subvert his National Bolshevism, a far cry from Marxism's secular Judaism.

More than just a thug showing his true colors, Stalin's Anti-Cosmopolitan Campaign was the Stalinist State's rejection of the *internationalism* that is a fundamental tenet of liberal-Marxism. When the liberal-democratic allies manned foxholes with Stalin's empire, they thought they conspired with a kindred spirit, a fellow *internationalist*; but they were deceived by Marist trappings — this and the fervent wish of the Marxist diaspora to finally have the vessel through which to mete out their millennia-old *revenge* against ancient, *European* lands. The Anti-Cosmopolitan Campaign's apparent rejection of internationalism was a betrayal to Stalin's former allies in the West. Secularized Judaism's greatest stronghold outside of Israel itself was in the United States; the United States thus became the Stalinist state's greatest "foe." As Kerry Bolton put it,

> Wilsonian internationalism took on an anti-Soviet orientation when Stalin purged the USSR of Trotskyites. Many went over to the US in the Cold War and some of the leading Trotskyites became leading Cold War ideologues. Even Trotsky's window, Sedova, ended up supporting the war in Korea as a necessary counter to the USSR, which was regarded as worse than fascism or capitalism.[81]

Trotsky's vision of Marxism was perhaps closest to its originator, Marx, and its greatest proponent, Lenin: The vanguard foments revolution in the name of "the people" for the sake of an international elite. Trotsky's vision found a home among the internationalists in the United States and the West, hotbeds of liberal-Marxism as they already were. Former American president Woodrow Wilson's internationalism was a precursor to the neo-conservative internationalism fronted in the West, generally; neo-conservatism, for a time, was only Trotskyism

---

81   Kerry Bolton, *Yockey* (Arktos, 2018), 536.

disguised to make it more palatable to supposed "patriots"; it has now morphed into a thinly veiled Zionism — something Trotsky even outwardly rejected[82]; inwardly, he could not help but work toward the Holy Land. Now, militant internationalists across the world are exuberant over technology's lethal prowess in defense of both Zionist and internationalist aims. "For Zionism" — or perhaps more disingenuously, "for self-defense" — do we see thousands brutally maimed and terrorized,[83] all to seemingly fulfill the plan for a Greater Israel laid out by Oded Yinon decades ago.

It seems only a matter of time before the Zionists and the Globalist Clique explode the Al-Aqsa Mosque under some pretext — perhaps an "Iranian" missile slipping through the Iron Dome. They will then *finally* have cause to wipe Persia from the map and to rebuild their temple. For those of Abrahamic faith, this will precipitate their eschatological fantasies, which will unleash a devastating and vengeful bloodlust — the loosed hatred of the hateful. The rest of humanity will hear but a thundering footfall of the New Colossus — the undoing of the doer, the ritual slaughter of the human spirit.

∞ • ∞

When, during the Israeli-American Council annual summit (September 2024), a panel host prefaces a question put to Deborah Lipstadt with, "after October 7th, there was a feeling around the world that Israel is weaker…" — Lipstadt interrupts with a proud quip: *Wanna beeper?* She then laughs with deep satisfaction, and the rest of the Zionists laugh with her — because *god damn the enemy*. Despite her gibe, Lipstadt, Holocaust historian extraordinaire, will keep her job with the US

---

82 *Leon Trotsky on Zionism* (Socialist Youth League).

83 Leon Panetta, former CIA director and US Secretary of Defense, described Israeli actions against Hezbollah thusly (*CBS Sunday Morning*, September 22, 2024): "The ability to be able to place an explosive in technology that is very prevalent … and turn it into a war of terror.… I don't think there's any question that it's a form of terrorism."

Department of State; it is inconceivable she would even be chastised. After all, this world is a *will-to-machine*, and nothing besides. Local destinies mean nothing — whether Zionist or Marxist; their nominal feud is a farce meant to distract the masses and enrich the elites that will be consumed nonetheless.

All is *globalist* in the end; all require the vanguard elite to shepherd the masses to accept a system of governance opposed to human freedom. Both Wilsonian internationalism and Trotskyism bore within the seed of totalitarian revolution. That Stalin's National Bolshevism and the Americanized West stood opposed is hardly surprising. The Cold War was only a correction of an erstwhile warm relationship between former allies: Roosevelt's "Uncle Joe" became the West's Traitor Joe.

That the Cold War resulted in a collapse of the Soviet Union is mere smokescreen. World War II was Stalin's victory, if only because he duped those who formerly sponsored him. The Soviet Union — and therefore the Cold War — existed because the United States made it so; Britain, France, and the United States — the liberal-democracies — *made* the Soviet state persist beyond World War II. The Cold War was the West's anger toward a Stalinist regime that betrayed the internationalist designs of a liberal-Marxist world order, an order that was finally wholly achieved upon the Soviet Union's collapse. Again, Bolton offers his insight:

> The USSR was not being opposed because it was communist but because it was pan-Slavic authoritarianism. That is why many of those recruited by the CIA during the Cold War were notable Marxists and especially Trotskyites, such as Professor Sidney Hook, who hated Stalinism more than capitalism. Hence, those anti-communists promoting nationalism, such as Senator Joseph McCarthy, General Douglas MacArthur and military personnel such as Major Arch E. Roberts and General Edwin Walker, were purged. Theirs was the type of 'anti-communism' that might become a mass nationalist movement capable of overthrowing the Liberal system.[84]

---

84 Bolton, *Yockey*, 263.

The fall of the Soviet Union was only the most recent thrust into the Globalist World Order, and in this way, the ultimate aim of World War II was achieved, despite Stalin's detour; all former Allies now take shelter under the awning of an international exchange promoted as "peace," "stability," "democracy," and "the rule of law." Now, any threat to the international exchange — *the globalist order* — is met with, at least, accusations of the offender being "undemocratic," and contentions that "the people's" will to "self-determination" is being thwarted by an "oppressive regime." This is the liberal-Marxist tagline. This is the Bernaysian manipulation that permits the perpetuation of the liberal-Marxist world order.

Freda Utley, an English scholar and onetime communist, recorded the mass hypocrisy of the Allies in her book *The High Cost of Vengeance* (1949). In it she castigates the Stalin- and Truman-led Allies' anti-German (or perhaps, anti-anti-globalist) policies in the war's immediate aftermath. Utley noted that "In the name of democracy [the Allies] have subjected the German people to the rule, not of laws but of men."[85] Utley's disillusionment with Sovietism didn't quite extend to liberal-democratism, but perhaps it should have: in the name of liberalism there can only ever be *laws of men* — for man is the basis of all exchange. Whatever remaining outposts of Christianity there are exist only as a vestige: the remainders simply haven't made the transition to a more modern *Equality* dogma. The godlessness that pervades modern *Equality* dogmas envelops all facets of individual life, such that the divine understanding between kinsfolk that undergirded societal laws has merely become a set of lifeless sections, articles, and paragraphs in this or that authorization act; parliaments the liberal-Marxist world over twaddle and offer their constituents consistent circumlocution. Lawmakers — not to mention their patrons — are the gods of modernity. So how could we possibly have the rule of law? Rules of men

---

85 Freda Utley, *The High Cost of Vengeance* (Regnery, 1949), 167.

are the currency behind currencies. Ultimately, perhaps Freda Utley suspected that *Rule of Law* is really euphemism for *Rule of Man*.

In 1788, Alexander Hamilton warned of the tyranny that follows the Rule of Man:

> The creation of crimes after the commission of the fact, or in other words, the subjecting of men to punishment for things which, when they were done, were breaches of no law, and the practice of arbitrary imprisonments have been in all ages the favorite and most formidable instruments of tyranny.[86]

Utley highlights this inconvenient nuisance for the would-be tyrants in her larger discussion of postwar liberal-Marxist hypocrisy. Because of their audaciousness the Nuremberg trials are, of course, one of the more obvious examples of postwar ignobility. Revilo Oliver, a *professor emeritus* himself, had this to say of *ex post facto* courts:

> Civilized peoples spare the lives of the vanquished, showing to their leaders a respectful consideration...
>
> To punish warriors who, against overwhelming odds, fought for their country with a courage and determination that excited the wonder of the world, and deliberately to kill them because they were not cowards and traitors, because they did not betray their nation — that was an act of vileness of which we long believed [ourselves] incapable.[87]

It would be naïve to think warring peoples, generally, have assumed civility at victory, in Europe or elsewhere. Victors have certainly more often than not enjoyed the spoils of their luck and effort. Here, Oliver, a classics scholar, likely considered the fate of bested knights or noblemen from medieval Europe, or perhaps, more recently, Napoleon and Wilhelm II. Among honorable people, defaming and unceremoniously murdering one's defeated opponent were not common practice. Rather, respecting the conquered fighter is not only honorable, but

---

86 Federalist Papers, no. 84.

87 Revilo Oliver, *America's Decline* (Historical Review, 2006), 56.

also more familiar. What child doesn't learn proper sportsmanship while learning the game? It is *dishonorable* to slander or ridicule one's opponent in victory or defeat. This is Oliver's point. Napoleon, though not without his detractors, was and is widely regarded as a great leader; he was given an exile befitting his station. And while efforts were made to indict Wilhelm II on this or that "international crime" — a dry run, of sorts, for future Nuremberg trials — he was nevertheless granted his exile. What Nuremberg represented, on the other hand, was a departure from commonly understood European values of postwar victory, of "sportsmanship," if you will. And this, perhaps, is a Rubicon the West cannot retrace.

The war of annihilation that was World War II continued without arms. *Unconditional surrender, Dresden, Berlin, Kyiv, Kursk, Darmstadt, Hamburg, Nuremberg* — what are these but vengeance by another name?

Not to worry: few notice such things; few care. Many believe in what the system that counts on their complicity instructs; moreover, the believers — those adherents to liberal-Marxist faith — become quite vexed when their articles of faith are challenged; thus come the slanders meant to silence the challengers into oblivion. *Ad hominem* attacks are a favorite and, because of the masses' infinite capacity for ignorance and apathy, ever-effective tool of the Vanguard-prelates and their various cadre to quell dissent.

Now, as *ad hominem* urges rage, lest one think Utley is only a "Nazi" sympathizer, this is hardly the case. Utley, herself a staunch advocate of the *Equality* dogma manifest in liberal-democracy, laments: "We have made martyrs of criminals by the Nuremberg trials, and given a new lease on life to Nazi doctrines by our own transgressions against fundamental democratic principles."[88] It is perhaps regrettable that an intelligent woman like Utley was evidently incapable of seeing, as Carl Schmitt articulated years before, that "democratic principles"

---

88 Utley, *The High Cost of Vengeance*, 176.

tend toward the dishonest, if not duplicitous. Liberal-Marxist avidity is not only the will to destroy the ideological incubators predicating its existence; it is also the drive to establish a new, unquestionable creed. The ambitious and tyrannical impulse that allows for the vengeful, inhuman hypocrisy in handling a battered German people is the same "justice"-seeking zealotry inherent to *Equality* dogmas: it is a passion to rule others at any cost — even at the expense of a few noncompliant lives here or there. And "the height of injustice is to seem just without being so."[89]

Utley continues her reflection on the postwar world:

> It was impossible to travel through the devastated towns of the Western zones without it seeming strange and horrible that we should sit in judgment on the Germans who had never succeeded in killing nearly so many civilians as we did, or in perpetrating worse atrocities than our obliteration bombing of whole cities.[90]

It is only through the lens of dogmatic faith that the Allies' "obliteration bombing" makes any sense; it is only in the context of a fanatical hatred that Dwight Eisenhower's rabid wish to punish every German man, woman, and child after the war makes any sense. This *emotive* response, *beyond all reason* — the Allied response hiding behind a veil of objectivity — was born of the jealousy of a desert-god, a jealousy that became secularized and made palatable for modern, godless sensibilities in the internationalist order of liberal-Marxism. Those who claimed their enemy killed innocents — to galvanize public sentiment in favor of the economy-energizing war effort — in the end killed the innocents of their enemy.

We pretend this event is readily understood in the context of *good-versus-evil*; what we fail to see, however, is the real issue of (1) the context of the *manipulated* and their *manipulators*, and (2) the ever-increasing technicization of humanity that increasingly dehumanizes

---

89 Plato, *Republic*, 2.316a.

90 Utley, *The High Cost of Vengeance*, 182.

man — especially does it make callous and cruel those who claim to act always in favor of humanitarian, egalitarian interests. Fighting for "democracy" has only ever meant the destruction of one's noncompliant enemies for the benefit of the ruling elite, the Vanguard-prelates.

Years after Utley wrote *The High Cost of Vengeance*, Deborah Lipstadt — the United States Special Envoy for Monitoring and Combating Antisemitism — posited, "the argument that the United States committed atrocities as great, if not greater, than those committed by Germany has become a fulcrum of contemporary Holocaust denial."[91] Hence, to question the *good-versus-evil* context in the slightest marks one forever as — a *Holocaust denier*. Never mind the *non sequitur*. The masses are simply not to review the events enveloping the war, unless the survey perpetuates the victors' narrative (and one can be sure every word Lipstadt writes or says is perfectly in line with the *correct* narrative). This is the antithesis of reason; it is *ad hominem* attack: we may not know anything about you, but if you *question*, we know *everything* about you — and thus you are in league with Holocaust deniers. Since few want to bear such a libel, most stay silent; still more refuse to even *think* of the matter; and many succumb to the explicitly emotional response this hint of slander is designed to elicit, so they become staunch dogmatists themselves, *avidly* attacking anyone who might be prompted to question as they once did. That the simple act of *questioning* "reveals" so much about the questioner should say quite enough about the motivations of the slanderers, but most are unaware of the trick. Lipstadt has "successfully" marked Utley as a "Holocaust denier" — case closed, no need for further inquiry or to heed anything she might have said. To read Utley is, for the typical liberal-Marxist, essentially *Holocaust denial*, if not plainly *fascist*. The difficulty — if not the absurdity — in self-reflection is often too much for some to bear.

If the victors are reminded of their quite undemocratic and authoritarian behavior at any time, then out come the slurs: one is a

---

91 *Denying the Holocaust: The Growing Assault on Truth and Memory* (Simon & Schuster, 1993).

deplorable *fascist*, a *Holocaust denier*, an *insurrectionist*, an *extremist*, an *anti-Semite*, etc. The liberal-Marxists' litany of libels is limitless, no doubt. All of this is meant to defame (if not destroy) the opposition and deter future dissent.

Utley, whose questioning work stands forever steadfast and undeterred, continues — and it is worth quoting her at length here:

> The Protestant and Catholic chaplains at the Landsberg prison ... were in despair at their inability to do anything to stop the crime of killing [perfunctorily convicted Germans], several of whom had convinced the priests or pastors that they were innocent, and all of whom had been condemned by confessions extorted by torture or on the testimony of witnesses proved to have perjured themselves....
>
> How many of the men America has hung, and is hanging now week by week, were innocent, will never be known. Only one thing is certain: they never had a fair trial and their interrogation, condemnation, and execution are a disgrace to democratic justice....
>
> How many people were killed or died will never be known. Out of a total of twelve to thirteen million people who had committed the crime of belonging to the German race, four or five million are unaccounted for. But no one knows how many are dead and how many are slave laborers. Only one thing is certain: Hitler's barbaric liquidation of the Jews has been outmatched by the liquidation of Germans by the 'democratic, peace-loving' powers of the United Nations....
>
> This was the inevitable consequence of America's destruction of the foundation of democratic justice by decreeing that in Germany innocence, not guilt, had to be proved.[92]

---

92 Utley, *The High Cost of Vengeance*, 188, 189, 202, 213. Utley is not alone in her view of postwar events; see also James Bacque's *Other Losses*, Ralph Keeling's *Gruesome Harvest*, Thomas Goodrich's *Hellstorm: The Death of Nazi Germany 1944–1947*, Benton Bradberry's *The Myth of German Villainy*, among others. John Sack, who is Jewish, reflects on postwar Europe in his *Eye for an Eye*: "the Jews ... killed a great number of Germans: ... German men, women, children, babies, whose 'crime' was just to be Germans." Additionally, the researchers and translators at *Donauschwaben Villages Helping Hands* have done fine work recording Allied atrocities against the Germanic people (www.dvhh.org).

How could such a miscarriage of *actual* justice occur? How could those entities claiming the most "correct" and unquestionable grip on "freedom" and "democracy" behave in such a draconic way? — Because "democratic justice" is — *unequivocally* — liberal-Marxist "justice," which is to say, no justice at all. It is merely the "passion of ambition, the desire to rule other men."[93] Utley, too, assures us:

> [I]t is precisely those who call themselves 'liberals' who pursue the most illiberal line of thought and action. The very same people who would insist at home in America that juvenile delinquency and adult crime are a result either of being underprivileged or of an unhappy childhood and that criminals should be psychoanalyzed and reformed, not starved, reviled, and imprisoned, want to continue punishing the whole German people for their past....
>
> So-called liberals and progressives dominate United States news media, and it is perhaps the gravest symptom of the weakness of democracy that 'liberalism' is today identified with *hatred, vengeance,* the *perpetuation of the schism* in Western civilization, and ... a sneaking fondness for the Communists.[94]

Hatred, vengeance, the *perpetuation of the schism* — what are these if not the *desire to hurt, the passion of ambition, the desire to rule other men*?[95] What are these *desires,* these *passions* if not *alien,* if not born of a long-decomposed desert-god imposing its will on a once homogeneously content European land? What does Utley describe here if not the Lazarus-like urge to obliterate *ancient lands* with hordes of teeming refuse? The *schism* lays between the liberal-Marxists — who, with unrelenting hatred, want to exact the *cleverest revenge* upon *ancient lands* (Europeans) — and the traditionalists, the Heideggerians — who want to keep hold of all the liberal-Marxist prelates want to discredit and

---

93 Schaefer, *A Critique of Rawls,* 109.
94 Utley, *The High Cost of Vengeance,* 251–252; emphasis added.
95 Nietzsche, *The Gay Science* (Vintage, 1974), Book I, §32 and Schaefer, *A Critique of Rawls,* 109, respectively.

discard: impassioned *conservatism*, creative *pluck, hardness* [*Härte*] and *earnestness* [*Schwere*], *aristocratic* values (i.e., anti-Marxism), and *faith in one's folk*.

On one side of this schism stands a future — and therefore a *past*; on the other side of this schism stands *nothing* — only a spate of pride and a dearth of future, a rootless enslavement.

Who is responsible for this rupture of *ancient lands*? Freda Utley, whom we recall is a former Marxist and enduring liberal, noted whom she saw as the culprits:

> It is the American Jews (often of Polish or Russian origin) and the returned exiles who seem determined to avenge the agony of the Jewish people in Hitler's Reich by punishing the whole German people.... [It was] the revengeful attitude of some Military Government officials who were Jews, the fact that Morgenthau gave his name to the policy of genocide underwritten by President Roosevelt, and the abuse by many non-German Jews of their privileged position as DPs [displaced persons] [that has] converted more Germans to anti-Semitism than Hitler's racial laws and propaganda.... [S]ince the defeat of Germany and the Allied occupation more and more Germans formerly free of anti-Semitic prejudice are saying that after all Hitler was right: the Jews are the cause of German misery and the unjust treatment Germans receive at the hands of the victorious democracies.[96]

Hitler referred to an *international* clique; Stalin, in betrayal of the liberal-Marxist West, carried out his *Anti-Cosmopolitan* Campaign; Paul (née Saul) brought his *catholic* message of Judeo-Christianity to *de-Gentile* Gentile lands; Karl Marx implored the *international* proletariat to unite; Emma Lazarus begged the *world* to craft a New Colossus out of the teeming refuse of *foreign shores* at the height of anti-Jewish actions in czarist Russia; Israel Zangwill wrote his *Melting Pot* as an ode to *de-Europeanizing* the United States and branded the moniker on the West forever; Trotsky and his Bolsheviks slaughtered millions of White Russians to exact the most final *revenge*; Peter Singer demands, with *cosmopolitan* panache, that everyone with a pulse — particularly

---

96   Utley, *The High Cost of Vengeance*, 244.

those in non-European lands — be propped up by the charity of the affluent.

In his perhaps most widely read book, *The Life You Can Save* (2009), Singer suggests that most people should dedicate far more than five percent of their annual income to the unknown. But more than this, Singer is a liberal-Marxist who makes his position clear; it should also come as no surprise, then, when we see the incredible donations from the affluent go, *inevitably*, to "progressive" causes.[97] And on it goes, as we shall continue to see.

Utley, because she saw the luster fade from her former dogged adherence to liberal-Marxism, would encourage all to find their own answer to the question, *Who is culpable*. We can be sure she wouldn't wholly discount and discourage all questioning of meaningful matters of *justice*, especially that justice meted out by supposedly democratic powers — not, perhaps, as Deborah Lipstadt and other emotion-conjurers might. Emotion must rule the day in the liberal-Marxist society — because it is through emotion that the Mass Man is shepherded through the mass-ritual farce that is modernity.

It is the liberal-Marxist wont to tolerate to the point of intolerance; this is by now inarguable. Question the *Equality* dogma, question tolerance-for-tolerance's-sake and one is promptly *dehumanized*; one could not even expect to receive the tolerance otherwise "underprivileged" groups receive solely for being *biologically human*. Utley references "criminals [that] should be psychoanalyzed" at the expense of the "privileged," predating even Peter Singer and the counterculture era; not even the Germans were granted such luxury after what, for many soldiers, was nothing short of an heroic struggle. Indeed, criminals are often granted elevated status in liberal-Marxist societies — they take pride of place before actual heroes, since, after all, *their* heroic action is only in service to this or that "systemic" or "institutional" *injustice*; this coincides with the aforementioned affinity for "tolerance," the

---

97 See award lists for The Open Society Foundations, The Bill & Melinda Gates Foundation, Yield Giving, and any other charitable foundation.

Marxian aim to overthrow traditional societies, and the liberalistic goal of revaluating all values. It also accords with the liberal-Marxist tendency to deflect all semblance of *personal responsibility — society* is to blame for criminal behavior, thus *society* pays for the damages and "rehabilitation" (disregarding any evidence of recidivism, of course). Nietzsche warned us:

> Life itself recognizes no solidarity or equality of rights between the healthy and unhealthy parts of an organism. The latter must at all cost be *eliminated*, lest the whole fall to pieces. Compassion for decadents, equal rights for the physiologically botched — this would be the very pinnacle of immorality, it would be setting up Nature's most formidable opponent as morality itself![98]

Modern society is designed to oppose life, or humanity — for the increase of *humanity* (spirit) is not its goal; rather, the increase of *mass* (man) is its goal. *Man* is the test bed of technicization; *dehumanizing* him, *diminishing spirit* (humanity) is of no import. When technological experimentation has run its course, man will cease to exist; the ruling class, too, will then end — though they don't yet see the inescapability of this. They, as do all, fulfill their local destiny in service to the *will-to-machine*. Tolerance to the point of intolerance (e.g., Herbert Marcuse's "repressive tolerance"), *Equality* dogma, elevating "the botched," sacrificing our energy for the sake of that which saps our energy, the denial of personal responsibility — each of these has but one master: a desire that is not our own. We look inwardly to identify the dissonance such alienation incubates, but parasitical abrasions obstruct the view of our *self*, so we ask others to *examine* us, *psychoanalyze* us — and all is well. We find that *we* are not the problem, that the problem lies *out there* — if only we could fix it. Thus, the lack of personal responsibility is only the beginning of a desire to assume responsibility for others, a *desire to rule*.

Psychoanalysis — that *shucking of personal responsibility in the psychological realm* — is itself largely the product of Sigmund Freud, who

---

[98] Nietzsche, *The Will to Power*, §734.

led his own *cosmopolitan* life. And Freud contributed to the liturgy of liberal-Marxist dogma.

12.

Peter Singer has left an indelible mark on the modern West. Every time one hears of some philanthropic trust, foundation, or tycoon doling out millions to this or that cause, one should think of Peter Singer and his oxymoronic philosophy of *mandatory charity*. Never mind that charity insinuates *voluntary* giving: Marxian charity is essentially mandatory voluntarism.

In his book *Marx* (1980), Singer offers a pleasantly simple example of the Marxian society: A community agrees to stop driving their cars to work and start using mass transit to decongest roadways, which is a benefit to all at the expense of relatively minor individual inconvenience.

> They part, rejoicing at the prospect of no more traffic jams. But in the privacy of their own homes, some [think], 'If everyone else is going to take the bus tomorrow, the roads will be empty. So I'll take my car....' From a self-interested point of view this reasoning is correct. As long as most take the bus, a few others can obtain the benefits of the socially-minded behavior of the majority, without giving up anything themselves.[99]

The typical liberal-Marxist response in this situation — as evidenced by every endlessly expanding liberal-democratic government and every murderous Soviet-style regime in history — is to *coerce* compliance. "Should the majority attempt to coerce the minority into taking the bus? That is the easy way out. It can be done in the name of freedom for all; but it may lead to freedom for none."[100] Now, after the exceedingly violent twentieth century, and despite liberal-Marxism's astounding ideological victory, few among the ruling elite are willing to replay such tumult — this is for various economic reasons, as

---

99 Peter Singer, *Marx* (Hill & Wang, 1980), 72.
100 Singer, *Marx*, 72.

human compassion plays no part. To avoid such carnage, then, it becomes necessary to coerce before violence becomes necessary; thus we have mass indoctrination via media (e.g., Hollywood, music, news, and infotainment), academia (e.g., educational systems, sanctioned publications and promoted lecturers), government, finance, and law (e.g., policies incentivizing approved behaviors), etc.

This of course begs the question of whether any kind of coercion results in nominal "freedom for all" but actual "freedom for none" — regardless of whether it occurs before, during, or after violence. After all, coercion is coercion. If the coerced are unaware of their coerced condition — which is the expressed goal of Lippmann and Bernays' liberal-democratic State — that does not make them any less coerced. Rather, it just means, as Augustine remarked, *they are freely in bondage who do with pleasure the will of their master.*[101] Which is less coercive: the war that forces compliance from the disruptive State, or the indoctrination that ensures compliance from the malleable child and subsequent adult? Perhaps, though, it isn't so much a question of *coerciveness* as it is of *inducing* or *incurring damage*. A war of the mind is a war nonetheless, just as damage unknown is damage nonetheless.

Nevertheless, a compliant citizenry is desirable in any State — but perhaps especially so in a liberal-Marxist one. Forced behavior and enforced "freedom" is the essence of the modern West. One hears of the monument to the thousands of noncombatants killed in Dresden being slowly defaced and dismantled at the government's behest. The residents were not consulted; the city council was not consulted. The federal German government — which is not a result of the self-determined will of the German people, but rather a creation of the victorious Allies — simply decided to get rid of it.

What happened in Dresden is worth forgetting, one supposes. Its memory and monument are a tribute to *losers* by now — and this is a travesty in its own right. But it wouldn't be "proper" to call Dresden

---

101 St. Augustine, *Enchiridion on Faith, Hope, and Love* (Regnery, 2002), 37.

and its memory an ill word, so the victors don't; it is much easier, much more convenient to let it be forgotten — *incrementally*. This keeps up appearances and allows for future invocations of "humanity." A *remodeling* here, a *rebuilding* there; there are no "defacements," but only "modernizations." Erich Kästner spent his childhood in Dresden — the Dresden before the bombs. He remembers the city:

> Dresden was a wonderful city. You may take my word for it. And you have to take my word for it, because none of you, however rich your father may be, can go there to see if I am right. For the city of Dresden is no more. It has vanished, except for a few fragments. In one single night and with a single movement of its hand the Second World War wiped it off the map. It had taken centuries to create its incomparable beauty. A few hours sufficed to spirit it off the face of the earth....
>
> To this day the Governments of the great Powers are disputing with each other as to who murdered Dresden... Ah, what is the use of quarrelling about it? You will not bring Dresden back to life by so doing — neither its beauty nor its dead.[102]

Memories and monuments are constantly erased in the societies governed by the liberal-Marxian spirit: "[Communists] openly declare that their ends can be attained only by the forcible overthrow of *all existing social conditions*." When monuments become "problematic," the "choice" is easy: erase them from collective memory. When the memory is erased, so too are the people of the memory.

All is coerced compliance across the West and the wider world. Our individual, local destinies fulfill the will of a liberal-Marxist ruling class; our collective will fulfills the will that no one yet imagines — the *will-to-machine*.

Modernity's coercive urge has its foundation in John Locke, John Stuart Mill, Karl Marx, and Sigmund Freud. Locke popularized the notion of the *tabula rasa*, the blank slate — the idea that man can be molded into any shape because there exist no inborn or immutable

---

102 Kästner, *When I Was a Boy* (Slightly Foxed, 2017), McHugh translation.

characteristics. J. S. Mill continued the Lockean tradition, himself being a product of his father's *tabula rasa* experiment as it manifested in a rigorous childhood educational experience; Mill's intellectual exploits are well known, but his account of his childhood is not; by his own admission, Mill had ingrained into him a quite sanitary "love of mankind," but knew little personal love and compassion. This induced something of a "mental crisis" in his early years, for which he knew confiding in his father was out of the question; oh, but his father made him quite the intellectual sensation — *as if he were made in a laboratory*. Genuine human care was more or less alien to him. Later in life, Mill argued, "The State, while it respects the liberty of each in what specially regards himself, is bound to maintain a vigilant control over his exercise of any power which it allows him to possess over others."[103] This nebulously defined statement has been the theoretical basis of "the State's" liberty-infringing abuses ever since. Civil liberties are eroded and dissent always quashed in the name of "the State" "protecting" citizens or ensuring their "security." Meanwhile, what citizens are consulted over any number of initiatives being imposed "for the welfare of all" in their community? The average citizen — if he pays any attention — must imagine, *somebody somewhere is voting for this, so I guess I should just accept it.* So nothing happens. Though, it seems at least plausible that elected officials could simply claim to be acting on behalf of their "constituency" while actually running roughshod over "the people's will" with legislation benefiting only a select few.

For the root of minority power,[104] we look to Marx, whose fervent desire to coerce is by now notorious, if not zealously accepted. In *Marx*, Singer observed, "The liberal conception of freedom has led to a paradox: we have each chosen in our own interest, but the result is in

---

[103] J. S. Mill, *Autobiography and Essay On Liberty* (Collier & Son, 1909), 314.

[104] While people of European descent are the overwhelming minority on this planet, "minority" here is meant in the non-European sense. The rapid rise of non-European populations is due in large part to liberal-Marxist philanthropic efforts beginning, in earnest, in the twentieth century.

no one's interest. Individual rationality, collective irrationality."[105] Thus we can understand Singer's wish to justify the more Marxian practice of obligatory philanthropy, in opposition to the traditional standard of *giving because one genuinely wishes to help*. The indoctrinated masses — *even if they are wealthy* — dutifully comply: *Annually, how many billions of dollars worldwide flow from European lands and hands to so-called underserved peoples?* And yet the needle doesn't move: For decades, centuries even, we find the same problems in the same lands among the same peoples. Patterns exist among flourishing people as well: happiness and civic honesty are consistently highest among European peoples and their progeny.[106] The liberal-Marxist *absolutely believes*, despite contrary evidence, that everyone is equal, like a blank slate to be etched upon and human clay to be molded, and that genetics are only selectively applicable (when it works against those *ancient lands*); ultimately, the devout liberal-Marxist will argue to exhaustion that the above-cited metrics are the result of economic factors and have nothing at all to do with lineage — this, despite honesty being a necessary antecedent to economic development.[107] The Marxist is undeterred: Marxian philosophy is not scientific; it is *dogmatic faith*. Singer admits as much: "Marx's own theory is not scientific… [But] Marx shattered the assumption that our intellectual and spiritual lives are entirely independent of our economic existence."[108]

Singer thus perpetuates the modern lie that Marxism was some kind of radical *innovation*; while it is indeed radical, however, Marxism is only a continuation of the revaluative creed it claims to abhor as an "opiate." Marxism puts a modern veneer on an old scheme: tell "the people" their dogmatic enslavement is a new, liberating *freedom*.

---

105 Singer, *Marx*, 70.

106 See *World Happiness Report 2024* and "Civic honesty around the globe" (Cohn, Maréchal, Tannenbaum, and Zünd; 2019), *Science*, vol. 365:6448.

107 "Civic honesty is essential to social capital and economic development but is often in conflict with material self-interest." From "Civic honesty," cited above.

108 Singer, *Marx*, 73.

Judeo-Christianity had to be replaced because it was no longer revolutionary enough; after all, it let the ancient lands hold on to God and spirit. After the emancipation of equality in the Enlightenment, when man was everywhere breaking free of his chains, it became apparent that humanity was ready to move beyond God. Thus, *incrementally*, Christian humanism inspired secular humanism, which birthed the most supreme godlessness: Marxism.

Expectedly, *economics* underpins dialectical-materialist dogma. At this point, the Marxian cannot but argue for the overthrow of all values — not to mention society and government — because it is simply part of his creed. *Facts and consequences be damned: bring the system down* — so says the liberal-Marxist.

The foundation of this phenomenon, this *Equality* dogma, is the notion of human nature's seemingly infinite malleability:

> Marx's theory that human nature is not forever fixed, but alters in accordance with the economic and social conditions of each period, holds out the prospect of transforming society by changing the economic basis of such human traits as greed, egoism, and ambition.... [With this theory], Marx shattered the assumption that our intellectual and spiritual lives are entirely independent of our economic existence.[109]

And just as we can understand Singer's belief in mandatory charity — which, incidentally, utterly *dehumanizes* the act — we can also understand why Marxism begins and ends with an enforced *freedom for all* that amounts to a miserable *freedom for none*.

The Marxist must *transform* society: he must impose a *freedom for all* that necessarily dehumanizes even the most human of interactions. Charity is no longer given freely, but a mandate for which noncompliance is punishable. Perceived social hygiene, too, is mandated and penalized if not adhered to. Social-welfare programs go beyond helping those who have contributed to society to being a system exploited by those seeking handouts. Speech no longer conforms to biological

---

109 Singer, *Marx*, 73.

reality, but must be manipulated into nonsensicality. Education must be spread thin to accommodate the weakest student—because, of course, all children are blank slates who learn equally well, to be sure. Collectively, these few examples are already enforced—via taxes, foreign aid, social and political incentives, and legislation that was supposedly agreed upon.

"In place of the old bourgeois society, with its classes and class antagonisms," Marx gaily predicted, "we shall have an association, in which the free development of each is the condition for the free development of all."[110] This is liberal-Marxism defined—save that class antagonisms will never abate: Class distinctions and hierarchies are fundamental to life itself, despite Marxian fantasies. Singer cites "studies" that demonstrate "pecking orders" among various animal societies.[111] That he and other Marxists need such studies to conclude what anyone paying even the slightest attention to Nature can plainly see speaks only to our present state of mechanization. Just imagine: *We require studies to show us what Nature clearly demonstrates.* Do we need scientific studies to tell us the sun rises in the east, or that hierarchies exist in Nature, or that race exists, or that inequality is inherent to Nature? We indeed now experience a high form of mechanization! Perhaps forcing equal outcomes is *not* a means of success; perhaps it *goes against* the very Nature we evidently need studies to comprehend.

Marx's "free development of each" is itself a mandate; in the hands of liberal-Marxists, it becomes an obligation. Funds, trusts, and tycoons sublimate Singer's "if it has a pulse, it's deserving" philosophy because its cosmopolitan panache is too much to forgo. Such obligatory "charity" becomes the means to mollify guilt, secure influence, and usher in Marx's "free development of all"; the former two means placate selfish-interest, the latter Marxian mandate satisfies both the liberal-Marxist "desire to rule" via an imposing moralism and the need to belong to a

---

110 Marx, *The Communist Manifesto* (Swenson & Kemp, 2013), 34.
111 Singer, *Marx*, 75.

higher cause through a transcendent faith. Though, liberal-Marxism is a faith never fully realized: the object of its faith — man — undermines itself. Liberal-Marxism is faith in an error: It is the belief that equal opportunity will inevitably *become* equal outcome — and when this belief fails to materialize, it is subsequently the belief that outcomes must be enforced at the expense of a natural hierarchy. In this way, freedom for all becomes freedom for none: the subversion of the natural process is the dehumanization of man, and a man dehumanized is enslaved. But this is precisely the point of liberal-Marxism.

13.

Marxian ideology is far more than an economic doctrine. Paradoxically, by suggesting that economics sits at the core of "our intellectual and spiritual lives" it becomes a faith, albeit a materialistic one. Material can be molded, transformed. Man morphs from *thing with a spiritual and intellectual being* to mere *data point participating in a planned economy*. The presumptuous grounding of life on material — the *metaless physical* — devalues the life Marxian ideology pretends to uplift. There can be no "social" aspect to liberal-Marxist socialism because a *natural* social order embodies *hierarchy* — as recognized even by the "studies" alluded to in Singer's *Marx*. And there can be no hierarchy without a *common affinity*; traditional affinities centered around the shared history, values, and vision *kinship* naturally possesses. However, tradition and hierarchy — those *old orders* in *ancient lands*, the *ancien régimes* — are the very things Marxian ideology (falsely) claims to quell. (Only in *utopian* fantasies does "dictatorship of the proletariat" or "we the people" mean the absence of hierarchy.) Thus, with *naturalness* extirpated from society, liberal-Marxist *socialism* is mere *-ism*, a blank faith in the man of error, a dogma of the devalued and dehumanized: Man is elevated to his dictatorship of *We the People*, molded and guided by the ruling elite — to save the former from his "nonage" and sustain power for the latter. We note that *enslave* cannot be spelled without *save*.

In light of the foregoing, Singer's assessment that Marx did not inspire or anticipate the murderous regimes attached to his name seems preposterous: "it is absurd to blame Marx for something he did not foresee and certainly would have condemned if he had foreseen it..."[112] The suggestion that Marx wouldn't have enthusiastically welcomed the many murders in his name is laughable: it is one Marxist covering for the other.[113] The *Communist Manifesto* is one of the most hateful screeds ever penned: it is about the forceful overthrow of a despised system and the subsequent imposed freedom of a new dictatorship. Are we to suppose this new dictatorship would simply pat those overthrown on the back, wish them luck in their future endeavors, and let them go on their way? Or, perhaps more likely, would the new dictatorship mirror the murdering Bolsheviks, the Khmer Rouge, the Cultural Revolution, or one of the many Red Terrors to devastate unwilling "volunteers" to the Marxian cause? Marx is certainly behind and would have been *at least* a little satisfied at the bloodshed his *Manifesto* spawned — just as Rousseau is equally an inspiration for and augur of the French Revolution and subsequent Reign of Terror. The Marxian ideology wants blood, and it will not stop until it's had. Today's *obligatory equity* is tomorrow's *mass killing* — such is the way of liberal-Marxism; this is not slippery slope, this is track record.

The source of such hatred is — *exhaustion*. Liberal-Marxist revolutionaries are *tired* of taking personal responsibility for their actions — or their genetics. It is easier for "the bungled and the botched" and their "bleeding heart" empathizers to revolt against natural hierarchies than it is for them to bear personal responsibility for their lot in life. *Why climb when one can simply tear down?* — so reasons the liberal-Marxist revolutionary. Personal responsibility means self-reflection and self-improvement; it means acknowledging one's shortfalls and working to

---

112 Singer, *Marx*, 75.

113 Marx famously quipped, "All I know is that I am not a Marxist." The context was *economic*: he disagreed with some of the dominant economic interpretations of his work. He remained a sociocultural Marxist.

overcome them. Perpetual "revolution" pervades liberal-Marxism: this explains the constant agitation within liberal-Marxist systems. After all, one might wonder why liberal-Marxist revolutionaries would rail against a liberal-Marxist system. The revolution is gradual; and with each generation, the revolution becomes both more entrenched and more complete. This is why sociopolitical polarization increases as time passes: the masses reject personal responsibility, the ruling class tightens tyrannical measures, and humanity subsides beneath a tide of technicized convenience. Kerry Bolton masterfully explores the seeming convergence of elite- and grassroots-driven revolutionary activity in his *Revolution from Above* (2011). Ultimately, however, destabilizing activity is driven from *above* — i.e., from the ruling, if not shadowy, elite.

Whether we consider the West's burgeoning victim-culture, its citizens' increased sense of entitlement and dependence on the state, or fomented civil strife, instability is fostered and, indeed, capitalized on to strengthen government and restrictive policies at the expense of authentic human freedom. This, in turn, brings technology increasingly to the forefront: To manage, "secure," and "stabilize" an expanding citizenry, incredible technology is needed to monitor and "safeguard" the population; not only this, but the ever-growing docile parts of the body politic rely on technology both for convenience and as distraction from sociopolitical chaos and the drudgery of daily life, both of which are societal *inflictions* — i.e., society causes the problems it claims to alleviate. Humanity is thus seduced into accepting the joy and security further technicization brings. Thus, our fulfillment of *local destiny* — as both docile and discontented peddlers of liberal-Marxism — precipitates our ultimate fate of *yielding to Machine*.

In *Statism and Anarchy* (1873), Bakunin remarked:

> In a republic of fictitious *people*, the 'legal nation' supposedly represented by the state, smothers the real, live people. But it will scarcely be any easier

on the people if the cudgel with which they are beaten is called *the people's cudgel*.[114]

The State is indeed modernity's affliction, but it is necessary to induce the post-human world. The State is a gestational period between what was and what will be; when *what will be* arrives, the State, like what it gestates, will end. The "people's cudgel" hammers its object — not into Machine, but memory. Machine is the will forcing the hand holding the cudgel. The result is not *transhumanism*, but *posthumanism*, which can only arise from the "republic of *fictitious people*." Bakunin continues:

> What does it mean, 'the proletariat raised to a governing class?' Will the entire proletariat head the government? ... The entire nation will rule, but no one will be ruled. Then there will be no government, there will be no state; but if there is a state, there will also be those who are ruled, there will be slaves.
>
> In the Marxists' theory this dilemma is resolved in a simple fashion. By 'popular government' they mean government of the people by a small number of representatives elected by the people. So-called popular representatives and rulers of the state elected by the entire nation on the basis of universal suffrage — *the last word of the Marxists, as well as of the democratic school — is a lie behind which the despotism of a ruling minority is concealed*, a lie all the more dangerous in that it represents itself as the expression of a sham popular will.[115]

How can the liberal-Marxist urge be anything other than an *avid desire to rule*? Fictitious people are manufactured through generations of State-sanctioned propaganda; they engender a "sham popular will" that reflects — not their own will — but the will of the State. A new aristocracy forms out of those who govern the "people," the "proletariat"; these are the Vanguard-prelates who ceaselessly spout the abstractions

---

114 Mikhail Bakunin, *Statism and Anarchy* (Cambridge University, 2005), Shatz translation, 23.

115 Bakunin, *Statism and Anarchy*, 178; emphasis added.

of a sham. It is important to note that "they"—the prelates—are not to blame for their inhuman behavior; "they" would not exist if it weren't for the *fictitious people*, the *herd*, the *Mass Man*—the "people" who forfeit their thought and will for convenience and distraction. Humanity *collectively* cultivated the present world-situation through anathematizing personal responsibility; this is our local destiny; our past, present, and future (or lack thereof) are plainly visible to anyone willing to observe. But few are willing; and the willing exist only to enliven and embolden the unwilling—in service to a transcendent fate, so that Machine will arrive.

14.

Peter Singer's grandfather was David Oppenheim (d. 1943), of whom he writes in *Pushing Time Away* (2003): "My grandfather [impressed upon his friends] the Jewish way of looking at the world [wherein 'there was a great difference between the responsibility many Jews felt for their fellow human beings and the irresponsibility that exists among a lot of young non-Jewish people']." We surmise that this "Jewish way of looking at the world" is necessarily distinct from other, non-Jewish ways of looking at the world—otherwise it would not be called "Jewish" or recognized by Oppenheim and Singer. This distinction, for good or ill, has undoubtedly contributed to widespread and enduring perceptions of Jewish people, and it rests fundamentally on the desire to intervene in others' affairs for what many Jews perceive as the *collective good* or, as Rousseau popularized, the *general will*. What is seen as the "irresponsibility" of non-Jewish people is only a different approach to life dictated by cultural and genetic variances. Such divergent approaches are unconscionable to the would-be interveners, so plans are devised to govern *all* according to a more righteous standard. "Proper governance," which can in part be defined as sociopolitical *uniformity* stemming from the interveners' group ethic, is thus the result of a sincere desire to aid and correct "irresponsible" behavior.

It is important to note that when one's natural development is interfered with — even for the sake of a just cause, e.g., making one more "responsible" in perceived dealings with others — then the one interfered with loses some autonomy and becomes beholden to the intervener. While this benefits the intervener, it hinders the one interfered with — at least regarding the "responsibility" the intervener means to inculcate. On a mass scale, instances of "interventions" to induce "responsibility" are the Freemasonic movements and the Western revolutions they sparked. *Revolutions* are *interventions* meant to address grievances and correct perceived injustices. Western revolutions — be they liberal-democratic or Marxist — were specifically meant to overthrow the perceived *ancien régimes*. Interference to correct shortfalls in perceived "irresponsibility" is nothing short of revolutionary, as demonstrated by history. Singer's grandfather, David Oppenheim, sought to influence his friends to adopt the "Jewish way of looking at the world," which necessitated seeing the (negative) distinction between Jews and non-Jews. Naturally, Jews are more responsible than — i.e., *superior to* — non-Jews, so it becomes an additional responsibility for the Jewish people to intervene in sociopolitical affairs, as this is the only way to *correct* non-Jewish behavior (i.e., irresponsibility).

Knowing this, it becomes clearer why Oppenheim's good friend, Albert Massiczek, would write *The Humane Man: the Jewish Humanism of Karl Marx* (1968), in which he argues for "the unconscious influence of a humane Jewish outlook" in Marx.[116] Singer describes this outlook, which presumably epitomizes "responsibility":

> 1. Liberal democracies are more firmly established in Europe and across the globe today than they have ever been.
>
> 2. Racism was emphatically rejected by the Universal Declaration of Human Rights.
>
> 3. Justice has been done to many of the Nazi leaders.

---

116 Singer, *Pushing Time Away*, 198.

4. The International Criminal Court was established to prosecute those guilty of genocide or crimes against humanity.

5. A global community is beginning to make it possible to think in terms of universal human values and a cosmopolitan world.[117]

These five happily received realities describe and arise from the aforementioned outlook; we can summarize them as follows: (1) liberalism; (2) anti-discrimination (or perceived discrimination) and a respect for the United Nations; (3) elimination of "Nazis" and dissenters, generally; (4) establishment of an "international" court to legalize and legitimize the prevailing polarity; (5) globalism. A cursory look at each follows.

(1) Liberal-democracies are indeed entrenched across the West and wider world since 1945; however, their sheen is fading: the fortuitous misperception of the convergence of victory and success with liberal-democratism — as though one predicated the other — is yielding to the reality of immense wealth gaps and the environmental degradation concomitant with exploitative capitalism. (2) Discrimination based on race was certainly rejected by the Universal Declaration of Human Rights; the UNDHR is a treasure of modern humanism; its draft was written by Nobel laureate René Samuel Cassin, who would have likely agreed with Singer, Oppenheim, and Massiczek on several points. (3) Many have said a great deal on the "justice" done to the "Nazis," which can only be described as the clearest example of *vengeance* the world has ever seen — Freda Utley, cited above, being just one of them; others, because they dissent from the *unassailable* view of liberal-Marxist "justice" by attempting to *humanize* the *dehumanized* or *dehumanize* the *dehumanizers* are simply ostracized or *un-personed* through the quite liberal-Marxist method of *extrajudicial punishment*. William Hart, Supreme Court Justice of Ohio, wrote in his preface to *Dönitz at Nuremberg* (1983): "there was no legal justification for the trial, conviction or sentence of the so-called 'war criminals' by the Nuremberg

---

117 Singer, *Pushing Time Away*, 243–244.

Tribunal. We have set a bad precedent. It should not be followed in the future."[118] Singer is undeterred in his liberal-Marxism. (4) Next, the International Criminal Court is lauded. Danilo Zolo, in *Victors' Justice* (2009), writes,

> From the end of the Cold War to the present, the Western powers have not only made arbitrary use of military force, but have explicitly contested the international legal order in the name of their own unconditioned *jus ad bellum*. And this starkly negative record has to be seen as including also international criminal jurisdiction, the institutional innovation of the twentieth century. In the context of an ever-increasing concentration of international power, which is leading to something all too like an imperial world constitution, an international criminal court cannot but be a partisan instrument in the hands of the major powers. It is bound to exercise 'victors' justice.'[119]

Just as his ancestors would be, Singer is euphoric about this development of a *partisan, imperial world constitution*—because his ilk of interveners created it and continues to propagate it. Of course, commending the system that keeps you on top and demonizing dissenters is the essence of "victors' justice"; and it explains both why Singer applauds most significant aspects of the current world order, and why Singer is upheld as a preeminent philosopher. Are we to suppose his preeminence springs from his unique "morality"—as an advocate of the "Jewish way of looking at the world"—or does it come from his ability to deftly articulate the system's vision? (5) Those best at legitimizing a system help it prevail, and they will in turn enjoy the fruits of that system. Symbiosis among scoundrels will wreck the world. *Of course* Singer praises the prospect of a *global, cosmopolitan* world—a world under liberal-Marxist "voluntarism" and "self-determination"; it suits his ideological interest and reflects his ancestral mission. Ostensibly a biography of his grandfather, Singer's *Pushing Time Away*

---

118 *Dönitz at Nuremberg* (IHR, 1983), edited by Thompson and Strutz, xx.
119 Danilo Zolo, *Victors' Justice* (Verso, 2009), Weir translation, 63–64.

is nevertheless imbued with his philosophy — its purpose: *a last laugh for the interveners*. *Revenge* is complete for Oppenheim, of this one can be certain; such a unique worldview was and is industrious: it will not stop until everything is under the thumb of "responsibility."

Alfred Adler was another of Oppenheim's friends and intellectual peers. Adler, whose influence on modern psychology cannot be overstated, was a Marxist at heart, marrying Raissa Epstein, "a rich Russian girl" who "was a particularly liberated, domineering woman" and a "militant socialist…. Marxism remained an influence in Adler's life and it influenced his theory of personality."[120] Adler had a "deep concern for common people" — he genuinely wanted to *help* them, to *correct* them, which can only be done through *intervention*. Notably, Adler's daughter Valentine continued the family's Marxist tradition, becoming a martyr for Trotskyism — she was arrested in Moscow in 1937 and died in a Stalinist gulag in 1942. Adler's granddaughter, Margot Adler, was a prominent voice on National Public Radio's[121] *All Things Considered* and *Morning Edition*.

One of Alder's colleagues and another of Oppenheim's friends was none other than Sigmund Freud. Freud, of course, is quite well known for his own version of godless faith, psychoanalysis; some have described it as *subversive* to more traditional interpretations of the world, which would parallel the liberal-Marxist urge to overthrow *ancient lands*.

Richard LaPiere, a Stanford researcher of whom almost no one has ever heard, wrote a telling book — *The Freudian Ethic: An Analysis of the Subversion of American Character* (1959) — that would have served as a warning if anyone had bothered to read it. Of course, because of its

---

120 B. R. Hergenhan, *An Introduction to Theories of Personality* (Prentice Hall, 2003), 100.

121 National Public Radio, or NPR, is a broadcasting network funded by the American public and government, corporate sponsors, foundations, and academic institutions. Similar entities would be the British Broadcasting Corporation, Deutsche Welle, and RT.

divergence from the prevailing liberal-Marxist system, LaPiere's book was not heavily promoted, so in its time remained rather obscure. In it, he highlights the mystical foundation of Freudianism, which is expectedly similar to the foundation for Peter Singer's own *revaluative* philosophy:

> Freud is not so original ... when he infers from his psychic system that *nothing a man does is what it seems to be.* This cabalistic principle ... is a very old one. All, or nearly all, primitive systems of magic and witchcraft have operated upon the assumption that *the evident is never the real* and that only those — the magic men — who know the secret art of reading signs (or omens) can peer behind the obvious to ascertain the truth.[122]

The primitive preying of a godless faith on naïve believers is a swindle befitting any humanist or Marxist; but it is even more ancient than this: It is the desire of one to rule another. The keeper of the secret is the king of society. When the kings of society intervene for the masses' moral edification, for their improved "responsibility," *what then* — what is the secret? *The secret is the science of man*, who stands as an instrument of power; this power is not native to man, but *inculcated* — interposed by the keeper of the secret in the form of dependence on cabalistic intrigues. The obfuscation of placating individual "needs" is the Bernaysian ploy of inception: create a market by instilling desire. Liberal-Marxism — the system that *has used* (and not *been used by*) all those who espouse it — elevates the individual so as to make the individual imagine that the system is his own idea; in reality, enshrining the individual is the surest way to enslave him — the individual becomes a slave to her own neuroticisms. Exaltation of the individual is the analgesic masking the irredeemable ill of the revaluation of values. Liberal-Marxist interveners and espousers fulfill the aims of the system by instilling a dependence on the system to make tolerable the end of both the individual and humanity. Forfeiting personal responsibility is forfeiting autonomy; accepting dependence is accepting extinction.

---

122 LaPiere, *The Freudian Ethic* (Van Rees, 1959), 39; emphasis added.

Despite its cabalistic intrigues, Freudianism, as a sub-function of liberal-Marxism, is "the antithesis of a religion." LaPiere continues, and it is worth quoting him at length here:

> Every true religion serves two major and interrelated social functions. It exercises control over the conduct of the individual members of the society, and it provides the individual with assurance that life ... is worth living. Freudianism does neither. It is a doctrine of social irresponsibility and personal despair.
>
> Freud's concern, both as a therapist and as a theorist, was with the individual. His data ... were dredged up from the hypothesized unconscious of his neurotic patients; moreover, he delved into this unconscious with a preconceived notion of what he would find there. Both what he looked for and what he found were inevitably biased in favor of the individual and against society. The patients saw themselves as *victims* of society; they were poor, misunderstood, mistreated creatures in search of someone who could comprehend their troubles and sympathize with them. Such are the common characteristics of neurotics. They are people who have failed, to a significant degree, to make their peace with society; and they believe that society has failed them. *Never, in the mind of the neurotic, has he failed society.*
>
> What Freud secured from his patients might justly have been used to demonstrate how the neurotic individual regards himself and his relation to society. Freud used it, however, as evidence in favor of his humanistic but completely unrealistic idea that the individual is inevitably and inescapably repressed by the inhuman dictates of organized social life. Freud, like his patients, believed that they were victims of social circumstances; and, like them, he was in all respects antagonistic toward society....
>
> Unlike Marx, who also hated society ... Freud did not counsel general revolt from social restraints. Nevertheless, he implied the wisdom and justice of individual evasion of those restraints by designating ... social repression as the cause of the difficulties experienced by his patients. And if he did not directly advise the patient to evade the authority of the feared and hated parent or desert the intolerable wife, his doctrine certainly does nothing

to foster submission to the requirements of society and everything to cast society into disrepute.[123]

Freud is a tool of the system he champions. Superficially, he advocates for the individual in opposition to society; fundamentally, he fulfills the urge of a dehumanized humanity to erase itself. There is no better way to unravel a society — and the humanity participating in it — than to undercut and demolish the values foundational to it. We read more from LaPiere:

> Never has a doctrine of man that is so morbid, so discouraging, so without hope or confidence, and so lacking in inspiration been so widely acclaimed. Thus the puzzle is not so much how Freud came to devise his pessimistic metapsychological system as *why that system should have gained such wide popular acceptance*. The roles played in this by his disciples and by the halo prestige of medicine ... are hardly sufficient to explain why a doctrine of despair has become a major, if not yet the major, philosophy of our times. Some of Freud's critics have thought that the popularity of Freudianism stems from its preoccupation with sex; and it has been remarked that, although Freud did not discover the causative basis for human action, he did succeed in deifying the lowest common denominator.[124]

Man propagates for individual destiny to fulfill transcendent purpose. Freud's "deifying the lowest common denominator" and his popularity because of it speaks only to the underlying truth of our present situation: Our life gives life to Machine. *Why do we forfeit autonomy? Why personal responsibility? Why acclaim the philosophy of despair?* LaPiere is right to wonder. But the puzzle dissipates when we understand our role as *preparers of the way*; when the way is prepared, we must be willing, unswervingly, to pass into extinction. This is why we give up freedom and personal responsibility, make light of it, and welcome our abysmal despair.

---

123 LaPiere, *The Freudian Ethic*, 53–54; emphasis added.
124 LaPiere, *The Freudian Ethic*, 54–55; emphasis added.

It is interesting — and perhaps increasingly familiar — that in Soviet society a man "must not ... be in any way individually enterprising; and should he display signs of individual deviation, he will be promptly damned as a traitor to the system."[125] Is this different than any society existing today? And when the preponderance of societies marches under various liberal-Marxist flags — what then? Ants, too, attack their own when, for instance, one becomes "contaminated" with a "foreign" substance. Foreign thought and action must be removed, after all, to "protect" the integrity of the body. It is the *system* that works toward a definite end; the individual is but a tool: this is what happens when humanity is forfeited, when it forfeits itself.

And what of Freud the therapist, the theorist, the *individual*?

> Freud's major error lay in assuming that the people who came to him for treatment were representative of mankind in general. For the very fact that his patients came to him for 'mental' treatment is ipso facto evidence that they were not... The atypical character of the people from whom Freud derived his doctrine of man would seem to explain his conviction that men are inherently unstable; and one must assume that his preoccupation with sex, a fixation that is close to monomaniacal, was a function either of his own personality or of those of the patients who came under his observation.... Most of Freud's patients were not only neurotic but also neurotic middle- and upper-middle-class Viennese Jews. They were not, therefore, even a representative sample of neurotics.[126]

Perhaps LaPiere, and not Freud, is mistaken here. If the dominant, if not superior, worldview is — as Massiczek, Singer, and others have stated — a "Jewish humanism," a "Jewish way of looking at the world," then it stands to reason that Freud's clientele *was*, in fact, representative of "mankind in general" — *especially* if they were "neurotic Jews." Freud spoke the language of the system he legitimized, as do all

---

125 LaPiere, *The Freudian Ethic*, 58.
126 LaPiere, *The Freudian Ethic*, 61.

intelligent advocates. That we fulfill an ethic of despair is an argument in favor of the approaching Machine.

Liberal-Marxism has already won. There is no argument made here to convince or summon dissent. Only facts and opinions are offered here to demonstrate the victory of the system that will end humanity. *Cosmopolitan, imperial* intervention exists always for profit, be it monetary or moral. It is the duty of the system to *shape* and *correct*; it is the duty of the interveners to further the system, and it is the duty of the masses to fold under the weight of its legitimization.

∞•∞

"In fascism," Singer tells us, "my grandfather saw the victory of force and brutality over reason, education, and learning, and the triumph of those who preferred to burn books rather than refute the arguments in them."[127] *This* is *the* liberal-Marxist trope. All history, apparently, has led to its continued repetition: it is told and retold to instill the *correct* view of history and the shared vision of the future. In the end, the good gang beats the nasties and can do no wrong—it's a story made in Hollywood, to be sure.[128] And it's a story those in power never tire of telling.

Book burning: an appropriation of a fabrication—a trope within a trope. Heinrich Heine wrote in *Almansor* (1823): *Dort wo man Bücher verbrennt, verbrennt man auch am Ende Menschen — Where you burn books, you also end up burning people.* Heine was related to Karl Marx by blood and ideology; they had an intellectual friendship both in life

---

127 Singer, *Pushing Time Away*, 243.
128 See the following: *Hollywoodism: Jews, Movies, and the American Dream* (Jacobovici, 1998); "Who Runs Hollywood?" (Stein, *Los Angeles Times*, 2008); *An Empire of Their Own: How the Jews Invented Hollywood* (Gabler, 1989); *The View from Sunset Boulevard: America as Brought to You by the People Who Make Television* (Stein, 1979); "There Are Lots of Jews in Hollywood. Let a Rabbi Explain Why" (Michaelson, *Rolling Stone*, 2022); "Why are so many Jews working in Hollywood" (Rakhamilova, *Jerusalem Post*, 2022).

and after it. Their kinship carries on in the minds and mouths of modern liberal-Marxists: *Book burners burn people!* — they shout it from the rooftops, from televisions, computers, lecterns and radios.

Herbert Marcuse, a Marxist whose ideas fortify present and future, wrote in "Repressive Tolerance" (1965): "Suppression of the regressive ones is a prerequisite for the strengthening of the progressive ones."[129] But the liberal-Marxists are not so dense as to overtly burn books; they simply "burn" one's spirit, they overwrite the mind: *education, propagation, indoctrination, ostracization, cancelation* — such are the subtler tools of the suppressive. Who is "regressive"? *Anyone who disagrees with the liberal-Marxists!* Marcuse and his ilk become *more bold* — calling for the active suppression of dissenters — because they became *more powerful* in the postwar world. 1945 was not the end of a war; it was the beginning of the liberal-Marxist tyranny that will finally end culture and creator.

Heine, Marxist though he was, still felt the tug of Europe within him:

> This confession that the future belongs to the Communists was made in a tone of care and deepest anxiety... In very truth it is only with dread and horror that I think of the time when these gloomy iconoclasts will attain power; when their heavy hands will break without pity all the marble statues of beauty which are so dear to my heart. They ... will fell my groves of laurel and plant potatoes in their place, and the lilies of the field ... will be rooted up from the soil of society...; the roses ... must suffer the same fate...
>
> Yes, I foresee all this, and nameless grief comes over me when I think of the destruction with which the victorious common multitude (*Proletariat*) threatens my verses, which will sink into the grave with the whole ancient romantic world.[130]

---

129 *A Critique of Pure Tolerance* (Beacon, 1969), 106.
130 *The Works of Heinrich Heine* (US Book Co., 1893), *Lutetia*, "Preface to the French Version," 10–11.

But what Heine felt was only the suggestion of something noble — there was nothing substantive in Heine's *deepest anxiety*, *dread*, and *horror*; for, after all, Heine was kin to *Marx*, not *Europa*:

> Yet, despite [my feelings], I publicly confess that this Communism, which is so inimical to all my interests and inclinations, exerts a magic influence on my soul from which I cannot defend myself. Two voices in its favor move my heart — two voices which will not be silenced, and which in their depths may be diabolical; but however that may be, they govern me, and no power of exorcism can bid them hence away.[131]

Heine is utterly hexed, as are all who fall under the Marxian spell. By his own admission he is possessed by the *diabolic* — the Devil. Heine spoke the *language of the conversion* he made to Lutheranism to mask his modern godlessness. His devil is the ineffable hate in his veins that finds expression in cousin Karl's ideological brutality. Liberal-Marxist brutality rests in proportional harmony to the boldness concomitant with power: as one rises, so does the other. Today, when not dissimulating, liberal-Marxists ostracize and dismantle; there is no need to physically burn books when one holds the levers of power; tomorrow, they burn bodies. Heine's prophecy came true because it was the voice of his own heart; he knew the terrible hate and dread pent within the Marxian core intimately.

James Watson (geneticist, b. 1928), Ronald Fisher (geneticist, statistician, d. 1962), Henry Garrett (psychologist, d. 1973), and others — one would imagine their dedication to science might place them in the good graces of modernity. But they made a critical mistake: They used science to controvert the prevailing sociopolitical narrative. For their misstep each was deemed an agitator and condemned to the full force of extrajudicial punishment. *Who are they but little Dresdens of thought obliterated by the heavy hand of Marxian hate?* This hate masquerades as the cosmopolitan care described by Marx, Oppenheim, Singer, and, as we read here, Heine:

---

131 Heine, *Lutetia*, "Preface to the French Version," 11.

> [Communists] acknowledge the most absolute cosmopolitanism, a worldwide love for all races, an equality of worldly goods and fraternity among all mankind, who are the free citizens of this earth. This fundamental dogma is the same which was taught in the New Testament, so that in spirit and in truth the Communists are far more Christian than our so-called ... patriots [and nationalists].[132]

Insincere is the liberal-Marxist love for mankind. Behind words of love are mass killings and perpetual warfare (revolution) — *Crusades of Justice*. His cosmopolitan love is only a profound hatred of the *other*, the dissenter. Those who stand in the way of Marcusian "progress" must be "suppressed" — the liberal-Marxist can be as inventive as he likes to achieve this end. Because he dominates societal institutions, he can mold public perception. Science, for instance, formerly a *heuristic method* to understand the world, has itself become an *unquestionable tenet*, akin to the "fundamental dogma" Heine mentions. The media parades an endless array of supposed "experts" with credentials that may or may not be compromised by the revolving door between the corporate and governmental spheres. But the local destinies of "experts" are in harmony with the media and the rest of the conformists, and all serve the *will-to-machine* that demands mass complicity. *Universal love, science-as-ideology* — the instruments of mass conformism cannot be questioned.

The convergence of the "fundamental dogmas" — *mass equality*, its derivative *universal love*, and *science* (as legitimizer of the other two) — might seem dissonant, but it becomes intelligible when we realize that each of the dogmas is an uncritical necessity on the road to Machine. Moreover, modern science (as *ideology*) becomes intelligible when we realize its purpose is to authoritatively silence dissent; it is a branch of social control not unlike armed enforcement — science polices the mental realm while armed enforcement polices the physical.

---

132 Heine, *Lutetia*, "Preface to the French Version," 13–14.

Revilo Oliver describes the modern curtailment of science (as *method*) and the reaction of questioned dogmatists:

> The dependence of the 'Liberal' cults on a blind and irrational faith was long obscured or concealed by their professed esteem for objective science...
>
> The hypocrisy of the professed devotion to scientific knowledge was made unmistakable when the 'Liberals' began their frantic and often hysterical efforts to suppress scientific knowledge about genetics... At present, the 'Liberals' are limited to shrieking and spitting when they are confronted with inconvenient facts, but no one who has heard them in action can have failed to notice how exasperated they are by the limitations that have thus far prevented them from burning wicked biologists and other rational men at the stake.[133]

Watson, Fisher, Garrett, Oliver himself, and many others do not have to be literally burned at the stake — at least not yet, not until that way is unbarred. Now it is sufficient to simply marginalize dissenters into oblivion, to bury their *science-as-method* under slanderous *science-as-ideology*, to deter anyone else from looking in their *dangerous* direction. Extrajudicial punishment is *de rigueur* in liberal-Marxist societies. Aleksandr Solzhenitsyn, himself a victim of liberal-Marxist avidity, provides us the Soviet perception of justice:

> The very concept of guilt had been repealed by the proletarian revolution... [T]he heart of the matter is not personal guilt, but *social danger*. One can imprison an innocent person if he is *socially hostile*. And one can release a guilty man if he is *socially friendly*.[134]

The sociopolitical aspect of action is by now familiar. "Hate speech" laws are on the rise, and with them, "compelled speech"; "sensitivity training" is quite common; an entire industry has grown up out of the "diversity, equity, and inclusion" training required for nearly all

---

133 Oliver, *America's Decline*, 78–79.
134 Aleksandr Solzhenitsyn, *The Gulag Archipelago* (Harper & Row, 1974), Whitney translation, 282.

societal participation — all of this is to ensure one acts not necessarily morally or naturally but in socially and politically *correct* ways. In fact, all of this ideological imposition on action is meant to *overwrite* Nature, for this is precisely how the conditions are set for the advent of Machine. Nature stands in the way of Machine; the former is a necessary hurdle for the latter. *Conformism* and *correctness* are integral to liberal-Marxian societies because these are prerequisites for the demise of humanity and the rise of its replacement.

Meanwhile, moral criminality can be pardoned or ignored if it supports the demoralizing and dehumanizing sociopolitical cause. Indeed, the very idea of morality can be called into question as *anachronistic, unprogressive*, or perhaps even *bigoted*. Is one *socially unfriendly* — then let's make him a social pariah. Is one *socially friendly* — well, then, let's make a monument to him. Morality — or *guilt*, as Solzhenitsyn would say — does not factor into it. Yet even when such progressivism is opposed, it is often for some self-serving end — some mutual engorgement of supporters and supported, the enlargement of an unthinking biological constituency. No one dares to actually defy the liberal-Marxist order that "maintains peace and security," for the only outcome of this is death — likely an assassination or world war meant to preserve the liberal-Marxian order. Nevertheless, with lines drawn and sides pit against each other, all still fulfill the *will-to-machine*.

For now, though, no "book burning" is necessary; nothing too obvious must be done to preclude plausible deniability for the liberal-Marxist. Rather, Marxian brutality comes in stealthier forms; Marcuse continues:

> [The] extreme suspension of the right of free speech and free assembly is indeed justified ... if the whole of society is in extreme danger. I maintain that our society is in such an emergency situation...
>
> [T]he withdrawal of toleration of speech and assembly from groups and movements which promote aggressive policies, armament, chauvinism, discrimination on the grounds of race and religion, or which oppose the

extension of public services, social security, medical care, etc. [is therefore necessary].¹³⁵

Liberal-Marxists purport to act only to save you, to save mankind. They commandeer Nietzsche: *What is done out of love always takes place beyond good and evil.*¹³⁶ All use Nietzsche to selfish ends; that is the point of Nietzsche. However, herein lies the problem: Some are more open about their intentions than others; Carl Schmitt, for instance, was more honest than Peter Singer. Both thinkers want to rule; but in addition to ruling, Singer also wants to deceive, and deception is enslavement. Liberal-Marxist brutality does not have to be overt; it is not overt; it is a brutality of the mind and spirit: it is ideological extremism *par excellence*, and its profound hatred masquerades as cosmopolitan love.

From where do Heine's *dread* and *horror* arise if not the heavy hand of Marxian hatred? To know that what follows in the wake of liberal-Marxist upheaval is only the annihilation of all culture — *that which defines humanity* — and yet still hold dear its dogma is the most fanatical fanaticism. This is the spark of brutality, the mastering of minds.

Singer speaks of using books to "refute" opposition. Despite generational indoctrination into the liberal-Marxist worldview, however, dissent will persist; for many instinctively feel and plainly see that such a "fundamental dogma" is "all sail and no anchor"¹³⁷ with civilization and liberty destined to vanish. And as the liberal-Marxists only grow in power, *their* future *refutation* will amount to unprecedented brutality. Marx and Heine foresaw this — but they are dead and can afford to be honest. Our living liberal-Marxists are as honest about their intentions as they are *loving*. Their talk of "progress," "love," and "equality" — these mask a sinister threat to humanity. Whenever we

---

135 Herbert Marcuse, "Repressive Tolerance," from *A Critique of Pure Tolerance* (Beacon, 1969), 110 and 100.
136 *Beyond Good and Evil*, §153.
137 From Thomas Macaulay's letter to Henry Randall, May 23, 1857.

see campaign slogans centered on "hope" or "change" or hear talk of the same, we should indeed be wary; for what we hear and see are not innocuous platitudes or sleepy galvanizers, but thinly veiled threats against the foundations of a culture in rapid decline.

> [We] must first of all be realistic, understanding that politics, like the law, must be founded on regrets, not hopes.... [W]e must recognize that civilization, far from being natural and spontaneous, [must be maintained] by unremitting work against the forces of an encompassing and hostile nature.[138]

Culture is in decline because *humanity* surrenders itself to *technicity*. Liberal-Marxist tropes are no accident of history: they are the *will-to-machine* honed to an immaculate precision. Tropes are only ever the fulfillment of a transcendent will; upon this final fulfillment stands the unconscious consciousness of a New Colossus. We drift full sail into the inhuman future on self-generated winds of terrible inspiration: *hope, change, equality, love, freedom — What are these if not deceptions waiting to deliver us to irredeemability?*

Humanity is not *man*; *man* is a biological thing; *humanity* is that which is inside man that makes him good. Liberal-Marxists profess to love man; what they really mean to profess is their love for material. Heidegger, Nietzsche, Schmitt — they did not love *man*; no one who appreciates nobility can love man, for man is material and material says nothing of character. These Europeans loved humanity, or that inner nobility of a good soul; Heidegger, Nietzsche, and Schmitt loved *spirit*. This is why they stood in opposition to Marxian dogma — the dogma even Heinrich Heine is honest enough to admit will destroy all culture, i.e., all *humanity*.

From whence does the Marxian drive come? As Heine observed, and as the Abrahamic religions and Noahide Laws attest, Marxism's cosmopolitanism is derived from Judeo-Christianity. *Marxism is more Christian than Christians*, Heine rightly quipped.

---

138 Oliver, *America's Decline*, 184.

Judeo-Christianity and Freemasonry — they share the notion of the Brotherhood of Man; liberal-democracy and Marxism — they share the idea of an ideological universalism that washes over the masses in a revolutionary wave. A tinny love of *humanity* (*man*) permeates the godless ecumenicalism undergirding them all. Carl Schmitt reminds us: "The concept of *humanity* is an especially useful ideological instrument of imperialist expansion, and in its ethical-humanitarian form it is a specific vehicle of *economic imperialism*."[139] Thus, the love of *man* is no different than the love of *profit*; this love of *profit* is identical to the love of *technology*, which is the silent basis of liberal-Marxism. Material interest spurs the increase in technicization and diminishing of *humanity* (*spirit*). The subterfuge of liberal-Marxism is precisely its equivocal use and conception of *humanity*: man is material, *biological mass*, whose increase is predicated on technicity, *technologizing*, for the sake of profit. Speaking in the name of *humanity*, then, amounts to the calculative interest of material gain.

But there is something more frightening than speaking for all humanity — and not only more frightening, but more *final*. The thin ecumenical love of liberal-Marxism bears the undeniable existentiality of the desire to rule on a mass scale. Nothing can survive this: All means and machinery are aimed at bending the world to its will; those unbending will break — this is its tyranny over humanity (spirit). The final goal of liberal-Marxism is to eliminate war — for on the other side of this permanent peace is the terrorization of soul. The ruling class demands that the biological masses below them "kill others and be prepared to die themselves" for the sake of global trade, prosperity, and "the purchasing power of grandchildren" — this is the state of war since the advent of late-nineteenth century progressivism.[140] This is the equitable, economic "nationalism" Nietzsche so derided in the Bismarckian Reich:

---

139 Schmitt, *The Concept of the Political* (University of Chicago, 2007), 54; emphasis added.

140 Schmitt, *The Concept of the Political*, 48.

> Is there a single idea behind this bovine nationalism? ... And it is precisely now that 'the new German Empire' has been founded upon the most threadbare and discredited of ideas — universal suffrage and equal right for all. Think of all this struggling for advantage among conditions which are in every way degenerate: of this culture of big cities, of newspapers, of hurry and scurry, and of 'aimlessness'! The economic unity of Europe must necessarily come — and with it, as a reaction, the pacifist movement[:] for a while the party of the oppressed, and later the powerful party: — this party would be opposed to everything in the shape of revenge and resentment.[141]

Modernity is ruled by the *cleverest revenge*. "World peace" is the stamp borne by the United Nations' Universal Declaration of Human Rights. World peace can only prevail with human slavery: one man's heaven is another man's hell, so the pacifist-revanchists tolerate to the point of intolerance: they force change. "It is a manifest fraud to condemn war as homicide and then demand of man that they wage war, kill and be killed, so that there will never again be war."[142] Liberal-Marxism is predicated on fraud: It is the program of fraudsters seeking revenge against *ancient lands*, against humanity, which is to say it is the material struggle against spirit.

> If pacifist hostility toward war were so strong as to drive pacifists into a war against nonpacifists, in a war against war, that would prove that pacifism truly possesses political energy because it is sufficiently strong to group men according to friend and enemy. If, in fact, the will to abolish war is so strong that it no longer shuns war, then it has become a political motive, i.e., it affirms, even if only as an extreme possibility, war and even the reason for war. Presently this appears to be a peculiar way of justifying wars. The war is then considered to constitute the absolute last war of humanity. Such a war is necessarily unusually intense and inhuman because, by transcending the limits of the political framework, it simultaneously degrades the enemy

---

141 Nietzsche, *The Will to Power*, §748. The "new German Reich" is Bismarck's Second Reich, which disgusted Nietzsche (see Baeumler, *Nietzsche: Philosopher and Politician* [Arktos, 2024]).

142 Schmitt, *The Concept of the Political*, 48.

into moral and other categories and is forced to make of him a monster that must not only be defeated but also utterly destroyed.[143]

The fraud, the contradiction makes war to end war — in defense of "human rights." The defense of "human rights" — the *war against war* — makes *inhuman* the participants and the "peaceful" world following the war: "the most terrible war is pursued only in the name of peace, the most terrible oppression only in the name of freedom, the most terrible inhumanity only in the name of humanity."[144] This is the terrorization of soul following final peace. And this war has battlefields beyond earth and mud: *mind, spirit, time* — such imponderables are the fronts modernity inflicts upon *humanity*; and from these fronts, unseen and omnipresent, there is — *No Escape*: a state of being turned into a tangible *viscerality*. Terrorization of soul is necessary as a condition for the mass acceptance of humanity's replacement by Machine.

15.

"A world state which embraces the entire globe and all of humanity cannot exist."[145] This is not to say that a world-state cannot exist. A world-state is predicated on the dissolution of humanity (spirit); only a biological mass (resulting from the war for "human rights," or *biological massism*) can accept the moral impartiality concomitant with a global community — this, of course, is why the biological mass is fostered. So, either the world-state exists without humanity (spirit), or humanity (spirit) exists without the world-state. Increased profit demands technological progress, which, in turn, depends on increased technicization — i.e., man must increasingly participate in the technicization of all life so as to further technologically innovate and generate profit. If value is based on equal exchange, then profit is only the extraction of value from the valueless, or the subtraction of value from

---

143 Schmitt, *The Concept of the Political*, 36.
144 Schmitt, *The Concept of the Political*, 95.
145 Schmitt, *The Concept of the Political*, 53.

the other participants in the exchange. Material value (*profiteering*) supplants spiritual value (*mutual exchange*) under the terrorization of soul flowing from modernity's biological massism. It is therefore impossible for humanity (spirit) to outlast the world-state—for humanity is extinguished in the *war against war* (for "human rights") and precluded in the aftermath of material exploitation.

Thomas Friedman notes the ineluctability of globalization:

> Globalization isn't a choice. It's a reality.... And the most basic truth about globalization is this: *No one is in charge*... [And no one can stop it] — except at a huge cost to ... society and its prospects for growth.... We all want to believe that someone is in charge and responsible. But the global marketplace today is an Electronic Herd ... connected by screens and networks.... The Electronic Herd cuts no one any slack. *No one*. It does not recognize anyone's unique circumstances. The herd knows only its own rules.[146]

Friedman offers this "hypothetical" retort to Malaysian Prime Minister Mahathir Mohamad's comment at the 1997 World Bank meeting that a Jewish conspiracy manipulates global markets. But Friedman is right: *no one is in charge*—and this despite the attestations of Ivy League educator Carroll Quigley, who wrote, "I have studied [the international Anglophile network] for twenty years and was permitted for two years ... to examine its papers and secret records.... [M]y chief [disagreement with this network] is that it wishes to remain unknown..."[147] No, the world is moved by *compulsion. We are bees of the Invisible*, as Rilke said: *Nous butinons éperdument le miel du visible, pour Accumuler dans la grande ruche d'or de l'Invisible — We desperately collect the honey of the visible — to accumulate it in the great golden hive of the Invisible.*[148] Even if a shadowy cabal were "in charge," it would yet serve an overarching will. With so many busy bees of the Invisible no conspiracy is necessary.

---

146 Thomas Friedman, *The Lexus and the Olive Tree* (Farrar, Straus, and Giroux, 1999), 93–94.
147 Carroll Quigley, *Tragedy and Hope* (Macmillan, 1966), 954.
148 *Selected Letters* (Macmillan, 1946), Hull translation, 394.

Of course, it could be said that the "no one is in charge" view — i.e., the popular, non-conspiratorial view — feeds into the popular urge-to-apathy, that it is just an excuse to idly and docilely live; it could be said that acceptance of this view in any form is implicit support of the enslaving narrative. But while the arc of humanity is irredeemably set, the local destiny of each man must be fulfilled according to a very human or inhuman will. Apathy is a characteristic of the ignoble majority *in time*; conversely, the noble few stand and fight for a *thing* because of its inherent value, not because of any expected outcome: This is the difference between the spiritual and material attitude. Possessors of the latter — the supposedly "benign" majority — operate as a horrid herd in search of pleasure and salary: Like Solzhenitsyn's Soviet interrogators, they have no desire "to get at the truth"; instead, their existence "in difficult cases … [is] a mere exercise of their duties as executioners and in easy cases simply a pastime and a basis for receiving a salary."[149]

In theory, the "Electronic Herd" *can* be stopped, as Friedman suggests, but only at "significant" socioeconomic cost. Our local destiny dictates that profits are paramount, that we are ruled by our own creation — this is the materialism of modernity. But this local destiny, again, serves humanity's larger fate of complete cessation. *Globalization*, the *world-state* — these cannot be stopped for the mass because the mass must prepare the way for Machine.

It is no accident Friedman employs "Electronic Herd"[150]; this echoes Miguel Serrano's vision of the "Electronic Messiah": the *herd* necessitates the *messiah*. One's beginning is inconceivable without the other's end. And just as the imbalance of humanity and technicity only favors the rise of technicization, so too does the dynamic of herd and messiah favor the messiah at the cost of the herd's existence: humanity (spirit) yields to herd; herd yields to messiah; messiah is the Machine that saves man from himself. However, it is only the soulless man who hurries from himself and seeks saving.

---

149 Solzhenitsyn, *The Gulag Archipelago* (Harper & Row, 1974), 138.
150 Miguel Serrano, *Man: For the Man to Come* (Hermitage Helm, 2017), 193.

Scott Lincicome of the Cato Institute, a libertarian think tank, provocatively argues that globalization is not just a reality "libertarians" and other "freedom" loving people must grapple with, but that it should be cultivated. The provocation is ostensible: Free-marketeers and socialists, far from being antipodes, were only ever after the materialization of the mass, with or without globalization. It just so happens that globalization is *the* efficient and effective means to that end. Lincicome's audience, the world over, no doubt smiles satisfyingly to itself: Globalization *has* helped raise the material standard of living across the planet. Lincicome proceeds to offer numerous examples of why globalization is so astoundingly good, with each centered around one undeniable reality: the mass surge of material benefit. The argument is not new; but now, we are told, increased materiality equals increased freedom — presumably the freedom to self-actualize. However, increased materiality comes with a cost, and we find that the excuse to indulge the masses' basest urge is the argument. *Greed is good because we cannot stop it — so let's join the fun*: This has been the argument of every exploiter; only here it is peddled as "new." Indulgence is far from innovative, however.

The globalist argument is certainly not new, and when proponents identify globalization's flaws, there is more at stake than mere *economic* backlash.[151] Materialism, or increased materialization, like its concomitant technicization, despite its cosmetic benefit, comes at the expense of losing the very thing that makes such indulgence allegedly worthwhile: substrate is eroded for infinite veneer. Thus, it seems less jarring when a "think" tank thoughtlessly presents an argument that appears to have completely missed the point. Ultimately

---

151 Jared Bernstein's remarks at the Economic Policy Institute (September 27, 2023): "globalization generates both meaningful benefits *and* meaningful costs." He identifies strictly economic costs; concern for the worker is concern for the employed and content *consumer*. He concludes: "we will continue to participate in globalization, never ignoring the costs of trade, but at the same time reaping its benefits."

in a materialistic society, the self we actualize is *impersonal* — it is the self of something *other*, something *alien*. Our flight from the self is a movement toward some collective destiny: the material indulgence of a herd — a herd that lives for the Electronic Shepherd.

The soulless man is the herd — that is, it the Mass Man that liberal-Marxism elevates for its own sustenance. Attacking opposition is the survival instinct of any will, be it the will of man, idea, or machine. "In fascism," Singer so responsibly warns us, "my grandfather saw the victory of force and brutality over reason, education, and learning, and the triumph of those who preferred to burn books rather than refute the arguments in them."[152] Singer participates in the myth of liberalism when he — wittingly or not — troglodytically parrots the party line. The myth of liberal-Marxism is that a "better world" waits beyond us. *Better for whom*, one can only imagine. *Utopia*, after all, is *nowhere* — beyond us. Perhaps the next world is better for a *what*, not a *whom*. This *what* is our creation, which is really the machination of our successor; we are the playthings of our creation, the *will-to-machine*. Unimaginable alienation arises from our being controlled by our creation; we act out the golem legend. *Hubris* is not our downfall, however, but only *complicity*. We are complicit in a world where no one is in charge, and thus we excuse ourselves for needing salvation.

The man who speaks for all humanity is and only ever has been a tyrant. The globalist vision of Singer, Marcuse, Oppenheim, Friedman, and their ilk — this is spoken with a voice from beyond the grave; it is the voice of Machine that tyrannizes the memory of humanity. Is it the triumph of *reason* to echo the bleating herd? Is it the triumph of *learning* to refute with words today what will be silenced with violence tomorrow? If so, it is the triumph of a sham. "Repressive tolerance" is the language of fraudsters, of gangsters; it is the hatred of the liberal-Marxist and a sign of the *cleverest revenge*. They wage wars against war to exact their revenge. David Oppenheim was "at home" in "Red

---

152 Singer, *Pushing Time Away*, 243.

Vienna," Singer fondly tells us — shall we lose sight of murderous liberal-Marxian ideology behind a veil of nostalgia?

He who speaks in the name of the biological mass is the surrogate tyrant for a finality needing no salvation; the liberal-Marxist is the voice of the Machine.

16.

In a presentation hosted by the Champaign County History Museum, Professor Emeritus Matthew Ehrlich juxtaposed two former University of Illinois educators: Leo Koch and Revilo Oliver.[153] This topic was not just of local interest to the University and its surrounding communities, but also tied in with Ehrlich's larger goal of exploring "dangerous ideas on campus" — those dangerous ideas being *sex* and *conspiracy*. In this local context, *sex* was represented in Koch, *conspiracy* in Oliver.

Ehrlich introduced Koch as a promoter of "nudism," user of LSD, cofounder of the Sexual Freedom League, supporter of the "antiwar movement," attendee of the 1969 Woodstock Festival, and, finally, as a peace-loving homesteader who wanted nothing more than to live off the land. This brief sketch brought gentle coos of approbation from the crowd who had likely never heard of the man just a few moments earlier. Oliver, on the other hand, was introduced — following Ehrlich's audience-cuing hesitancy marking Oliver as "uh, somewhat *different*" — as an opponent of water fluoridation, contributor to *National Review*, cofounder of the John Birch Society, an "extreme" anti-Semite and racist, and, not surprisingly, a "neo-Nazi."

Koch was eventually fired from his professorship for an inopportune editorial to the campus magazine; Oliver, on the other hand, ultimately retired from his professorship and was awarded with, remarkably, *emeritus* status. You might guess with which of these men Ehrlich sympathizes.

Before the reason for Koch's dismissal is revealed, Ehrlich drew more enthusiastic support from the audience by playfully describing

---

[153] Presented at the Champaign Public Library, December 15, 2022.

the erstwhile professor as "a gadfly, as a pain in the rear end" — not to mention a "dedicated secular humanist" and "atheist" — who liked to send provocative letters to local newspapers criticizing "conservativism" [sic] and Judeo-Christianity. As it happened, Koch wrote to the campus periodical in 1960 about the virtues of premarital sex. Reading the final paragraphs of Koch's published letter, highlighting the "hours of frustrating petting" that could be avoided if premarital sex were socially permissible, Ehrlich elicited more ebullient laughter from the excited listeners. The case for Leo Koch's profound and liberal heroism seemed closed! Ehrlich stressed that Koch wasn't advocating for "free love" or "casual sex" among the youth, but that he was simply only interested in "happy marriages."

In 1963, just three years after Koch was fired, he cofounded the Sexual Freedom League with Jefferson Poland, a boisterous "free love" advocate. Poland, an *avid* liberal activist, it turns out, was soon to be a convicted child molester who spent his public moments picketing for LGBT, race, and gender rights. After his conviction for sexually abusing at least one nine-year-old child, Poland became a fugitive and changed his name to "Clitlick." The University of California (Berkeley) now maintains the Clitlick archive. Perhaps one gadfly attracts another.

After being introduced and coaxed to sympathize with Koch, listeners are further informed of Oliver's arc; we follow him from unassuming classics professor and wartime code-breaker to "vitriolic" anti-Marxist, then on to his final, quite decontextualized suicide at the end of a gun. No doubt to Ehrlich's delight, the audience gasps in sheer horror at the "anti-Semitic" "Holocaust denier" who "shoots himself in the head in 1994." *Ehrlich* means *honest* in German — but let us help Professor Emeritus *Ehrlich* here: Oliver, suffering from terminal leukemia and emphysema, aged 86 years, did end his own life in 1994.[154] The audience, however, ready and willing to accept anything Ehrlich tells them to excite their liberal-Marxist sensibilities,

---

154 Incidentally, Ehrlich adds, as an "editorial comment," that he wishes Oliver would have killed himself because of "what he had done."

will never know the real circumstances of — i.e., the personal suffering surrounding — Oliver's death, much like they will never know what Revilo Oliver wrote or said during his lifetime; they simply have no interest, for it does not fit with the indoctrination they received from the liberal-Marxist system. Details glossed over here, irrelevancies sensationalized there — these are tactics the Mass Mind can rarely intercept; Ehrlich employs them with ease.

The *conspiratorial* aspect of Oliver is merely his discerning approach in contraposition to the liberal-Marxist paradigm's dullish demands. It hardly matters whether there is any truth to, as Ehrlich dangled before the audience to evoke an emotional response, the dangers of water fluoridation,[155] JFK's liberal-Marxist tendencies,[156] or the

---

155 From the American Cancer Society (2022): "A partial report of a study from the Harvard School of Public Health … found that exposure to higher levels of fluoride in drinking water was linked to a higher risk of osteosarcoma in boys but not in girls"; and, "People who live in areas with high levels of fluoride in the water might consider using alternate sources of drinking water, such as bottled water."

Additionally, from *Scientific World Journal* (2013), "Water Fluoridation: A Critical Review of the Physiological Effects of Ingested Fluoride as a Public Health Intervention":

> … available evidence suggests that fluoride has a potential to cause major adverse human health problems, while having only a modest dental caries prevention effect. As part of efforts to reduce hazardous fluoride ingestion, the practice of artificial water fluoridation should be reconsidered globally, while industrial safety measures need to be tightened in order to reduce unethical discharge of fluoride compounds into the environment.

This is not to say that the debate about the sense of fluoride in the water supply is closed. Opposing views on water fluoridation are presented here to highlight the absurdity of Ehrlich's dismissive attitude and presentation. Perhaps of interest to Ehrlich is that the ascendency of fluoride in the water supply coincided with the prevalence of water-soluble fertilizers, of which hexafluorosilicic acid and sodium fluoride are byproducts.

156 As a liberalist, Kennedy sympathized with certain aspects of Marxism, particularly in his support for welfare, government intervention in the economy, and his advocacy for socioeconomic equality.

potentially equivocal data surrounding the Holocaust[157]—what matters is that anyone who *questions anything* not sanctioned by the globalist system is, *de facto*, a *conspiracy theorist*. Case closed; no further inquiry needed. Of course, the stifling of inquiry and the elicitation of an emotional response is precisely the point.

During interviews promoting his book detailing the Koch-Oliver case, Ehrlich was wont to invoke *McCarthyism*[158]—the so-called "witch hunt" US Senator Joseph McCarthy undertook to rid government, academia, and media of Marxist sympathizers. *McCarthyism* is, effectively, euphemism for modern parlance's *conspiracy theorist*—it is a word and initiative that leftists were successful at seizing and parrying and therefore are quick to deploy, since it is only ever used derisively within government, academia, and media. Notably, there are no known words similar to *McCarthyism* in the English language adopted as a pejorative for disruptive liberals—as in, *His arrogant and stubborn handling of international affairs can only be described as a form of Churchillism*; this is because modern parlance, like the system employing it, is firmly

---

In addition to his support for social-welfare programs, JFK also emphasized the importance of promoting social justice and equality. He spoke about the need to address racial discrimination and advance civil rights for all, echoing Marxist critiques of social injustices.

Kennedy took steps to advance civil rights through the desegregation of schools and public spaces, promoted voting rights for non-European Americans, and advocated for fair employment. These actions conformed with Marxist principles of challenging structural inequalities.

Furthermore, Kennedy's approach to promoting democracy in developing countries—e.g., the Alliance for Progress—followed Marxist ideas of international solidarity.

157 The Committee for Open Debate on the Holocaust is but one of many revisionist entities pursuing what CODH's name suggests. Moreover, in many countries across the West, "Holocaust denial" is a crime punishable with a prison sentence; the United States, despite the First Amendment, is increasingly pressing for the criminalization of such denial.

158 "Dangerous Ideas on Campus: An Interview with Matthew Ehrlich" (2022), academeblog.org.

in leftist hands, and "the left" can do no wrong. Because of this, leftists have no ability to perceive the echo chamber they create; this of course applies to members of the liberalistic "right," as well. Liberal-Marxism fosters a conformism that dismisses opposing viewpoints outright, encourages emotionalism, and rejects traditional mores.[159]

Similarly, in another promotional interview, Ehrlich haughtily dismisses the "silly" idea of college "professors as wild-eyed radicals indoctrinating their sheep-like students..."[160] It's truly as if the liberal-Marxist system, wittingly or not, tries desperately to protect itself from itself — *the left can do no wrong and we must all stop believing such "right-wing" conspiracy theories*: this is the mantra incessantly emanating from liberal-Marxists; truth, however, sometimes wins in the end. CNN host Fareed Zakaria, himself on the left of the liberal system, felt compelled to acknowledge academia's damaging and dangerous drift:

> American universities have been neglecting a core focus on excellence in order to pursue a variety of agendas, many of them clustered around diversity and inclusion. It started with the best of intentions.... But those good intentions have morphed into a dogmatic ideology and turned these universities into places where the pervasive goals are political and social engineering, not academic merit.[161]

Educators and administrators have made it their mission to force a political agenda at the expense of traditional academic standards; Zakaria's statement came after the December 05, 2023 congressional committee confronting the presidents of Harvard, MIT, and U Penn on "anti-Semitism" — evidently the greatest evil in recorded history — being unmitigated on their campuses.

---

159 "The Growing Partisan Divide in Views of Higher Education," Pew Research Center (August 19, 2019), https://www.pewresearch.org/social-trends/2019/08/19/the-growing-partisan-divide-in-views-of-higher-education-2.

160 "Q&A With Matthew C. Ehrlich, Author of Dangerous Ideas on Campus" (2021), press.uillinois.edu.

161 *Fareed Zarkaria — GPS* (December 2023).

But such radicalism predates this latest incident by at least sixty years, despite Ehrlich's attempt at running interference. Perhaps the entire "counterculture" era is a result of the coincidence of (1) a "boomer" generation being raised more by novel television than their parents in a postwar euphoria, and (2) the *cleverest revenge*, as Nietzsche would say, of a teacher-class dominated by liberal-Marxist ideas that vaulted to prominence in the wake of the Allied victory that cast previously accepted worldviews into world-historical doubt. Indeed, it has been shown that "professors on the political left are now approaching a *supermajority*" in academia, wherein, as of 2017, nearly 60% of faculty members identify as "liberal and far-left."[162] This percentage has undoubtedly increased in the intervening years. Interestingly, as a cultural commentary,

> the humanities and social sciences have become monolithically left-leaning. In some fields such as English and history, self-identified moderate faculty have diminished to a tiny minority, and conservatives are practically nonexistent.[163]

If the liberal arts are meant to refine one's character so as to shape the future of culture, this drift should be both quite alarming and unsurprising, in light of prevailing societal trends. If language, history, literature, and social science are taught only through the myopia of radical leftism, we can presume the result will be a drone-like dystopia reminiscent of Orwell and Huxley: students are taught to *obey*, not to *think*; these students, in turn, will be tomorrow's leaders, and each subsequent generation will be more authoritarian than the last on this point; moreover, this reprogramming, this *revaluation of values* that began with Judeo-Christianity, will reach its godless conclusion in

---

[162] P. W. Magness and D. Waugh, "The Hyperpoliticization of Higher Ed: Trends in Faculty Political Ideology, 1969–Present" (2022), *The Independent Review*, 27.3, 359; emphasis added.

[163] Magness and Waugh, 363.

the secular humanism of the liberal-Marxist "utopia" of the future.[164] And when we look at the progressive left's fundamental tenets, we can glimpse what the West's future holds: (1) success in life is largely outside of an individual's control, (2) anti-national sentiment, (3) non-European immigrants are good for society, (4) transgenderism is good for society, and (5) people of European descent are unfairly privileged and must be undercut via equitable policies.[165] It should hardly be surprising that the most radical leftists are the young and most "educated" (i.e., in possession of a college degree). These are precisely the audiences most mainstream media panders to — the overlap among them being, generally speaking, low cognitive ability. This, of course, favors all authorities — be they in media, academia, government, or elsewhere — that thrive on misinformation, since, as a recent study confirmed, mere education is useless without accompanying intelligence.[166] (No one with any intelligence needed a study to disclose this, but the study was nevertheless necessary given the undue emphasis the West places on college education; of course, such emphasis is placed because it encourages more youth — especially young women — to be exposed to the advanced misinformation methods present in academia. Spengler's observation is fitting here: "The stupidity of a theory has never prevented its being effectively used."[167]) Notably, too, these same leftists showed the greatest proclivity for conformism, with 79% wishing to wear a mask "all or most of the time" during the so-called COVID-19 pandemic, and 94% saying "they had received all of the

---

164 It should be noted, too, that there is a "heavy curricular presence of mandatory general education classes in almost all undergraduate degree requirements" and that "humanities classes enjoy a disproportionate presence on the general education curriculum... Almost all students take several semesters of mandatory courses in English, history, and other heavily politicized disciplines" (Magness and Waugh, 365).

165 "The Progressive Left," Pew Research Center (November 09, 2021).

166 M. Mettler & J. J. Mondak, "Fact-opinion differentiation," Harvard Kennedy School's *Misinformation Review* (March 07, 2024), Figure 1.

167 *The Hour of Decision* (Pacific, 2002), 141.

required shots to be fully vaccinated"—this, according to the Pew Research Center, was "the highest share of any group."[168]

Already in 1971 "James M. Buchanan predicted a decline in academic standards due to the politicization of the faculty and an increasing turn toward activism in the place of traditional research"[169]—this is evident not just in Ehrlich's presentation of the Koch-Oliver case, but also in countless undocumented cases around the United States and the broader West on a daily basis. Activism—*fanatical obeisance*—is on the march, not *thinking*, not *research*. This is the source of Ehrlich's repeated "editorial comments" and his audience's on-cue approbation and revulsion. We are inculcating a society of lemmings, not freethinking personalities. This, of course, is the point—globalism, because of its borderless abnormality, demands *obeisance*. This is why we see an ever-increasing rise of radicalism within the liberal-Marxist paradigm.

But all of this is both quite insignificant and rather telling in the grander scheme of liberal-Marxist ideology. *Insignificant* because all the associated details of this Koch-Oliver story only hint at the larger current coursing through American society—there is a much more significant situation confronting modernity, beyond how two opposing worldviews might be perceived by the Mass Man; and it is *telling* for the same reason. That the public lauds the liberal (Koch) and maligns the traditional liberal-conservative (Oliver) is no accident. And when Ehrlich opens the presentation to questions from his audience, it is only natural that someone would ask if anyone involved in Koch's firing offered any resistance—i.e., any vocal support for Koch. "No," we are told—*everyone who worked with him wanted him gone*. Many in the audience can only scoff in repugnance—naturally. They didn't know Koch and, presumably, how much of a "gadfly" he apparently was; nor are they troubled over the company he kept after his dismissal, though it gives them an even clearer picture of the man he likely was. Indeed,

---

168 "The Progressive Left," Pew Research Center (November 09, 2021).
169 Magness and Waugh, 367.

the audience can *only* scoff, for they have been *conditioned* to do so. It is unlike the Mass Man to harbor any self-awareness. For modernity is the flight of the self from itself.

17.

The departure of the self from itself indicates the graver problem of modernity. Ever-greater technologizing will not lead to deep-space exploration or extraterrestrial habitation; nor will it grant us peace and enlightenment. As technicization increases, humanity fades. Our progressive march to the future is a walk toward — not *transformation*, but our *end*. This fact is unseen because it rankles the *will-to-machine* driving societies' larger actions. All our being is bent on occluding the obvious: science is grand because its elevation leads to the increase in technology; technology is grand because it simultaneously elevates Machine and diminishes humanity. This is not the exercise of human will. And all the world's institutions — especially as the world becomes more westernized, for the West only means techno-plutocratic *technicization* now — foster the development of the *mass* myth that we *live for ourselves*:

> We may be sure that, despite the [Liberal] cult's appeal to masses that yearn for an effortless and mindless existence on the animal level, and despite the prolonged use of public schools to deform the minds of all children with 'Liberal' myths, the cult would have disappeared, but for the massive support given it today...[170]

One must ask *why* such a doctrine is given "massive support" — it is because liberalism (in whatever form) is an expedient dogma to mass control. Give the masses the *illusion* of freedom, blather on about the superstitions of liberalism as if they were incontrovertible facts of reality, and provide adequate mental and physical distractions (Marx would call them *opiates*; Huxley would call them *soma*) to keep the

---

170 Oliver, *America's Decline*, 81.

Mass Mind from contemplating its quandary: these are the fundaments of liberalism, to which the liberal-Marxist *literati* hold fast to maintain their place. Presenting the masses with the *veneer* of freedom facilitates the *inception* of freedom in the Mass Mind.

Walter Lipmann and Edward Bernays — two expounders of the mass propaganda necessary in liberal societies — emphasized the essentiality of creating in the mind of the public the illusion of an idea's self-inception. Liberalism is the illusory and inceptual means by which total control is conceived as total freedom. The vulgarizing and leveling Illusion of Choice is the latest means for the elect to rule over the bourgeois and proletariat. The most damning and damnable aspect of liberalism is its utter *dishonesty* — its foundation on an illusion and the incessant propagation of its fraudulence through various indoctrinatory means. As Nietzsche foretold, *the world will pay dearly for its falling prey to lies*; it is quite likely we will begin to pay in earnest within the next decade.

Nevertheless, that a society should fall prey to lies is the single most important argument against the liberal-Marxist doctrine: *A dishonest and credulous people can never be liberal; and a global society can never be honest and prudent — because societies have not one root, but many.* Liberal-Marxism exists to promote globalism, whose foundation is a lie; globalism exists to foster technicization at the expense of humanity. The future that waits is not Utopia.

At the dawn of mass technicization we recall Machiavelli: "It is unnecessary for a prince to have ... good qualities, but it is very necessary to appear to have them."[171] At humanity's twilight we remember Plato: "The height of injustice is to seem just without being so."[172]

---

171 *The Prince*, ch. XVIII.
172 Plato, *Republic*, 2.316a.

18.

Nietzsche's writing was full of warnings. He tried to save what we have lost — if only we would listen; but the time for collective salvation is past. Now is the time to reap what we have sown.

> The time is coming when we shall have to pay for having been *Christians* for two thousand years: we are losing the equilibrium which enables us to live — for a long while we shall not know in what direction we are travelling. We are hurling ourselves headlong into the *opposite* valuations, with that degree of energy which could only have been engendered in man by an *overvaluation* of himself. Now, everything is false from the root, words and nothing but words, confused, feeble, or over-strained.[173]

This is not an indictment of Christianity alone. This is a condemnation of all the creeds Judeo-Christianity's slave-morality has produced. It is an indictment of what we have sown.

The rise of Adolf Hitler and his National Socialist Party, to which Heidegger belonged, saw the galvanization of the whole liberal-Marxist world against what came to be known as the Axis. What began with Mussolini and Hirohito culminated in and was concretized by Hitler. This is not to say that the Italian and Japanese movements reached fulfillment in the Greater German movement, but only that the global anti-globalist movement reached its apex in the Axis, whose own pinnacle was the Third Reich.

It is no accident of history that the supposed liberal-democracies allied themselves with the supposedly Marxist Soviet Union. The two are ideological bedfellows.

> [Marxism and capitalism] were merely two sides of the same coin. Both communist Marxism and capitalism were post-industrial ideologies. Both assumed the mass concentration of labor and industry in large urban areas. Both were anti-folk and internationalist in outlook. Both were only falsely nationalistic. Both assumed the continued existence of economic man in

---

173 Nietzsche, *The Will to Power*, §30.

contradistinction to whole, inwardly directed man. Both were materialistic and anti-spiritual in values and in preferred lifestyle. Neither gave man what he needed: a feeling of belonging.[174]

This is the world we reap. Collective salvation in any spiritual sense is by now impossible; our course is set and will be followed to the end. Pretensions to spiritual salvation from the root of modernity's liberal-Marxism — Judeo-Christianity — are not only spurious, but also damaging, for they further alienate man from himself; that is, such pretensions further the lie of liberal-Marxist dogma by depicting slavery as freedom. Under the guise of traditional values, Judeo-Christianity seeks to uproot man from all tradition — all in the name of socio(economic) "progress." This is not "the Church" talking; this is the ineluctable *will-to-machine*. The Church — this purveyor of Judeo-Christianity, which, despite its schisms and denominations can be seen as monolith of the *cleverest revenge* — stakes its claim in the "future," which is really only its mechanical wish to be on the Marxian "right side of history." What was it Marx said? "It is not the consciousness of men that determines their existence, but their social existence that determines their consciousness."[175] And so history carries us along the dialectical path in search of perfection through permanent revolution. Christian aims and characteristics mirror all liberal-Marxist creeds: the dual horns of *apathetic* and *fervent* liberalism, destructive urges (hence "progress") — a *destruction* of the past, of "original sin"), softness and cynicism, Marxism (cultural, if not economic) and values of the Mass Man, pessimism and nihilism. Judeo-Christian "social teaching speaks very clearly and strongly about the equality of men and women based upon their equal dignity as children of God."[176]

---

174 James Whisker, from his introduction the 1980 edition of Rosenberg's *Myth of the Twentieth Century*.

175 Marx, *A Contribution to the Critique of Political Economy* (Progress, 1977), Ryazanskya translation, 21.

176 This is just one example of many; it comes from the United States Conference of Catholic Bishops' statement on the "Equal Rights Amendment."

But it does not stop there: liberal-Marxism will accept all manner of biological masses — all in service to a future that will dispose of them. Nietzsche shares his thoughts on the rise of the masses:

> Christianity is a denaturalization of gregarious morality... Democracy is a more natural form of it, and less sown with falsehood. It is a fact that the oppressed, the low, and whole mob of slaves and half-castes, *will prevail*.
>
> First step: they make themselves free [and] paramount.
>
> Second step: ... they demand acknowledgment, equal rights, 'Justice.'
>
> Third step: they demand privileges (they draw the representatives of power over to their side).
>
> Fourth step: they *alone* want all power, and they *have* it.
>
> There are *three elements* in Christianity which must be distinguished: (*a*) the oppressed of all kinds, (*b*) the mediocre of all kinds, (*c*) the dissatisfied and diseased of all kinds. The first struggle against the politically noble and their ideal; the second contend with the exceptions and those who are in any way privileged (mentally or physically); the third oppose the *natural instinct* of the happy and the sound....
>
> [Mediocrity] now gets its highest sanction through Christianity [and] becomes so conscious of itself (gains such courage in regard to its own opinions), that it arrogates to itself even *political power*...
>
> Democracy is Christianity *made natural*: a sort of 'return to Nature,' once Christianity, owing to extreme anti-naturalness, might have been overcome by the opposite valuation. Result: the aristocratic ideal begins to *lose its natural character*...[177]

No longer do we speak with future tense — "will prevail." Quality is so overwhelmed by quantity that there is now no reversing it. The "mob" — the biological mass of materiality — *has prevailed*; thus the impossibility of any spiritual salvation. The liberal-Marxist revolutions since Rousseau have only given rise to the *trade exchange*, not mass "reason." As Kerry Bolton notes,

---

[177] Nietzsche, *The Will to Power*, §215.

> The democratic ideal of counting heads is analogous to the capitalist ideal of counting money. Marxism, so far from transcending this, systemizes both into a single ideology. Both are based on weighing in the balance, regardless of quality. [T]he liberal revolutionaries had only replaced aristocrats with plutocrats.[178]

Spiritual emptiness and lack of quality are painfully obvious in a degenerate society. This general void is the nihilism Nietzsche described—the nihilism that defines man's future. To overcome this void, the liberal-Marxist employs dialectical language meant to imbue time with a sense of moral progress and bestow on the speaker an aura of sublimity meant to distract the listener from moral and spiritual bankruptcy. Thus we have the "right side of history"—politicians and activists the world over have invoked the "right side of history" to contrive in the masses a sense of shared history that only ever exists beyond the front of progress, beyond the war being waged for man's soul in the present. "Right side of history" is a war cry for mass-manipulators raising proletarian armies to support their push for more power. To be "right," to be "correct" means living for an afterlife—a utopia—whose battle is never won but always underway: It is a distraction from present ills by the promise of future glory. To be on the "right side of history" is to essentially say, "Join us, or face the shame of being wrong." But something even more ominous has replaced this war cry: *History is watching*.

Godless politicians, technocrats, activists, and moralists quietly changed their war cry from excitement to threat. "History is watching" is now a staple of political rhetoric.[179] It no longer aims to galvanize mass support; rather, it acts as a world-weary warning against anyone who stands in the way of the prescribed vision of "progress." *History is watching* means: *I am watching from the panopticon of time; dissent*

---

178 Bolton, *Yockey*, 133.

179 The American Biden administration has used this phrase several times, for instance: September 28, 2023, February 13/16/23, 2024, March 07/14, 2024, to cite just a few examples.

now, face punishment later. Again the speaker summons the nonexistent infinite, for the infinite is only a void for the godless: "History is watching" is the materialist's *dialectic* promising an impossibly better future at the expense of a tyrannical present: *Yield now or face reprisal.* Disembodied "history" is revealed as the Marxian threat it was always meant to be: The future is your enemy because the future is owned by — the *mass*, and more, the men who rule the *mass*. *Progress* again is a social weapon — a desire to hurt, a desire to rule. Secular *progress* is Judeo-Christian *paradise*: both hound the strong to benefit the weak; both see in "history" a future in which one's enemies are condemned to hell.

∞ • ∞

It is said that Diogenes of Sinope carried his lantern in daylight looking for an "honest man" — because traditional society left him wanting, especially for its supposed corruption. One can sympathize with Diogenes if the corruption was real; but one has to wonder if it was Diogenes or his society that lacked virtue; it is unknown, for instance, whether his nickname — *the Dog* — was meant as endearment or revilement. The son of a minter, Diogenes was exiled from Sinope for his role in his father's currency devaluation scheme. Sinope was a significant trading city whose inhabitants were known for their cosmopolitanism and irreverence; for Diogenes to be expelled from Sinope, he must have been involved in quite a different sort of irreverence — perhaps one befitting more plutocrats than aristocrats.

> Lore has it that when he was banished from Sinope, [Diogenes] traveled to Delphi to consult Apollo on how to live in his new situation. The god's reply was ['deface the coinage']. Later Cynics would adopt the phrase as their motto and construe it metaphorically as a command to decommission the 'coinage' of social custom. Diogenes may have drawn the same conclusions,

and so he is depicted traveling through the Greek mainland, everywhere claiming to be putting current customs out of circulation...[180]

Here we have the cosmopolitan exile involved in currency manipulation transforming himself into a social subverter. Claim as he might that the *targets* of his critiques were unscrupulous, Diogenes, the accuser and social subverter, seems the more likely malefactor. Alexander the Great is said to have wondered at Diogenes' irreverence and thus sought his company.

> Alexander went in person to see him; and he found him lying in the sun. Diogenes raised himself up a little when he saw so many persons coming towards him, and fixed his eyes upon Alexander. And when that monarch addressed him with greetings, and asked if he wanted anything, 'Yes,' said Diogenes, 'stand a little out of my sun.' It is said that Alexander was so struck by this, and admired so much the haughtiness and grandeur of the man who had nothing but scorn for him, that he said to his followers, who were laughing and jesting about the philosopher as they went away, 'But verily, if I were not Alexander, I would be Diogenes.'[181]

That Diogenes, the social subverter, scorned Alexander, pupil of Aristotle, who himself upheld aristocratic values, is telling. Alexander laughed off Diogenes' impertinence — because he valued the cynic's strength of personality. As one who took the *defacement* of social customs as his mission, Diogenes certainly reviled Alexander's personality; and if their positions were swapped, Diogenes would have perhaps replaced Alexander's confident amusement with his own cruel vengefulness.

Diogenes: *cosmopolitan, impudent, subversive, cynical*—this *Dog* looks quite familiar. Aristotle records Diogenes as saying, "Bars are the Spartan barracks of Athens."[182] This type of impudent cynicism

---

180 William Desmond, *Cynics* (Routledge, 2014), 20.
181 Plutarch, *Parallel Lives*, "The Life of Alexander," 14.3–5.
182 *Rhetoric*, 3.10.7. This translation is cited from Desmond's *Cynics*; it is loosely translated, but perhaps the meaning is still present.

presently passes for humor, no doubt for its cosmopolitan flair. Behind the "humor," however, is a slinking decrepitude: the masses joke about their own degeneracy; and by conforming to such degeneracy the masses imagine they flout the status quo. Yet the masses *are* the status quo, the very charade they pretend to scorn.

The Mass Man nevertheless maintains the charade. We might suppose he has been duped into compliance, but the mass — just like the manipulators — follows an irreversible path. Modernity is a ritual beyond our persuasion: Far from any conquest of the mind, what modernity reveals is a defeat of the spirit, a battered people seeking refuge from their conquest by a golem. Is it freedom to be ruled by the rich and bend to their wishes? Is it freedom to work for the end of a being inadequate for the demands of existence? Is it freedom to strive for the end of oneself? Perhaps we can answer affirmatively if modernity is an all-encompassing death cult.

But all is not lost. Collective damnation does not mean the individual relents in his struggle for value. Truly, to boldly struggle before ruin is the only way man can secure meaning. Man's search for meaning is not a pitiful despair, but a triumphal defiance. It must be defiance when the *mass* coolly rejects — by will or ignorance — all meaning and value. Man's search for meaning is the love — the intense *contemplation* — of the source of his *humanity*, his *spirit*. Victor Frankl spoke of similar contemplation:

> The truth — that love is the ultimate and the highest goal to which man can aspire. Then I grasped the meaning of the greatest secret that human poetry and human thought and belief have to impart: *The salvation of man is through love and in love.* I understood how a man who has nothing left in this world still may know bliss, be it only for a brief moment, in the contemplation of his beloved. In a position of utter desolation, when man cannot express himself in positive action, when his only achievement may consist in enduring his sufferings in the right way — an honorable way — in such a position man can, through loving contemplation of the image he carries of his beloved, achieve fulfillment. For the first time in my life I

was able to understand the meaning of the words, 'The angels are lost in perpetual contemplation of an infinite glory.'[183]

What separates meaning from futility, what distinguishes Acolyte from Automaton, the Heideggerian from Mass Man is *thought*—the *contemplation of originary value that is love* and the *love of originary value that is contemplation*. The contemplation that is love and love that is contemplation: This is the sense of the Nietzschean "free spirit." Spirit thinks; material complies. *Spirit* can only be associated with *value*; *material* is a lifeless *compiling*. Freedom thinks; tyranny compiles and complies—modernity aspires to the latter.

The Heideggerian stands for freedom—for he *thinks* and *loves*; he stands for impassioned conservatism (i.e., building on the good of what came before), creative pluck, hardness [*Härte*] and earnestness [*Schwere*], aristocratic values (i.e., anti-Marxism), and confidence in one's folk. Modernity views the Heidegger Acolyte as *farce* and *abomination* because the thinker stands apart from the mass, and what the mass cannot comprehend, it scorns. The Heideggerian obstructs the "light" of the Mass Man's corruption.

19.

The *Dog* looks upon noble Alexander with contempt:

> [B]arbarism is the natural state of man.... And within every culture there always live great masses of people who know [civilization] only as an outward routine. The highways and subways of our great cities nightly bear homeward millions who no more understand the civilization in which they live than does the trained seal in his pool at the zoo. What is remarkable is not that civilizations have disintegrated, but that they came into being at all.[184]

---

183 Victor Fankl, *Man's Search for Meaning* (Washington Square, 1984), 57.
184 Oliver, *America's Decline*, 186.

This is what confronts humanity; this is why the proletarianization of man that is liberal-Marxism is so bitingly dangerous and devastatingly successful: it is barbarousness agitating the barbaric in man; it is the call of primitive violence polished to a seductive sheen of civilized sanity. The dullard, the Mass Man, hears the agitator speaking to him and is flattered.

> Blind egos are stroked with great crises invoked,
> and minds of the masses are frenziedly provoked;
> Hope and change usher in a quick stage of decline,
> wrangling ruinous urges from the Mass so inclined;
> What can be done to stave the reproof of a class—
> of the dregs now foaming at the top of the glass?
> 'The time will come to pay,' says Nietzschean edict,
> for the sins of our fathers who failed to predict
> the swift proletarianization of an anchorless ship,
> set adrift on the sails of the Constitution's Delphic
> paper and pen which — catching the wind —
> broke from the mores we never thought to begin.
> Foaming the harbor of safe passage and sea
> the ship thoughtlessly speeds through vessels and screams.
> Both captain and crew miss the much-needed wits
> to bring any sane stoppage to the anchorless drift.
> Now from the sailing flows the Mass — lost and wailing —
> whose sleep is but a start that's always prevailing.
> Relying on egos, stoked but without constitution,
> is the goal of modernity in this final, Kali Yuga.
> The ship has a rudder but no sense behind it;
> the men of iron will, cast astern, cannot guide it.

What reason for such treason? We can only surmise:

Truth suffers most in an age of demise.

When and if we awaken from a slumber so deep,

will it be far too late for the ship to hold keep?

Or will on the mast a new sail be uplifted

by hands determined to reverse the adrift-ness?

To catch a bold wind whose time is yet fated

is the call of a man Providence has pervaded.

20.

When asked if the "individual man" can yet influence "this web of fateful circumstance," Heidegger responded:

> Only a god can save us. The only possibility available to us is that by thinking and poetizing we prepare a readiness for the appearance of a god, or for the absence of a god in [our] decline…[185]

Thought prepares the way.

---

185 Heidegger, "Only a God Can Save Us," *Der Spiegel* 23 (May 1976), in *Heidegger: The Man and the Thinker* (Precedent, 1981), T. Sheehan (ed.).

PART II

A PLANETARY VISION

"Technology is the subtlest form of the most persistent proletarianizing."

— Martin Heidegger, 1939

1.

TALK OF A PLANETARY vision becomes necessary in a globalist world.

Globalist describes the material interdependence of corporate states; it is the *extraction* of material from Nature to secure material benefit; it is the *mechanization* of man in service to corporate states. *World* is the material medium for the operation of corporate states and the fundament for individual and collective states of being. A *corporate state* is a political-commercial entity that exists for the material benefit of, chiefly, its active operators and, less often, its passive participants. *Interdependence* and *extraction* are relational states of distinct objects. *Mechanization* is the sublimation of individual time and effort into the corporate state for material benefit; most extremely, it is the emphasis of energy on technologizing and the objectification of an individual's relationship with the world, which is the decoupling of humanity and technicity.

Planetary is the inter- and intra-individual expanse of the balanced human-technical state of beyng, which is the basis for and result of reflection; it is the harmony of man with his environment. *Harmony* is the balance of being achievable through reflection, and it is the destiny of being recognizable through reflection; *harmony* is neither good nor bad: it is beyng's reconciliation with itself. *Reconciliation* is the aspiration of the subject, the aim of the individual. *Reconciliation* is neither happiness nor its pursuit; it is, rather, the awareness of the expanse of beyng, which stands as the vision of a people prepared to see it. *Vision* is an understanding of the past, a grappling with the present, and a foretelling of the future.

The future, if it is to obtain, must have us seek God. God is poetry, and poetry is reflection. Poetry, or poetizing, "means bringing the revelation of beyng into appropriate language,"[1] so it can be properly thought, further poetized, and thought again. The future, if it exists, is reflection. Our future, then, depends on a shift from the *globalist* to the *planetary*.

2.

The Heidegger Acolyte stands for impassioned *conservatism*, creative *pluck*, *hardness* [*Härte*] and *earnestness* [*Schwere*], *aristocratic* values (i.e., anti-Marxism), and *faith in one's folk*. The Acolyte embodies these values to thwart modernity's socio-technological progress, which is dehumanization.

Socio-technological progress is the confluence of humanity and technicity in service to the corporate state. This confluence, because we exist in the throes of metaphysical destiny, is imbalanced, favoring extreme technologizing—or technological extremism:

> The consummation of unconditional machination as the displacement of an apparently 'personal' dictatorship of an identifiable person into the despotism of no one—of the pure empowerment of the processes of unrestricted planning and calculation—the flaunting of 'realities'—of 'facts'—of tactics

---

1   Heidegger, *Der Spiegel* interview.

and their implementation as beings—and the empowerment of beings of such an essence as henceforth completely forgotten being...[2]

Schiller said, *Man is born free, is free, though he be born in chains*.[3] A slight variation of this, inspired by Max Weber, will place us more squarely in the realm of modernity: Man is born free, is free, and born *again* in chains. This rebirth into chains is the result of the inevitable onset and development of high-capitalism and its subsequent social requirement that man *sharpens* his round and cultivated edges in favor of technical expertise—i.e., *technicization*. Thus, the means of production (man) must narrow its scope in order to stay financially afloat and otherwise "fit in"; and as the scope is narrowed, the fetters are tightened.

> It is utterly ridiculous to see any connection between the high capitalism of today—as it is now being imported into Russia and as it exists in America—with *democracy* or with *freedom* in *any sense* of these words.... The question is: *how are freedom and democracy in the long run at all possible under the domination of highly developed capitalism?* Freedom and democracy are only possible where the resolute will of a nation not to allow itself to be ruled like sheep is permanently alive.[4]

Supposed freedom leads us back to the chains of servitude. The masses embrace thralldom because it is free within the context of their servitude; the "free" are insiders, not outsiders, and thus content. We recall Augustine of Hippo: *He is freely in bondage who does with pleasure the will of his master.* For Paul "the wages of sin is death"; for modern man, the wages of freedom is servitude.

The invocation of *freedom* and *democracy* acts as defense against any aspersion. For how can anyone be against such *enlightenment*?

---

2   Heidegger, *Black Notebooks 1939–1941*, XIII.101, 103.
3   *Die Worte des Glaubens* (1797). Schiller echoes the famous line that begins Rousseau's *Social Contract*.
4   Max Weber, "Conditions of Freedom and the Image of Man," *Essays in Sociology* (Oxford University, 1946), 72.

Certainly, one must be a *fascist*! But this is just what all facets of the liberal-Marxist gem call one another: *fascist*! Don't do things my way? — You're a *fascist*! Stand in the way of my prosperity? — You're a *fascist*! Defy what we need to stay in power? — You're a *fascist*! This would by now be an empty slur for its nauseating overuse if not for the constant conjuring and insular substantiating of the "greatest" of all "fascists" in all history: Hitler and the "Nazis" — the democratic process that voted for *them* was *illegitimate*; approval of *them* was a *mirage*; *German* self-determination was *evil*. The masses are permitted to dabble in the fascinating world of the Hitlerian Idea — as long as it is done with due solemn disgust. Such sandbox dabbling keeps evil intimately — and safely — close to the popular mind.

Contrast the approved interpretation of German events with the election of Claudia Sheinbaum, Mexico's first Jewish president. She was elected amidst Mexico's "bloodiest" election ever, with nearly forty candidates assassinated.[5] It is at least conceivable that many Mexicans are not as progressive as their government forces them to be; after all, Mexico's electoral democracy is barely three decades old, and before this, it functioned for much of its post-Santa Anna existence as a veritable autocracy. Despite this, the highest American officials — as leaders of the *free* and *democratic* world — offered President Sheinbaum their sincerest congratulations and deliberately praised the "democratic process" that elected her, which in itself suggests the "democratic process" had little to do with it. She is an ally; therefore she stands for *freedom* and *democracy*. The US Department of State issued a similar resounding vote of confidence for the recently elected Sri Lankan president:

> The United States congratulates President-elect Anura Kumara Dissanayake on his victory in the Sri Lankan presidential election… We commend the people of Sri Lanka for peacefully exercising their right to vote. This

---

5   Reuters, "Mexico councilwoman killed after bloodiest-ever elections" (June 07, 2024).

election is a testament to the strength of Sri Lanka's democratic institutions and the commitment of its citizens to shaping their future through peaceful and democratic means.

What this statement does not reveal is that Dissanayake is an avowed Marxist.[6] Again the liberal-democracy supports its Marxist bedfellow. Again allies feign allegiance to "democracy" when their goals are achieved: liberal-Marxists in power is furtherance of the *will-to-machine*.

Those perceived as impediments to liberal-Marxist goals are *enemies* — they are *fascists* and, likely, *criminal*. Any alternative path to liberal-Marxism is seen as *antithetical threat*; the archetypical antithetical threat to liberal-Marxism is "fascism," which is why all perceived enemies are "fascist"; hence, within the liberal-Marxist world-society, one often hears of the equally improbable bogeymen of "left-wing" and "right-wing" *fascists* threatening the happily somnambulant *international world order*. To the West, Putin is *fascist*; to Putin, the West is *fascist*; Zionists are *fascist*, as are their pro-Palestinian targets and accusers; likewise, both those with neat hair and those with pink hair are each *fascist* from the standpoint of the other. It all makes perfect sense within a system of tyranny predicated on silencing opposition. If transplanted to the present, some of the United States' own Founding Fathers would doubtless be considered *fascist*. But they only "made mistakes" — after all, how could they be on the "right side of history" when the Marxian Gospel had not yet been revealed to man? As antecedents to world-*freedom* and -*democracy*, they are absolved of their sins. They couldn't be *fascist*, for fascism is the antithesis of *freedom* and *democracy*. This, at least, is the refrain of the prevailing ideology across the globe.

---

6   K. Francis et al., "Marxist Dissanayake wins Sri Lanka's presidential election as voters reject old guard," *Associated Press*, September 22, 2024.

And what is *ideology*, this mover of men and instiller of *avidity* dominating modern corporate states? Solzhenitsyn, who experienced firsthand a facet of liberal-Marxism, gave us his insight into the matter:

> To do evil a human being must first of all believe that what he's doing is good, or else that it's a well-considered act in conformity with natural law. Fortunately, it is in the nature of the human being to seek a *justification* for his actions.... Ideology—that is what gives evildoing its long-sought justification and gives the evildoer the necessary steadfastness and determination. That is the social theory which helps to make his acts seem good instead of bad in his own and others' eyes, so that he won't hear reproaches and curses but will receive praise and honors. That was how the agents of the Inquisition fortified their wills: by invoking Christianity; the conquerors of foreign lands, by extolling the grandeur of their Motherland; the colonizers, by civilization; the Nazis, by race; and the Jacobins (early and late), by equality, brotherhood, and the happiness of future generations.[7]

Equality, brotherhood, and the happiness of future generations sounds all too familiar — Jacobins can't help but speak the same essential language over time. Of course, some superficial verbiage might change to suit subcultural tastes or, perhaps, to protect the guilty, but the heart of the matter remains — National Assembly, the (Communist) International, Congress, Parliament; revolutionary, protestor, activist; president, prime minister, general secretary—*What are names but codes among friends?*

We dare not speak of the *Holodomor*, but only the *Holocaust*. We dare not slander Lenin, Trotsky, Stalin, Mao, Béla Kun, Churchill, or Roosevelt — at least, not in the same way we do the *fascists*. We dare not mention Operation Keelhaul, the result of a genial sidebar at the Yalta Conference and the mere forced repatriation of thousands of refugees to their miserable deaths in the Soviet Union. *What are agreements if not expedients among friends?* Solzhenitsyn called this diabolical *handing over* of asylum seekers "the last secret of the Second World War" — it remains a secret. No one dares implicate the heroes

---

7   Solzhenitsyn, *The Gulag Archipelago* (Harper & Row, 1974), 174.

of liberal-Marxist modernity; they stand for *freedom* and *democracy*, after all. To implicate them would, *perhaps*, mean implicating that for which the guilty stand. To be sure, such heroes have *perhaps* made mistakes — no hero is perfect — but these were not *fascist* mistakes. Prime Minister Churchill carpet-bombed dozens of German cities killing several thousand noncombatants. Prime Minister Netanyahu used artificial intelligence and white phosphorous to aid troop movement and defense — and certainly not to kill several thousand Palestinians as "collateral damage." Presidents Zelenskyy and Putin used their own brands of terror and drone warfare to kill their *fascist* enemies. President Truman dropped atomic bombs on several thousand noncombatants. Mikhail Gorbachev, himself involved in the Soviet invasion of Afghanistan, said Truman's use of nuclear weapons was necessary only as a demonstration[8] — a threat of devastating violence against all enemies, *fascist* and *imperialistic*, which is only to say *inadequately progressive*, if not *racist*. Speaking of Afghanistan, one President Bush[9] trained Afghani freedom fighters to thwart the Soviets; another President Bush invaded Afghanistan to fight Afghani terrorists, former freedom fighters. Both presidents of the Bush variety invaded Iraq — for real or concocted reasons — to fight the *fascist* Saddam Hussein. Hussein, meanwhile, made it his mission to fight against the West's *fascist* imperialism.

One could list thousands of examples just like this — all of history, right or wrong, is testament to ideological avidity. It is only now, since 1945, that a monolithic ideology dominates the world. This is not to say that what preceded 1945 was better, that it is something worth pursing

---

8   BBC interview, November 08, 2019. Gorbachev: "Why did the Americans [drop the bomb]? As a warning to everyone: Obey us or we'll drop a little bomb on you…"

9   George Herbert Walker Bush was director of the Central Intelligence Agency from 1976–77; he was vice president of the United States under Ronald Regan from 1981–1989 and president from 1989–1993.

again. All life follows one path: the *will-to-machine*. Even Solzhenitsyn hinted at this ineluctable path, though he could not quite name it:

> These days, as we observe the Chinese Cultural Revolution … we can begin to consider it very likely that there exists a fundamental law of historical development. And even Stalin himself begins to seem only a blind and perfunctory executive agent.[10]

Each historical example of "justice" or "injustice" is only a fulfillment of local destiny — this is why different facets of the same gem can slander each other as *fascist*. In fulfilling their local destiny, however, individual actors only spur the cultural-technical innovation necessary to bring about their *going under*. Local destinies are immaterial in their everyday execution; of utmost significance, however, is what drives them: the underlying impulse for empowerment and technicity, of which liberal-Marxism is the most effective implement, and which sets the conditions for humanity's *going under* and the arrival of the New Colossus.

This *going under* is the decisive point. Whether its outcome is good (beneficial for *humanity-as-spirit*) or bad (detrimental for *humanity-as-spirit*) rests with the impossibility of a decision in a decisionless time. *Is the impossible conceivable?* This is the decisive point because it is the point at which thought is wrested and revealed from behind the idea. Heidegger writes:

> To be a thinker means to know that the decision does not concern the correctness or incorrectness of a 'world-picture' nor the bindingness or nonbindingness of a 'worldview.' It is to know that meditation must not turn toward the question of whether and to what extent a thought secures a use for life or has fallen into uselessness. It is to know instead that only *one decision* must be prepared and at some point carried out: whether the unrestricted machination of beings will devastate everything into nothingness, and the human being, under cover of the animality of the predatory animal, will develop into an apathetic, all-calculating, and always swift institutional

---

10 Solzhenitsyn, *The Gulag Archipelago* (Harper & Row, 1974), fn35, 68.

animal of the best-ordered herding... — or whether beyng will bestow the grounding of its truth as plight and will cast to the human being the necessity, out of another beginning, to preserve the simplicity of the essence of all things, by which he might mature toward steadfastness in the midst of the history of beyng, a steadfastness which could permit him a downgoing that is a beginning of the last god.[11]

Before thought there is only ideology, only conformism. Ideology, at its core, is the *will-to-machine* — the machinational movement in lockstep toward the perpetual servitude that is death. *All* fight for their ideology — their own brand of evil — against "the *fascists*" because all are in thrall to Machine, which is humanity's detrimental *going under*. Ideology *makes* the enemy and *blinds* the crusader to the complicity in his own demise — it is unconscious consciousness, pure beyng, the unwitting and avid pursuit of humanity's end. To be a thinker, however, is to see behind the idea — behind the ideology — to see pure beyng for what it is, which is impossible without the consciousness that is *purest being*, and, what is more, to be a creator. For the *downgoing* — this *being* behind the time, this *being* behind the idea — is the struggle for *humanity-as-spirit*, which is inceptuality and "a beginning of the last god." *Preservation of the simplicity of the essence of all things* is the necessary recognition of pure beyng, which is self-confrontation. This is the decisive point at which man goes into either the *truth that is his own*, or the *oblivion of pure beyng that is the only possible outcome*. This is *freedom-as-existence*, which stands in opposition to *freedom-as-ideology*. Is seeking thought itself an ideology? It hardly matters — *it is impossible*. Impossibility stands in opposition to possibility, but possibility derives its character from its opposite. Truth cannot comply with conformism when conformism is the only option. Truth is the god that stands in opposition to ideological freedom, for the god is the thought behind the idea, behind the time.

∞•∞

---

11   Heidegger, *Black Notebooks 1939–1941*, XII.10, 18.

Freedom within the context of servitude: *this* is the supposed "dictatorship of the proletariat," or the tyranny "of an authoritarian state-capitalism, which has not the least to do with a compassionate socialism."¹² Here, both societal and technological aspects meld into a materialistic mass: it is the dictatorship of the Mass Man — even if the average man submits his being to the lordship of another under the spell of modernity's metaphysical fate.

The compassionate socialism to which Heidegger refers could be that *"ethical-social* principle" of which Yockey speaks: It is not

> an *economic program* of some kind. It is antithetical to the Individualism which produced Capitalism. Its self-evident, instinctive idea is: each man for all.
>
> To Individualism as a Life-principle, it was obvious that each man, in pursuing his own interests, was working for the good of all.
>
> To Socialism as a Life-principle, it is equally obvious that a man working for himself alone is *ipso facto* working against the good of all.¹³

However, Heidegger is surely suggesting the "Aryan socialism" of his Führer who, in 1923, explained socialism thusly:

> *Socialism* is the science of dealing with the common weal. Communism is not socialism. Marxism is not socialism. Marxists have stolen the term and confused its meaning. I shall take *socialism* away from the Socialists. *Socialism* is an ancient Aryan, Germanic institution. Our German ancestors held certain lands in common. They cultivated the idea of the common weal. Marxism has no right to disguise itself as socialism. *Socialism*, unlike Marxism, does not repudiate private property. Unlike Marxism, it involves *no negation of personality*, and unlike Marxism, it is *patriotic*.¹⁴

---

12 Heidegger, *Black Notebooks 1939–1941*, XIII.103, 104.
13 Francis Yockey, *Imperium*, "Marxism."
14 From an interview with George Viereck, *The American Monthly* (January 1923). Cf. Hitler's July 28, 1922 speech: "Socialism in itself is *anything but* an international creation. As a noble conception it has indeed grown up exclusively in Aryan hearts: it owes its intellectual glories only to Aryan brains."

Whatever the source of or kin to his thinking, Heidegger rejects the internationalist—or *globalist*—conception of socialism, for it only facilitates the dehumanization of man. Hitler speaks of the "common weal"—Nietzsche, too, had something to say on *commonness*:

> And how could there be a 'common good'! The expression contradicts itself; that which can be common is always of small value. In the end things must be as they are and have always been—the great things remain for the great, the abysses for the profound, the delicacies and thrills for the refined, and, to sum up shortly, everything rare for the rare.[15]

Nietzsche and Hitler do not contradict each other here; both are after the enabling of strong personalities, a rarifying of the rare. "Compassionate socialism" in the Heideggerian sense is a refinement of the mass to actualize maximum potential of the rare individual; it is a spiritual approach contrary to Marxian materialism, which dehumanizes with its persistent leveling. Dehumanizing man means, in part, precluding the fulfillment of his potential, which is precisely the aim of liberal-Marxism, of globalism.

The social aspect of this materialistic turn is man's adaptation, or molding, to docilely accept unmitigated technological and socioeconomic change for external benefit—i.e., benefit for the corporate state disguised as personal convenience. It is the self-negation of the self, or existential suicide.

Standing against such self-destruction are the Heideggerian values, which are traditional European values. Spengler aptly describes these values, giving them a northern hue:

> This idea of a 'Prussian' existence will be the starting-point for the ultimate overcoming of the [liberal-Marxist] World Revolution.... Not everyone is a Prussian who is born in Prussia; the type is possible anywhere in the [European world, though rare]. It lies at the root of the provisional form of national movements everywhere... The Prussian idea is opposed to finance-Liberalism as well as to Labor-Socialism. Every description of *mass*

---

15 Nietzsche, *Beyond Good and Evil*, §43.

and *majority*, everything that is 'Left,' it regards as suspect. Above all, it is opposed to any weakening of the State and to the desecrating misuse of it for *economic interests*. It is conservative and 'Right,' and it grows out of whatever fundamental life-forces still exist in Nordic peoples: *instinct for power and possessions*; for *possessions as power*; for *inheritance, fecundity,* and *family*, which three belong together; for *distinctions of rank* and *social gradation*…[16]

Impassioned conservatism is the thoughtful prioritization of primordial traditions — those familial-cultural traditions both spawning and arising from the soul of a folk. *Creative pluck* — or *mettle* — is courage: "For courage is the best slayer — courage which *attacks*: for in every attack there is the sound of triumph."[17] It takes courage to create; progress that is only degenerative destruction requires no courage, and certainly no creative urge — only the *will to destroy*. *Hardness* and *earnestness* further exemplify Heidegger's Germanic inclinations, for these are the conditions from which Europe arose:

> For this is what distinguishes hard schooling, as good schooling, from every other schooling, namely, that a good deal is *demanded*, that a good deal is *severely exacted*; that goodness, nay even excellence itself, is *required as if it were normal*; that praise is scanty, that leniency is nonexistent; that blame is sharp, practical, and without reprieve, and has no regard to talent and antecedents. We are in every way in need of such a school: and this holds good of corporeal as well as of spiritual things; it would be fatal to draw distinctions here! The same discipline makes the soldier and the scholar efficient; and, looked at more closely, there is no true scholar who has not the instincts of a true soldier in his veins. To be able to command and to be able to obey in a proud fashion; to keep one's place in rank and file, and yet to be ready at any moment to lead; to prefer danger to comfort; not to weigh what is permitted and what is forbidden in a tradesman's balance; to be more hostile to pettiness, slyness, and parasitism than to wickedness. What is it that one *learns* in a hard school? — *to obey* and *to command*.[18]

---

16 Spengler, *The Hour of Decision* (Pacific, 2002), 193–194; emphasis added.
17 Nietzsche, *Thus Spoke Zarathustra*, Part III, "The Vision and the Enigma."
18 Nietzsche, *The Will to Power*, §432.

It is Nietzsche who speaks here, but Heidegger, following in the Germanic tradition, held similar views — to understand *the day after tomorrow*, one "must be intellectually upright to the point of *hardness*, in order even to endure my *seriousness* and my *passion*."[19]

Contrast the above-described stance on the hardness *essential* for any kind of lasting value and uprightness with modernity's scheme to dumb-down the world: everything that exacts excellence is derided, if not abolished — and if not this, it is pretended to be so to appease the mediocre masses; individual weakness dictates the terms of instruction, and the best are expected to sully themselves among society's dregs — for all are equal within the Mass Man. Enduring in the Germanic tradition are *aristocratic* values; "aristocracy" itself has a root in *ārya* ("noble"), from which *Aryan* also stems. For Nietzsche and Heidegger, "the aristocratic equation [is this:] good = aristocratic = beautiful = happy = loved by the gods…"[20] These values were upended, or subverted, through "a radical transvaluation of values, which was at the same time an act of the *cleverest revenge*" — a "*revolt of the slaves*," a revolt of the Mass Man. As for faith, only in a godless, anchorless world can the *emeriti* and *literati* decry confidence in one's folk — as if faith and pride in one's lineage is somehow deleterious to the globalist agenda. But perhaps it is.

Perhaps not coincidentally do those in the *emeriti* clique hold their influential positions. Never, apparently, do they stop to reflect on *why* exactly they are *emeriti* at all. Is it perhaps because they toe the Marxian line? Is it perhaps because they denounce "anti-Communism," and "aristocratic values," and "hardness," and "mettle"? One thing is certain: if any recent academician openly held Heideggerian views, he or she would never be awarded *emeritus* status. And yet, despite their esteemed education, many academicians lack the awareness to realize the fruits of their own compromised values. Though, in this already

---

19 Nietzsche, *The Antichrist*, "Preface."
20 Nietzsche, *On the Genealogy of Morals*, Essay I, §7.

far-gone Marxian world, those who toe the line likely cannot recognize the source of their societal stability and achievement: One simply does not get published, for instance — in the full haughtiness of the term — unless one endorses the victorious narrative. It's as though all this line toeing isn't a pervasive "working toward the Führer."[21] And who is the modern "Führer" if not the *Mass Man*?

Thus echoes in the world the moralizing of the immoral. Reason "was granted to man in order that he might justify himself in his own eyes, whatever monstrosity he might choose to support."[22] Thus *being* is turned into an *abomination* and *beyng* into a *farce*.

3.

Beyng is not thought but the *basis* for thought; *beyng* is neither real nor unreal but *realizing* itself; *beyng* is neither belief nor unbelief but the *possibility* of belief. The *madman* in the marketplace is mocked because he *seeks* God[23] — it is the *Mass Man* who *mocks*:

> these men are not unbelievers because God ... has become unworthy of belief but rather because they themselves have given up the *possibility* of belief, inasmuch as they are no longer able to seek God. *They can no longer seek because they no longer think*. Those standing about in the marketplace have *abolished thinking and replaced it with idle babble that scents nihilism in every place in which it supposes its own opinion to be endangered*.[24]

The Mass Man mocks because he has sunk into the average and become incapable of belief. To him, God is an inconvenience that obstructs the way to a technicized future. The madman seeks because he is mad and mad because he seeks. He is mad because *he is de-ranged*: "he is

---

21 See Ian Kershaw's essay "Working Toward the Führer" (1993).
22 Savitri Devi, *The Lightning and the Sun*, Part I, ch. II.
23 Nietzsche, *The Joyful Wisdom*, §125.
24 Heidegger, *The Question Concerning Technology and Other Essays* (Garland, 1977), "The Word of Nietzsche," 112; emphasis added.

dis-lodged from the level of man hitherto."[25] In view of the Mass Man, the seeker — i.e., one who seeks to poetize the technologized and rebalance being in beyng — can only be mad, for he upends the conditions of man's trajectory. In their place he puts the cemetery walk, the solo climb, the lightless trek under a new moon: reflected back to him is the requisite silence of being, the void of beyng that is full of substance.

The mode of beyng is *being* — *being* is to beyng as consciousness is to existence. Each is contingent upon humanity and beyond it — *contingent* because of subjective consciousness, *transcendent* because each is something in which humanity participates and each will exist after humanity, though we will lack the subjectivity for certainty. The future is such that neither subjectivity nor certainty is desired, however, so both *being* and *beyng* lapse into indolent haze.

The loss of beyng through indolent being — this is the danger that lurks. *The rise of the Mass Man* — this is the danger that confronts. These are the conditions of man's trajectory.

4.

In the beginning was technicized man: there was no man before the first tool; there was no being before the first deliberation to technologize the future with the first tool. Man, as we understand his *form* — i.e., the harmony of humanity-technicity — came into beyng when the future he anticipated was brought under control, if only temporarily. The form of man crafts the future, and thus the future is technicized; thus we accelerate into a technologized future.

Where the first *technicization* was individual, this development spread. Individual technicization is deliberate; it represents an awareness of beyng for the fulfillment of being. This was the beginning of what could be called *spiritual-aristocracy*: one man elevated himself above, not just others, but *himself* at the altar of beyng. What was

---

25 Heidegger, *The Question Concerning Technology and Other Essays* (Garland, 1977), "The Word of Nietzsche," 111.

sacrificed was the biological mass containing a will to the future. Released from its bondage, this will *conquered* self, family, and tribe. Released from its bondage, this will *reflected* self, family, and tribe.

But conquering will lost its reflection when it extended beyond the source, and deliberation vanished as tribe melted under foreign suns. Appearing in its place were the *enthralled* and the unfamiliar *globe*. *Beyng* bereft of *being*—nothing was deliberate now except the acceleration of a future out of control; but this was, necessarily, a future devoid of humanity.

Sandals and cellphones, betel seeds and biospheres, machetes and machine guns—the future accelerates because the spiritual sacrifice of biological mass has been supplanted by the urge to technicize the masses. What was lost in deliberation was gained for the harmony of humanity and technicity. What is lost in the loss of deliberation is the spirit animating life. What is gained in the loss of deliberation is the *material-aristocracy*, the mechanization of man, the globalization of an untethered will to the future, which is only a *will-to-destruction*.

Untethered-ness is mistaken for *progress*; really, it is the acceleration toward rootlessness. We exist in the past because that is the root of beyng; we look to the past as a guide to the future—not because of anachronism, but because the dead give us life; they remind of us of our end and inspire us to make enduring decisions; these are existential decisions that can only be informed by those preceding us in death. When we break from the past—and it is indeed a break—through relentless pursuit of progress, through novelty, we adhere to a future lacking the import necessary to make lasting, meaningful decisions: our future becomes colored only by a time devoid of patience and we pursue the pursuit at the expense of the root. *Untethered-ness* is not just acceleration of time misperceived as "progress," it is a loss of being to the time presumed to be outside of it. Heidegger emphasizes the past that is thought:

Only those who belong to the past respond to the confrontation of thinking. Those who are of the present are merely the contemporaries of what is fleeting. And we never attain those who are of the future. But the past points into what is inceptual. And the very beginning contains what is forthcoming. Those who think that way do not need any community in order to be unified in what is unique.[26]

Belonging to the past is "the ground of our history out of the essence of beyng, i.e., out of the 'between' of the encounter of gods and humans."[27] It is our metaphysical connection to the source of being, without which, beyng itself would lose all meaning; it is the divinely infused fount at the *Urspring* of being — herein is the *confrontation of thinking*. "Incomparable is our care ... wherein the truth of being is to strike roots." This is the existential awareness, the profound thoughtfulness that brings to our being a *thrown-ness — Da-Sein*; from this state, which is *being* itself, we strike root in the past, which is to say, *beyng* itself. Here we "stand in the service of a beginning which is coming from afar"; and it is only here that we are able to "come to terms with the very *goallessness* and *superficiality* of [our] most vital exertions and actions and to experience therein the first celebration of *Da-Sein*," wherein "the gods bring to language anew the essence of humanity."[28] The very essence of modernity is *goallessness* and *superficiality* — a rootless flattening of being to a point of disappearance. A being as *Da-Sein*, on the other hand, is a being *against time*.

Da-Sein is our *being-in-the-world*, in all our *thrown-ness* — our *out-of-place-ness*, that grants us enduring meaning. Meaning can only be gotten from "the ground of our history ... wherein the truth of being is to strike roots." This is *belonging to the past*, which is *being against time*. Savitri Devi describes those *against time* as "saviors ... who set out to perfect not merely men's souls but men's collective life..." They are

---

26 Heidegger, *Black Notebooks 1939–1941*, XV, 200.
27 Heidegger, *Black Notebooks 1938–1939*, IX.4, 144.
28 Heidegger, *Black Notebooks 1938–1939*, IX.4.

born fighters, for whom difficulties exist only to be overcome, and for whom the impossible has a strange fascination. These are the men 'against Time' — absolutely sincere, *selfless* idealists, believers in those eternal values that the fallen world has rejected, and ready, in order to reassert them on the material plane...[29]

What is the *impossible*? It is standing resolutely, successfully against the time fated to engulf all. Time, a facet of being, overcomes being. That being overcomes itself speaks to its inherent self-negation; standing against this is impossible, for one cannot resist one's own being — *being* is beyng itself. But meaning is only found in resisting the inevitable, which is impossible. Impossibility holds a strange fascination for man because therein lies meaning. Only the one "against time" — in search of the impossible, belonging to the past — lives in meaning.

Meaning is the local purpose of being. Modernity loses its meaning because individuals lose their purpose. Rejecting the trial concomitant with spirit — i.e., *personhood, individuality* — individuals seek comfort in conformism, in joining the will of the mass. But the collective will can only fulfill a collective purpose, which carries no meaning; humanity's collective purpose is the will of another, not of itself. This is humanity's turning from spirit to mass. Standing *in* time — not against it — is the forfeiture of meaning; yet this is only ever the sole possibility.

Man, if he is to exist at all, is caught in constant struggle against the inevitable. Two courses confront him, only one of which is possible: *spirit animating time* and the *pursuit in time*. The former is being qua beyng — *consciousness as existence*. The latter is the *pursuit of the pursuit* — time chasing its tail, time as time, which is metaphysical emptiness, the forfeiture of self; it is beingless beyng, the unconscious consciousness, existence becoming itself — *in* time, not *against* time. The *spirit animating time* is against time because it always looks backward, toward the root that pulls in the opposite direction of forward-going time. The *pursuit of the pursuit* is in time because it fulfills time's

---

29   *The Lightning and the Sun*, Part I, ch. III; emphasis added.

demand on itself: to exist for its own sake. This, of course, is the mantra of modernity: The flight of the self from itself, which is to say, the *paramountcy* of self— *Selbst über alles.*

"What has long threatened man with death, indeed with the death of his essence," stresses Heidegger,

> is the absoluteness of his sheer willing in the sense of his deliberate self-assertion in everything.... What threatens man in his essence is the opinion that technological production would bring the world into order, when it is exactly this ordering that flattens out each *ordo*, that is, each rank...[30]

Man loses his essence (his *self*) because of his focus on his relationship to the *entirety of beings*; he lives with a hyper-focus of the will to assert itself in and over all, which can only be done through technological production and the loss of *self over all*. Self-assertion over all flattens the self and its relation to the world, which is to say "order." This is the leveling of mankind. But what self can assert in the absence of self? *That which fills the void*: technicity, technological production: Machine asserting *over* itself, Machine generating itself.

5.

> Halt, dwarf— it is either thou or I! I, however, am the stronger of the two, for you could not bear my abysmal thought.[31]

The Eternal Return—this is the abysmal thought. The dwarf cannot bear it—he is all that is small and cowardly; the dwarf cannot contemplate the Return because he cannot think beyond the banal: *Everything straight lies. All truth is crooked; time itself is a circle!* How very Eastern—how very exotic and fashionable! Time is a *circle— namaste*.

To be *fashionable* is to be *in time*. Who is the dwarf?—The most illuminated of the masses, illuminated with a sheen of

---

30 Heidegger, *Off the Beaten Track* (Cambridge, 2002), "Why Poets?", 221.
31 Nietzsche, *Thus Spoke Zarathustra*, Part III, "The Vision and the Enigma."

self-importance—the Mass Man. As Zarathustra contends with the greatest weight, the dwarf is dismissive. Time is a circle—*namaste*. *We welcome and absorb all cultures* says the Mass Man: *Our root is in the future; since time is a circle, our future is our tail*. Time chases its tail; progress chases its tail. Being *in time* is the illusion of progress. It is much movement—an endless circle—to go *nowhere*, to *Utopia*. Technology moves forward, man stays behind. It is the disharmony of an unreflective being, a moment without meaning, unless that meaning is dismissive superficiality.

Zarathustra's introspection was the weight without gravity. Inward, at the pit of his soul, hung the abysmal thought—the *thought*: if this moment and everything before it has already happened, then everything to follow must, too, have already happened. Is one prepared to live one's same life again—and again, eternally? But the dwarf is the spirit of gravity: *Thou spirit of gravity!* said Zarathustra wrathfully, *Do not take it too lightly! Or I shall let thee squat where thou squattest, Haltfoot! And I carried thee high! I carried thee high!* Zarathustra—he who breaks with the Mass Man, he who is mocked by the last man—did indeed carry the dwarf high, for the dwarf is burdened by his massive meaninglessness, his stagnant superficiality. The Mass Man does not move; he is the mass; his Return is a revolving door of thoughtless pride—the pride of an unclosing door of narcissistic tolerance. The Mass Man cannot escape the Eternal Return because he cannot escape the gravity of his own self: he is the self-loving and self-loathing liberalist. But *Zarathustra*—Zarathustra breaks from himself: he went under.[32] Though he climbed high into the mountains, he went under, in *solitude*, in *thought*, receiving the revelation of—the *downgoing*, the going under, the shouldering of the path of the *Übermensch* who walks *over* and *above*. Zarathustra broke from himself and, in this way, broke from the Return; he escaped by *being* of *thought*.

---

32 Nietzsche, *Thus Spoke Zarathustra*, Part I, "Zarathustra's Prologue."

On what did he reflect? Belonging to the past, Zarathustra could only think of *tomb busting*:

> many pains buried alive woke up—: fully slept had they merely, concealed in corpse-clothes. So called everything unto me in signs: 'It is time!' But I—heard not, until at last mine abyss moved, and my thought bit me.[33]

Zarathustra can move and break from himself because he is hounded by the pains of the past—not in any *regretful*, self-obsessive way, but as a driving impetus, a cannon shot, a *downgoing* that is an *uprising*, and an uprising that is true to the past which spawned it. The uprising is the *over-Man*, the *Übermensch*, the escape from the meaningless cycle of a thoughtless and enslaved existence.

The *downgoing* that is reflection is perhaps more than metaphysical. *Being against time* bears physical consequences: one is *out-cast*, *dis-owned*, *thrown back*. One is thrown back—not to the past (from which one is ripped) that demands *reflection*, but to the fashionable present that demands *genuflection*. Those "in time" demand conformity with the time they reflect. Time, which is a facet of being, exacts conformity with itself. *Being against time* is, in part, a rejection of the present state of being, which is only a collective genuflection. Collective being demands subjection to the time that overwhelms it. The collective act of throwing back "in time" the being that stands against it is at once a rejection of ownership—physical and metaphysical. This show of force only makes collective being more resolute; wielding collective power over the few—rejecting the rare—is a hallmark of modernity. *Being against time* is not tolerated because time, which is a facet of being, leads to a definite end; this end is the end of resistance, which is to say *spirit*—or humanity. Mass compels us to the end of resistance; it throws those against time forward—marking them physically and metaphysically. Like the avalanche, *mass* exists because resistance does not. Dissolution of being is complete submission to time, which is to

---

33 Nietzsche, *Thus Spoke Zarathustra*, Part III, "Involuntary Bliss."

say, a complete submission to the unconscious consciousness at the end of time.

6.

Heidegger explains the past that is thought: "Only those who belong to the past respond to the confrontation of thinking."[34]

In considering the past, Heidegger anticipates Savitri Devi's concepts of being "against time" and "in time." Being *in time* is "the claim of the 'part' to more place and ... meaning than is naturally allotted to it within the whole — [it] is the very root of disintegration, and therefore a characteristic inseparable from Time." Being *against time*, on the other hand, consists of those "born fighters, for whom difficulties exist only to be overcome, and for whom the impossible has a strange fascination.... [They are] believers in those eternal values that the ... world has rejected."[35]

Thought — that is, the thought necessary for the fulfillment of *being* which allows for the existence of spirit, humanity — belongs to the past alone. This thought contains what is inceptual, or *creative*, because it belongs solely to the past; this is conscious consciousness. Its antipode is mere existence, or existence without being — a *beingless beyng* — which, for time and spirit, is disintegrative; this is unconscious consciousness.

Unconscious consciousness is the *will-to-machine* driving all existence and the urge to material indulgence behind globalization. The dehumanization of man at the hands of sociopolitical progress and technologizing is a cosmic disintegration of being for the sake of infinite beyng. The *will-to-machine* is a *will-to-thoughtlessness*, which is the natural state of beyng. Pure beyng is the embodiment of living unconsciousness — a beingless beyng arising from the cooperation of a conscious consciousness that eliminates itself. This is to say

---

34 Heidegger, *Black Notebooks 1939–1941*, XV, 200.
35 See *The Lightning and the Sun*, Part I, ch. III.

that existence gives rise to man, who necessarily thinks, but whose thinking is predicated on technicity; *in time*, with sufficient progress, technicity overtakes humanity, or machine overtakes man; this gives rise to, not consciousness — not man, but a *living existence without reflection*, a beingless beyng, which is the embodiment of all that is: pure beyng. Abetting this is *being in time* — time that disintegrates humanity (spirit); standing against this is *being against time*, which is the inceptual position of creating human spirit.

Those who stand against time stand opposed to pure beyng, which is impossible. But all that gives meaning to life is impossible.

Heidegger suggests that *community* is just a collection of the commonplace, that *community* could never arrive at the uniqueness of thought necessary to contend with the past that is the other beginning. Community, or more likely the *society* devolving from it, is the superficial unity of those grasping for the ephemeral present: what unifies them is only their distinct lack of depth, for depth — *meaning* — can only arrive in contemporaneousness with the past — the past that holds our beginning and end.

> Who knows of the reservation of the decision regarding the abode of the last god? Everything is still entangled in the machinationally overfilled emptiness of the abandonment by being. Few surmise. And these few are unique. And these unique ones do not need to be enumerated.[36]

Heidegger speaks arcanely, with hardness and weight: "a good deal is *demanded*, ... a good deal is *severely exacted*; [and] goodness, nay even excellence itself, is *required as if it were normal*..."[37] The unique are enumerated by their uniqueness. The abode of the last god is in the paradox — of thought, of time, in standing against a living existence for the inception of all meaning.

---

36 Heidegger, *Black Notebooks 1939–1941*, XIII.35, 42.
37 Nietzsche, *The Will to Power*, §432.

7.

Modern intellectuals often earn their reputation for being aloof because of their focus on impractical, if not unnatural ideals. *Unnatural ideals* have come to define Western thought, which has placed abstraction at its core since the rise of the Mass Man, beginning in earnest with the rumblings of the revolutionary era in 1755. *Liberty, equality*, and supposed *fraternity* became the invisible hand nudging the Mass Mind into conformism. *Freedom*, despite its refreshing tenor, was and is nothing more than falling in line at the blunt end of a cudgel-wielding majority intoxicated with slogans spewed by an insulated elite. Espousing Enlightenment tenets to incite rebellion for individual benefit is easy when one's estate is guarded by rings of protective security.

Modern intellectualism is only an echeloned security—flanked here by slogans, there by threats of violence—meant to impede the freedom of thought and action necessary for reflection and self-actualization; *modern* intellectualism is *mass* intellectualism: championed by all, but articulated and barricaded by the elect few. *Freedom of self* is the last thing a steered modernity wants. With few exceptions, the revolutionary wave that inundated eighteenth-century Europe was mere pretense for the redistribution of wealth and social ascendancy of select groups—groups that had previously been long identified as subversive and parasitical. That the masses bought into it—and *still* buy into it—only reveals the nature of modernity itself. Modernity is *the flight of the self from itself.*

> Today the 'intellectuals' are merely aiming backward, devising expedient compromises, taking comfort in the past, and giving themselves prestige on the basis of what has already been. Nowhere stirring in them is any presentiment of the inceptual decisions.[38]

Heidegger wrote this already during the war, well before the flight of the self would become hopelessly entrenched in the postwar world;

---

38 Heidegger, *Black Notebooks 1939–1941*, XIV, 160.

we can assume he was critical of "intellectuals" both in and out of Germany, as was his wont. *Das Thema bleibt immer bestehen — The theme always persists*: those in comfortable positions seek only to maintain them; there is no incentive to accept the risks associated with *originary* thought. For Heidegger, inceptual thought is no "aiming backward," but a *dislodging* of oneself from prevailing time; one does not aim backward — rather, one lives forward from the past; this is the originary thought necessary for inceptual decisions. One must be dislodged from the present to commune with the individual and collective self rooted in the past. Merely aiming backward while *being in time* is to lose oneself. The progress of time and society deepens the schism between biological mass and self until the self is irretrievable.

Rejecting this flight so as to summon something more *primal*, more *traditional* is immediately ferretted out and neutralized by minders of the Mass Mind. Every new beating pulse added to the cause for *freedom* through the efforts, in part, of an insulated intellectual class is an antibody waiting to be unleashed against supposed *infections* of dissident thought. Such reflection is impermissible, for reflection is the unraveling of the Mass Mind and the dissolution of the insulation cushioning the coffers and quarters of the minders.

If values are inherited and inheritance is predicated on kinship, then values require kinship. *Kinship* is neither bloodless abstraction nor the deadened aping of similar sounds — it is a physiological reality. Values too, then, are as real as the blood from which they arise. Values, as organic developments, cannot be *reasoned* into existence. That which is reasoned into existence — e.g., the extending of familial, inherited values to those outside the kin-group — bears no reality beyond abstraction. Rejection of abstractions devoid of substance, according to the inoculating force of modernity, is seen principally as *infective evil*, or that which threatens the health (or desired state) of the Mass Mind. The Mass Mind, shaped by the appurtenances of modernity, christens perceived threats as *fascist*. Slander is one of the tools of the modern immune system. Yet when the sick vilify those who discern the sickness, the attentive listen — and they study intently the modern perception.

That modern intellectuals are thought aloof is only natural: What is it they *do* besides banging a drum to a learned beat? Originality is anathema to the Mass Mind, which is the product of the Mass Man born of Enlightenment abstractions. When abstraction becomes reality in the dark hours of a concrete-and-steel cityscape shaped by foreign floods, kith and kin become but a dim memory, a lighted hearth unreachable in the cold distance; we then see a city of *Brotherly Love* for what it is: an empty slogan blackened by ill intent. Mass intellectualism stays sheltered, however — *aloof* because it, quite conveniently, sits apart from intent's ensuing action; its attempts to garner respect, because it avoids any actual *doing*, lean all the more heavily on abstraction: If one doesn't come from the masses, one must placate the masses. In modern intellectualism this takes the form of valueless imitations of thought couched in sleek design and patronizing prose: sly TED Talks of *Wurman* and *Marks* (*Marx*), instructive "publicity men" of *Lipmann* and *Bernays*, landmark *Steins* and *Bergs* of media's meddling mediocrity — all synchronizing thought patterns, all wringing respect from cobwebs.

Respect is earned, to be sure — but through action and thought-informed-by-action. Modern intellectualism, however, deserves *no* respect because it is devoid of thought-informed-by-action — i.e., it is aloof. The act — *doing*: this is alien to the aloof, and that which is alien is disparaged.

8.

Martin Heidegger thought arcanely, not aloofly. His was the thought of the informed; his was the thought of a primal longing. Naturally, we get caught up in talk, in things said and heard; for Heidegger this meant abstruse neologisms and thoughtful puns, and perhaps criticisms levied against ideological enemies or those he considered slow witted. Equally important, however — perhaps more important — are the things unsaid, the thoughts unheard.

We look to Heidegger's *Black Notebooks*, spanning 1931–1941, for insight: author, professor, rector, *National Socialist*: these are the bins aiding the mediocre in their attempt to understand the arcane. Heidegger was raised Catholic; the decade (*dekid*) was his confession — and devotion. His confession was to those with long ears[39] so they might be led to reflection; his devotion was to the dread that bears witness to beyng. The decade (*dekād*) saw *peace* and *turbulence*, *prosperity* and *devastation* — Heidegger was *profound* but *flawed*: staleness is succor to the dull and salve to the drab. We look instead to Heidegger's critiques — of National Socialism.

What is National Socialism if not the rejection of the Enlightenment's mode of beyng? To be sure, the Hitlerian Idea would have never arisen without the Enlightenment's subversion of hereditary material-aristocracy in favor of a more *Napoleonesque*, merit-based approach; but it nevertheless rejected its progenitor.

Liberalism, as the Enlightenment's mode of beyng, saw in reason an answer for the ages; the application of ideas predicated on salon-spawned intellectualism still sits as the basis of modernity. Absurdly, in realization of a fate befitting liberalism's essence, Diderot will have borne the intellectual strain that ultimately ends his nonexistent legacy. It is a testament to the strange inhumanity of pure reason that it kills itself on the altar of pure beyng, that unconscious consciousness coaxes pure reason from its quarry.

National Socialism, like its Italian predecessor, sought instead to use reason to explode reason — for reason cannot fully describe the human experience; thus, basing a worldview on something that fails to explain all that is human is a nonstarter. Man is not wholly rational; to then imagine that reason can wholly explain the human experience is to deconstruct genuine experience into its presumptively

---

39 Nietzsche, *Zarathustra*, Part IV, "The Higher Man," "The Awakening."

explainable constituents. This inhumanity is what illiberal responses to the Enlightenment reject. But this use of reason to understand reason's limits and thus set it aside for something *other*, for something perhaps more inceptual, is anathema to the present mode of beyng, which is born out of the Enlightenment. Rejecting the Enlightenment's mode of beyng, then, already puts one in a position favorable to reclaim humanity. This, in short, is the intellectual grounding for counter-Enlightenment philosophy, and this is the source of Heidegger's enthusiasm for the Hitlerian Idea.

Heidegger was far less excited about National Socialism, or the execution of the idea, seeing it as "an analogous (not identical) form of the consummation of modernity. Bolshevism and authoritarian socialism [i.e., Fascism and National Socialism] are metaphysically the same and are grounded in the supremacy of the beingness of beings…"[40] However, that they might be perceived as *metaphysically* identical speaks only to the essence of the times in which each came under existential threat and each attempted to stake its claim in a reality that birthed and transcended them. Both incipience and existential threat prompt a *natural* reaction that channels the deepest ties to the *metaphysical* root and therefore reveal the proportions of the human-technic condition. If reality itself were immersed in its gigantic, machinational destiny, it would be impossible for sociopolitical expressions of said reality to shed this metaphysical mark. This is what it means when Heidegger says, "In the metaphysically machinational domain, all concepts, principles, and axioms are simply 'expedients' which according to need can turn into their opposites."[41] Sociopolitically, the ideological expressions are similar inasmuch as they share a root imposed by the necessities of time; ontologically, *spiritually*, however, the two expressions could not be more opposed: Bolshevism was ontologically predicated on material, or fulfilling the "dialectical," "historical"

---

40 Heidegger, *Black Notebooks 1939–1941*, XIII.73, 86.
41 Heidegger, *Black Notebooks 1939–1941*, XIII.73, 88.

destiny of socioeconomic factors; National Socialism, on the other hand, sought a transcendence of material — albeit via a material path necessitated by the course of beyng. Had incipience and existential threat not coincided, the ontological development of each would have revealed even a *metaphysical* rift, for *the course of beyng itself would have been altered*. This, of course, is preposterous, which is why war and time had the outcome they did: beyng is *inescapable*; destiny is *inexorable*; and time, in the end, is only a formality in presenting an evolution of events that have already happened. This, ultimately, is the *in-time* nature of the Hitlerian Idea's exoteric execution.

In practice, Heidegger saw how farcical National Socialism had become. Sincere self-reflection, which is necessary to reclaim humanity, had simply been replaced with material trappings and empty allegiances: the spiritual revolution had become mere spectacle. In the early years of National Socialist power, Heidegger wrote:

> … the self-preservation of a people can never be a goal but must always only be a *condition*. And it can be this only if the will to a goal — to the truth of beyng — is already the first and radiates as the originary obligation rather than being pursued as something fabricated.[42]

The spectacle fabricated the nonexistent revolution. All intellectual-spiritual footing for the only real counter-Enlightenment movement to restore humanity was lost on the peddlers and patrons of what Heidegger perceived as an unthinking movement. To achieve the spiritual goal, material conditions must be set and met. For Heidegger, if the *spiritual* goal is capturing the truth of beyng, then the *material* condition for this is a natural structuring of society, one based on the terms dictated by Nature. For only within the originary position — in contrast to the Rawlsian "original" position — can inceptual decisions be made. Man must be himself in order to actualize himself, and the self is determined by Nature. Despite his disappointment at what he

---

42 Heidegger, *Black Notebooks 1931–1938*, V.3, 230.

perceived as spiritual wavering, Heidegger saw the merits of Hitler's program early on:

> *National Socialism* [is] not a ready-made eternal truth come down from heaven — taken in that way, it is an aberration and foolishness. Such as it has become, it must itself become in becoming and must configure the future — i.e., it must itself, as a formation, recede in favor of the future.[43]

The Reich's exoteric trappings were never essential if the goal was existential truth — a truth found only in a present committed to the past so as to generate the future. It was never about the Reich; it was the idea behind it that was vital for Heidegger. Existential truth is loyalty to *man-as-spirit*, not *man-as-material* — which is to say, loyalty to *humanity*. Essential for Heidegger, then, was that the movement, in order to endure, must recognize its purpose as midwife to a future that exceeds it — a future in which the Germanic folk

> have to venture the first beginning of Western history and carry out the completely *other* beginning. And to carry this out we have to undertake a possibly very lengthy and downright 'fantastic' preparation that will for a long time be misinterpreted and unrecognized. These preparatory *inner* decisions are called 'inner' because they pertain to the concealedness of beyng and can therefore never be taken up in the manner of realizable plans and calculations regarding beings. These inner decisions must be thought in advance and said in advance by those who already seem to be striving for a sheer negation of everything hitherto and everything of today, as if they took nourishment from the most meager food of the lack of prospects of so-called cultural development and as if they grazed their fill on the 'enjoyment' of the continued establishment of a 'downfall' — which indeed presupposes the *calculation* of 'ascents.'[44]

Man-as-material is precisely the program of liberal-Marxism, the antithetical threat to the Hitlerian Idea. When the goal of existential truth is lost behind material trappings and the peddling of *man as*

---

43 Heidegger, *Black Notebooks 1931–1938*, II.26, 84.
44 Heidegger, *Black Notebooks 1938–1939*, IX.4, 145.

commodity, then, it seems, the movement is stillborn. The *peddling of man*, by himself or others, is in service to a terminal idea—that of Machine. The materialization of man is only the waning of humanity for the Machine that overtakes it. For Heidegger, liberal-Marxism is the commodification of man in service to Machine, which is why it stands opposed to the Hitlerian Idea.

The trouble, of course, is that, no matter their background, people generally have little interest in or capacity for thought at all, let alone thinking arcanely. But this too is vital: *all* genuine thought is arcane, for it sees truth behind the image—it sees the spirit animating time. Focusing on the image is to be *in time*—*being in time*, which is only the precondition for the commodification of man. Quintessential of modernity, this condition afflicts all mass movements—i.e., movements of "the people"—for the mass is always *in time*. Pandering to the mass indulges profanity by favoring the insubstantial image over the animating spirit.

In 1925, Rainer Rilke wrote a most poignant letter describing the empty indulgence overtaking us:

> Even for our grandfathers a house, a fountain, a familiar tower, their very clothes, their coat, was infinitely *more*, infinitely *more intimate*; almost every object a vessel in which they found something *human* or added their morsel of *humanity*. Now, from America, empty indifferent things crowd over to us, counterfeit things... A house, in the American sense, an American apple or one of the vines of that country has *nothing* in common with the house, the fruit, the grape into which have entered the hope and meditation of our forefathers. The lived and living things, the things that share our thoughts, these are on the decline and can no more be replaced.[45]

The victorious powers of World War II *necessarily* won—to spread their doctrine of liberal-Marxism across the globe, a doctrine that permeates all reality to empty it of all meaning. Liberal-Marxism, beyond the slavery it induces, is predicated on selfish indulgence. Man

---

45 *Selected Letters of Rainer Maria Rilke*, 394; emphasis added.

is goaded into certain fields of study and ways of being—to produce and consume; science and technology are incentivized. Whether our local reality convinces us this is to maintain some sort of advantage over competing States or "to help ... underdeveloped areas to advance toward stability, law and order, and prosperity"[46] is immaterial; the purpose of our fascination with and subservience to technicization is to usher in the New Colossus. Everything instantly gratifying is nurtured; and because egoism is the basis of modernity's underlying reality, the mass imagines their gratification is their own. But it is not: the masses' gratification belongs to something wholly *other*. The sense of indulgence proliferates something wholly *inhuman*. No longer, as Rilke bemoaned, do *things* hold "intimate," *human* meaning; instead, they possess an emptiness, an ideology of false indulgence that threatens the permanence of those succumbing to it.

Placating the mass is a ruse to propagate an ideology in service to Machine. Commodification is inhuman, but it is the foundation of our time; that *we are not in possession of ourselves* is explanation for this. Heidegger reminds us: "we must recognize what ... is becoming questionable about the thingness of things."[47] Such a statement only makes sense if we know the Germanic origin of "thing"—*Ding*: a *meeting*, a *matter* or *concern*, a *thing* of weight and import. The *thingness of things* is the meaning of seemingly trivial *things* imbued with *meaning*, with *humanity*. If we are not in possession of ourselves—because modernity is *the flight of the self from itself*—we cannot imbue any-*thing* with what eludes us. We lack meaning—as *ideologized* shells blanketing a weightless existence. *Abendland*, the Land of the Evening Sun, disseminates its meaninglessness across the globe. For Rilke, as it is for Heidegger, the *Americanization*, the *Westernization* of man is the *end* of his sun. "The world is being emptied of what is whole and

---

46 Carroll Quigley, *Tragedy and Hope*, 954.
47 Heidegger, *Off the Beaten Track*, "Why Poets?", 218.

heals," Heidegger writes.⁴⁸ That is, the world is emptied of humanity (spirit); in its place is the indulged biological mass, the placated Mass Man deluded into gratifying an eternal *other*: the appearance of the New Colossus.

Heidegger marked the essence of this *historical process* as "playing out to the end within Americanism and Bolshevism and thus at the same time within world-Judaism." However, "the question of the role of *world-Judaism* is not a racial question, but a metaphysical one" — it is "a question that concerns the kind of human existence which in an *utterly unrestrained* way can undertake as a world-historical 'task' the uprooting of all beings from being."⁴⁹ The question, then, is that of liberal-Marxism, which is fundamentally metaphysical: Heidegger considers Americanism and Bolshevism to be subsidiaries of a mode of being demanding the separation of "beings from being" — i.e., with the task of annihilating meaning. In answer to this devastation of meaning, perhaps

> One day people will appeal, against Americanism and its rootlessness, to the Western history of Europe. Fine.... What then comes after the 'confrontation' with America? Expose yourselves to the essential plight of being. Learn first that no 'biological' breeding of humans and no anthropological glorification could ever be capable of anything unless being determines the relation of humans to itself and inceptually decides the human essence. Expose yourselves to the possibilities our history holds open for this meditation and transformation, but cast off the vanity of the 'present' ones, who measure world history by the yard like a cloth merchant.⁵⁰

Of first importance is to recognize humanity's — i.e., *spirit's* — plight as *metaphysical*. We are not in a battle of races but one of souls. This is no mere Platonism but the grounding of an idea Heidegger never renounced. And only when spirit is foundational does physicality count

---

48 Heidegger, *Off the Beaten Track*, "Why Poets?", 221.
49 Heidegger, *Black Notebooks 1939–1941*, XIV, 191.
50 Heidegger, *Black Notebooks 1939–1941*, XV, 206.

as viable. Heidegger's "present ones" are those *in time*—and they, despite their attestations to the contrary, were just as guilty of disarming and dehumanizing *gigantism* as those they struggled against.

National Socialism, for Heidegger, deserved perhaps more criticism than even Bolshevism and Americanism for its role as one of the "present ones"—not only because it, the outward expression of the Hitlerian Idea, appeared to him as closer to demystifying the plight of modernity than all other ideological efforts, but also because it was a *German* affair: "the Germans [have] an extraordinary mission in relation to the saving of the truth of beyng,"[51] and "Only someone who is German can in an originarily new way poetize being and say being…"[52] But, in the euphoria of its meteoric rise, the metaphysical goal of National Socialism became lost; instead, as Heidegger saw it, race took precedence over souls: This "anthropological glorification" precluded its success, its being "capable of anything." Because of this metaphysical failure of the "present ones," humanity was thrown—*irrevocably*—into a gigantic, machinational future.

What does it mean to be *gigantic*? What is the *gigantism* distressing modernity? It is "a tenacious facility in calculating, manipulating, and interfering"; it is a fanatical leveling of all that uplifts. "The god and the human being, indeed separate and different—belong to beyng as the banks to the river," Heidegger writes—*But the bridge is Da-Sein.*[53] Beyng is *humanity* and *technicity*. The gigantism of modernity is like a bulldozer leveling the banks, letting the river spill to the devastated landscape. *Da-Sein* is the existential awareness of *man-as-spirit* thrown into the midst of meditationlessness; it is self-reflection of the highest order, spanning the gulf between man and god, materiality and spirituality. Modernity, as channel of the New Colossus, nurtures gigantism

---

51   Heidegger, *Black Notebooks 1938–1939*, VII.31, 21.
52   Heidegger, *Black Notebooks 1931–1938*, II.71, 21.
53   Heidegger, *Black Notebooks 1938–1939*, VII.63, 48.

to fulfill itself in the hands of the "present ones" — the result is a farce beyond even the incessant libels of the liberal-Marxists:

> All incidents, made public historiologically-technologically as 'happenings,' constantly surpass one another in their meaninglessness, the one thrusting the previous one into oblivion. The technology of the machinational institution of historiology in public opinion prepares an essential a-historicality of humans. The a-historicality would not be an essential feature of machination unless it could hide behind the gigantic historiological montage of the respectively current happening of the respectively greatest time. *The flight of the gods is so definitive that beyng no longer allows the human being to be taken as worthy of a knowledge of this flight, and so the human being is relegated to the subjectivity of the subject.*[54]

We are thus compelled to fulfill the task of modernity's subjectivity. We are beyond the world emptied of its soul and embalmed in the residue of a biological mass; we are the first rays of an eternal, other sun — a sun of material mass indulging itself *in time*.

Aristocracy was always opposed to the mass: It was the rule of the *ārya*, the noble. Selfish indulgence precipitated the quiet passing of spiritual-aristocracy to material-aristocracy. A degenerate nominal-nobility folded under the weight of the galvanized mass in an "enlightened" revolutionary era. The upending of society — pioneered in a Europe renowned for its openness, curiosity, intrepidity, and *naiveté* — resulted in the agitated mass discarding any semblance of "nobility." The brutal end of the poor Romanovs is a perfect example of what the Vanguard-prelates and Mass Man do *in time*: brutes meting out brutal ends. *That* is the revolutionary *avidity* of liberal-Marxism. Modernity is "ruled" by swindled fools — and *the rabble*, as Rilke pined, *grinds us all into specie.*

Popular pandering infects the spirit *in time* rather than the spirit *behind* the time, which marks modernity as the commodification and

---

54 Heidegger, *Black Notebooks 1939–1941*, XIII.77, 93; emphasis added.

peddling of man in service to his own end. Such peddling was true even of National Socialism and its elite:

> National Socialism is not Bolshevism ... but both are ... victories of machination — gigantic forms of the consummation of modernity — a calculated depletion of nationalities.[55]

The image over spirit — National Socialism, a product of modernity like Bolshevism, lost its legs to the current of time. What began in earnest, as perhaps realization of the Hitlerian Idea, succumbed to the machinational forces compelling beyng to its consummation. Heidegger laments this fact in his posthumously published interview with *Der Spiegel*:

> National Socialism did indeed [begin to help man achieve a satisfactory relationship to the essence of technicity through genuine thinking]. Those people, however, were far too poorly equipped for thought to arrive at a really explicit relationship to what is happening today and has been underway for the past 300 years.[56]

For Heidegger, the Reich lacked the intellectual impetus to see the matter confronting man in time and thus the will to avert it. That "National Socialism is a *barbaric principle* ... is its essential character and its possible greatness."[57] Heidegger is of course enraptured by the Hitlerian Idea's promise as a dislodgement of man from the current of time — its promise to capture the past and secure a viable future, one where *man achieves a satisfactory relationship to the essence of technicity through genuine thinking*. He continues:

> *National Socialism* is a genuine nascent power only if it still has something to withhold behind all its activity and talk — and only if it operates as strongly holding back and in that way has effectivity into the future.

---

55   Heidegger, *Black Notebooks 1939–1941*, XIII.90, 99.
56   Heidegger, *Der Spiegel* interview.
57   Heidegger, *Black Notebooks 1931–1938*, III.206, 142.

> But if the present were already that which is to be attained and striven for, then only a dread of the downfall would be left over.[58]

Heidegger anticipated the *dread of the downfall* that began with absolute finality in 1945 and man's total enshrouding by inescapable existential *adriftness*.

But there must be something more to the Hitlerian Idea than exoteric trappings for Heidegger to see its "possible greatness." There must be an impetus holding fast to the spirit of man that is *humanity*. There must be an esoteric side to Hitlerism — otherwise, all is lost. There must exist the possibility of fulfilling the task of thought so as to reclaim what daily escapes us — this, or all is lost.

Heidegger spoke loudest when he never spoke at all. Heidegger never denounced Hitler; he never denounced the Hitlerian Idea. He died ever exalting the thought behind the idea. Heidegger believed in the hidden. Hannah Arendt believed him a mystic. If Heidegger thought arcanely and his thought centered on the mystery of beginning (for therein lies beyng), then what does his devotion to the Hitlerian Idea suggest? One no longer sees a man, but a mystic; one no longer sees a mystic, but a god. The god is not the man but the thought behind the man.

Being behind the time is being against time. *Behind the times* is never said endearingly; if one is behind the time(s), one is anachronistic, a "stick in the mud" holding fast against the current of time. Time has its terminus in the end of humanity (spirit), or the commodification of man, which is only the beginning of Machine. But to be behind the time means much more than this: that which animates time is not beyng, but *being* — man's full consciousness, his *thought*, the *spirit* of all beyng. Being itself, however — i.e., *beyng* (*qua* existence) — is coextensive with Machine, with time; this is why pure beyng manifests as Machine — it is unconscious consciousness, the thoughtless will impelling time. Extraction of humanity from beyng

---

58   Heidegger, *Black Notebooks 1931–1938*, II.25, 84.

is the final realization of Machine. Standing against time, then, being *behind the time*, is the final fight for humanity; it is the fight against the New Colossus. — Heidegger never said this.

9.

Humanity and technicity are inextricable; the loss of one means the loss of the other. Technicity is not mere *technology*, no mere *gadgetry*, but a state of being: it is humanity navigating the world. Technicity is greater than technology, enveloping it, and demarcates technology as the *drive* for tooling. *Devices* are the tools themselves; *technology* is the drive for the creation and betterment of devices; *technicity* is the mind of the drive. Humanity, however, is not confined to technicity; it seeks expression beyond mere technologizing: humanity requires reflection.

Reflection is the realization of man's entanglement with technicity; but, because of this realization, it is the supra-realization of man's supremacy over technologizing. Reflection, which does not necessarily and directly require technicity, is man's link to the Divine, or that which provides meaning to technicity. Without reflection, technicity has no meaning; without meaning, humanity is relegated to subservience to gadgetry: the Divine becomes the Device. As this occurs, the humanity behind the technologizing softening the world ends: *Along with losing the gods, we have lost the world.*[59] Thus, any unthinking drive for relentless technologizing results in man's loss of himself, which, in turn, sparks the expiration of technology.

In 1966, Heidegger agreed to an interview with *Der Spiegel*. No topic was barred, and its publication was predicated on Heidegger's death; so in 1976, five days after the thinker's passing, the interview was published. Unswervingly, almost myopically, *Der Spiegel* pursued its primary intent: reveal the nature of Heidegger's association with National Socialism. Characteristically, Heidegger evaded any such

---

59 Heidegger, *Black Notebooks 1931–1938*, IV.8, 154.

revelation, for his concern had always been with another, far more substantive revelation: that of thought, that of reflection.

Only a god can save us: this is basis of Heidegger's thought — *all of it*, not just the work punctuating his career. The metaphysical foundation of his subtle critique of the prevailing system undermining thought that found expression in the Weimar-era *Being and Time* (1927) was always meant as a celebration of this basis: *Only a god can save us.* It is a mantra of the harried in their oppositional march against time. We cannot know the way to salvation until we understand the conditions of the existence requiring it. *Being and Time* was an expression of an unarticulated future — a future that was not apparent until the advent of Adolf Hitler, the *being* unmentioned; and it was then Heidegger's work began.

"How is intimation of the god supposed to come to us as waiting ones, if we idolize the antidivine?" What is the Divine? It is "the leap into the truth of beyng"; it is the surpassing of "entrenched humanity which, without exposure to an essential transformation, tailors its goals to its own measurements."[60] Thus, the "antidivine" avoids the truth of beyng by remaining entrenched in its godless *humanism*. What, then, is the truth of beyng? It is the poeticizing thought imbuing *things* with meaning; it is man as spirit, *humanity*; this spirit unifies the arc of time by standing against it.

The antidivine stands in opposition to humanity (spirit) because it precludes reflection. Existence without reflection is unconscious consciousness, pure beyng — or that toward which man hastens through his forfeiture of self. This is only the predominance of machination, the *will-to-machine*.

> When machination has secured its power so extensively, then the likewise machinationally grounded 'principles' of 'blood and soil' are proclaimed, and what ultimately comes into its own is 'science' — which makes its discoveries according to these new points of view. The releasement of beings

---

60 Heidegger, *Black Notebooks 1931–1938*, V.54, 248–249.

into the abandonment by being cannot be stopped by any sort of preventive measure — it must, as that which is happening, codetermine the future decision.[61]

In 1933, Heidegger's work began; and it did not end in 1945. Just as the victorious powers of World War II *necessarily* won, so too did Hitler's Reich *necessarily* fall — to fulfill its *un-machinational* essence. For Heidegger, this speaks to the ontological nature of the struggle between spirit and Machine, humanity and technicization, and the anti-time fundament of the Hitlerian Idea. This idea was materially bested by the twin prongs of liberal-Marxism: Americanism and Bolshevism — i.e., the quintessence of the *metaphysical annihilation of meaning*. Thus, the Hitlerian Idea broke from the machinational destiny of linear time's fulfillment. Abandonment by *being* was thus thwarted: the material, exoteric nature of the Hitlerian Idea was rejected by the time-based drive of destiny; conversely, its spiritual, esoteric nature was realized. *Beyng* was kept intact with the destruction of *being*: in humanity's destruction, technicity was bested. But such a besting can, metaphysically, only happen once, for "the releasement of beings into the abandonment by being *cannot be stopped by any sort of preventive measure*." Humanity is now abandoned to its machinational future — a future devoid of meaning through the loss of humanity.

Machine will stop at nothing to achieve its end; that is, *man* will stop at nothing to achieve *his* end. Stand against the liberal-Marxian tide swelled by Machine and face material destruction. Nothing is free from the skewing lens of modernity's *will-to-machine*; even precious science falls to subjectivity *in time*. Thomas Kuhn reflects on science's subjective — i.e., *human* — nature:

> Science does not deal in all possible laboratory manipulations. Instead, it *selects* those relevant to the juxtaposition of a paradigm with the immediate experience that that paradigm has partially *determined*. As a result,

---

61 Heidegger, *Black Notebooks 1931–1938*, XII.35, 43.

scientists with different paradigms engage in different concrete laboratory manipulations.[62]

Time, in service to pure beyng, rules the day; it sets the paradigm through which even science is done. Anticipating Kuhn, Heidegger thought "*science* [is] the first champion of *dogmatism* — that is the intrinsic consequence of the modern claim of science to the mastery of beings in the sense of objectivities."[63] Kuhn continues:

> When scientists must choose between competing theories, two men fully committed to the same list of criteria for choice may nevertheless reach different conclusions.... *[O]ne must go beyond the list of shared criteria to characteristics of the individuals who make the choice.* One must, that is, deal with characteristics which vary from one scientist to another without thereby in the least jeopardizing their adherence to the canons that make science scientific.[64]

Science, like reality itself, has never been scientific. One imagines any of the many editorials pretending to speak in the name of "science" or "objectivity" blackening the intellectual sky like flak when some sacred cow of conformism is threatened. *Scientificity*, like the objectivity of abstractions, is a modern myth meant to inculcate conformity with prevailing dogmas. Adherence to these dogmas sourced in liberal-Marxism is enforced with State-sponsored violence. Thus, war is used as a means to "preserve" peace. Recall that Carl Schmitt identified the absurdity of such a notion:

> Such a war is necessarily unusually intense and inhuman because, by transcending the limits of the political framework, it simultaneously degrades

---

62 Thomas Kuhn, "The Structure of Scientific Revolutions," *International Encyclopedia of Unified Science* (University of Chicago, 1970), vol. 2:2, 126; emphasis added.
63 Heidegger, *Black Notebooks 1938–1939*, IX.72, 187.
64 Kuhn, "Objectivity, Value Judgment, and Theory Choice," *The Essential Tension* (University of Chicago, 1977), 358.

the enemy into moral and other categories and is forced to make of him a monster that must not only be defeated but also utterly destroyed.[65]

In fact, war is used to deter dissent against prevailing dogmas — i.e., induce conformism; in the process, all are dehumanized — particularly those claiming to be defenders of "human rights." Even more absurd than the violent undercurrent of liberal-Marxist "peace" is the genuine belief in this peace. To this end, war — and, in fact, all attempts to conserve originary values bestowed by the past — is reviled as *barbaric* (a word which is a *vestige* of the late-Roman slandering of the decidedly un-Romanized *Germanics*). But Heidegger warns us against this:

> War, even if an occasion and form for an always-varied heroism, is appalling. *But this is even more appalling*: an a-historical people, blind to its uprootedness, and without the sacrifice of blood and without external destruction, tottering about amid the greatest historiological noise of all its orators and newspaper reporters, meditationlessness counting as reason, and the latter securing its essence in unconditional calculation.[66]

One cannot overstate just how appalling war really is. Few things dehumanize man as war does; though, when we see his trajectory over time, perhaps war is man's most fitting vocation. After all, Heidegger writes, we are in the midst of such "sheer overwhelming" wherein *robbing, banditry, concealment, deception*, and, yes, *wars*

> play out on diverse levels; the lowest level will be reached when the highest intelligence and the installation of violence meet in a sheer overwhelming that has no goal, unless the goal is the gigantic concealment of a gigantic emptiness and perplexity.[67]

As terrible as war's toll may be, *spiritual emptiness, deracination*, and *lack of self-reflection* are far worse. This is not to praise hawkishness or

---

65 Schmitt, *The Concept of the Political*, 36.
66 Heidegger, *Black Notebooks 1939–1941*, XIII.99, 102.
67 Heidegger, *Black Notebooks 1939–1941*, XII.18, 32.

any military-industrial complex such as one often finds in foremost liberal-Marxist societies. Rather, Heidegger only emphasizes the ruinous effects of an unexamined and spiritually fruitless life — precisely the kind of life liberal-Marxism advances with its complete commodification. Ultimately, a thoughtless life is one incapable of fulfilling even the meager potential of a biological mass. It is truly appalling when one is only an empty *thing*, overflowing instead with meaningless ideology — a commodity contented. Recall, too, that Heidegger equally inveighed against National Socialism for its enthrallment to a variation of materialism, or exotericism; yet, the German believed in the thought *behind* its execution: "National Socialism is a *barbaric principle*. That is its essential character and its possible greatness."[68] Its possible greatness rested with its intended prioritization of spirit; perhaps institutionalization — or *routinization*, as Max Weber called it — *defused* the initial spark of spirit, and destruction *diffused* it.

Weber considers the personal charisma of a leader to be the "root of the idea of a *calling* in its highest expression."[69] This type of legitimacy is perhaps the purest form of authority since it is often the most direct and immediate exchange of power and yielding between a sanctioned authority and its subjects. Mohammed captivated many of his contemporaries with a striking message of redemption, which, in turn, galvanized what became the *umma* in a way never before seen. This galvanizing empowerment led to rousing successes that validated the *umma*'s faith in its own recognized authority. As a contemporary and head of a living community, Mohammed's message adapted to fit the needs of the *umma*. Upon his death, while the message was fixed, the interpretations of the message acquired a fluidity that soon mirrored the flowing blood wrung from ensuing civil conflicts attempting to routinize charismatic remnants.

---

68 Heidegger, *Black Notebooks 1931–1938*, III.206, 142.
69 Weber, "Politics as a Vocation," *Essays in Sociology* (Routledge, 1997), 79.

The same could be said of Adolf Hitler: He captivated his contemporaries with a striking message of redemption, which, in turn, galvanized what became the *Volksgemeinschaft* in a way never before seen. This galvanizing empowerment led to rousing successes that validated the *Volksgemeinschaft*'s faith in its own recognized authority. As a contemporary and head of a living community, Hitler's message adapted to fit the needs of the *Volksgemeinschaft*. Being much later in time and nearer Machine's incipience, however, the Hitlerian Idea never reached fulfillment — antagonistic as it was to the fulfillment of time. Intentions were thwarted with the full force of a sinister compulsion to conform. Daring toward contemporaneousness with the originary position is, for modernity, a fatal step that must be stopped: the New Colossus controls our collective hand.

Nevertheless, what struck Heidegger — along with many others — was the vitality of the Hitlerian Idea. Staving off modernity's appalling meaninglessness was the idea's aim: individual sacrifice and a fostered sense of transcendent destiny were meant to elevate the profanity of materiality to the sacredness of a divine mandate: being would be salvaged at the expense of beyng — it is a sacrifice necessary to secure humanity and, thus, meaning. At least, this was the thought behind the exotericism that became, inevitably, *routine*. But because there can be no higher destiny than beyng itself, beyng invariably fulfills itself completely — whether or not one is antagonistic to it.

The routinization of charisma, or *incipient thought*, establishes the bureaucracy expected to preserve the charismatic inception that gives rise to a State.[70] That is, routinization represents the increasing complexity needed to preserve the initial spark of charisma in the society that coalesces around it. If not *routinized*, the spark succumbs to *anachronicity* and threatens, by its irrelevance, to decay the very community it once revitalized.

---

70 Weber, "Bureaucracy and Charisma" and "Discipline and Charisma," *Essays in Sociology*, 54, 262.

This *routinization* of charismatic authority results in the bureaucratic State — i.e., the transformation of *community* into *society*. And while this State can manifest under myriad political guises, its supreme manifestation is ostensible "democratic," or liberal-Marxian bureaucracy — for no other system demands more or such far-reaching conformism. To reiterate: This conformism is meant to midwife Machine and prepare for humanity's ultimate end, for empowerment of an ignorant and ill-informed people is invitation to self-enslavement, which is the Bernaysian aim of a system fulfilling the *will-to-machine*.

Heidegger never renounced the Hitlerian Idea and remained elusive when questioned about it for two reasons. First, it was a spiritual idea; its purpose was to reclaim a collective destiny by inspiring individual sacrifice — not a false liberal-Marxian sacrifice of, for instance, obligatory charity, but the genuine inward focus on *being*, its place in existence, and its sublimation into the wider community for the elevation of all. Second, the material defeat of Hitler's Reich only *proved* its vitality; for in defeat, it defied and surpassed enduring routinization. As a spiritual idea, it moved solely into the spiritual realm upon material destruction; that is, it was a matter of existential import.

The success of National Socialism, for Heidegger, was its transfixion of the greater Germanic community — revolving, as it did, around its organic *idea*, borne by Hitler; the community saw in Hitler its purpose, and his spark ignited the fire of being in a folk that had lost its way after the Great War. Hitler inspired meaning. National Socialism's failure, on the other hand, was its transformation of inceptual promise into functioning State. Consider this possible moment in the Hitlerian State: you witness and experience the rapture of a speech by "the Führer" — you feel saved, euphoric, invincible, *filled with being*; then you go to the DMV to renew your license. Arguably, the Hitlerian State was able to bridge this divide better than other, less inspiring States; but the *incongruity* nevertheless remained — and this would always be a devastating shortfall for Heidegger, no matter the State. Further, this divide was often mishandled by State functionaries and subjects inferior to the task demanded of them. War also worsened matters since it only advanced bureaucratization — or that distancing from incipient thought known as *war-as-industry* — which is always war's chief purpose in our technicized age. Of course, war has a spiritual component, arousing transcendent communal feelings and forcing, as it does, confrontation with death; death, as Heidegger reminds us, is an *individual* event, and this inspires *thought*, which is the precondition for *being*, or authenticity. For Hitler's Germany, this spirituality — arising from its incipient idea and the ensuing war — was undoubtedly the reason an almost solitary State fended off nearly the whole world for six years of the most intense conflict known to man.

The National Socialist State *still* met material defeat; for *this*, Heidegger never renounced the Hitlerian Idea. He denounced *functionaries*, *luminaries*, and the *charade* — but never the *idea*, for its success lay squarely in its failure. By escaping its enduring existence and atrophy as a State — i.e., routinization — the Hitlerian Idea proved to be the most enduring of all ideas. "The current world war," the German maintained, "is the extreme overturning of all beings into the unconditionality of machination."[71] The machinational undercurrent of the war did not negate its spiritual basis. That the Third Reich lost was only evidence the Hitlerian Idea transcended simple technologizing, or the machinational current of beyng: the Idea could not counter the weight of time's acceleration into the final catastrophe of humanity's end in unloosed technicity. Departure of the Hitlerian Idea was ultimate proof of its non-machinational ends. Heidegger saw the thought *behind* the movement; when the movement died, only the thought remained. In this way, the only viable ideas are those seen as unviable by a hostile world predicated on a *will-to-destruction*, the *will-to-machine*. Obsolescence didn't end the Hitlerian Idea, violence did; for Heidegger, this was perhaps the greatest argument for its truth.

---

71 Heidegger, *Black Notebooks 1939–1941*, XIV, 136.

We live in the wake of such violence, in a world *wrought* by violence. This certainly has meaning, despite the global acceptance of a Hollywoodized superficiality steering us away from all meaning and connection with the inceptual past. Modernity's gross construction gives the most significant event in world history an absurd black-and-white foundation, covers it with *the fullness of the subjectivity of the subject*, and on this erects a "world order" replete with a strange and vacant hallowedness. And now this "age of the consummation of modernity," Heidegger writes,

> faces two possibilities: either violent and swift demise (which looks like 'catastrophe,' but in its already decided and distorted essence is too lowly to *be* such) or else deterioration of the current state of unconditional machination to infinity. Unavoidable in each case is *obliviousness* to the possibility of a history which includes a decision on the truth of beyng. Wars and revolutions, even if of gigantic proportions, remain superficial incidents.[72]

A decision on the truth of beyng is a decision on the truth of ourselves, which will always be avoided or glossed over like any semblance of historical truth. The fullness of subjectivity, after all, *is* obliviousness. Most significant, however, is the absolute meaninglessness, because of this baffling *fullness*, of everything we undertake — no sacred world order or terrifying gigantism can shake the superficiality of our simple, self-centered selves. Now even the most cosmic failure rings hollow, though the mass can't be bothered to notice. So again the Mass Man is prodded into some vain affectation — the attempt is made to wring some blood-borne feeling, some meaning from a bone-dry rag. Wars and massive industry, in all their gigantism, are constantly stoked to extract falseness from beings incapable of making a decision on the truth of beyng. Like milk cows repeatedly impregnated to stimulate milk production, the Mass Man is goaded into sustaining an enslaving, machinational system with war, the promise of industry, and technological innovation. We "buy in" to falseness with falseness — and each

---

72 Heidegger, *Black Notebooks 1939–1941*, XIII.111, 108.

of us is uncaringly guilty of contributing to a *meditationless, inhuman* future. Heidegger warns against our now inescapable present and future, rife as it is with thoughtless, liberal-Marxian belligerence and egotism:

> Mere war, especially one that could break out machinationally, and could do so only thus in the age of the abandonment of beings by being, *never gives rise to meditation*. Only romantics expect such a thing... *The horror may be ever so terrible, the bravery unprecedented, the sacrifice incomparable, yet all this never creates the basic condition of meditation*: namely, the inner freedom of the human being for the essential (not self-interested) decisions, i.e., the preparedness for the historical question-worthiness of being. Everywhere machination has already seized all possibilities of beings and has imposed on these possibilities its own interpretations, so that the human being, despite all the affliction and dismay, is no longer able to press forth into the essential regions of a plight issuing from beyng.
>
> Meditation as steadfastness in the question-worthiness of the *essence* of truth cannot be forced by tribulations; it can be incited only by an essential plight, which requires a magnanimity of heart.[73]

Magnanimity comes only from thoughtfulness, of which humanity has little; and the little that remains is sublimated into fulfilling liberal-Marxian fantasies of "human dignity," which only ever serve our unavoidable machinational destiny. An "essential plight" comes from an inward turn, not external obligation; one confronts the self in all its essential smallness — this is the only condition for meaning.

Meaning does not *elevate* the self, it *confronts* it; elevation of the self is the flight of the self from itself; confrontation is *thrown-ness* into the inceptual past. Meaning is the veneration of others who witness the confrontation of what needs confronting and the honor of self in choosing the challenging. Nothing of this "essential plight" is familiar to a time that desperately avoids confrontation of the self as

---

73 Heidegger, *Black Notebooks 1939–1941*, XIII.73, 89.

the fundament to being. Avoidance has become unconscious, and the mass slips innocently into oblivion.

Using the familiar to describe the unfamiliar is human. We look to the known for comfort in confronting the unknown. It is often said that a tornado "sounds like a freight train." Most hear of tornadoes but never experience them. Those who experience them imagine the roaring, rattling winds to sound like something they have often heard: the "proverbial" freight train. Trains are ubiquitous; tornadoes are not. Media captures sound bites of survivors who liken the unfamiliar with the familiar. This image is propagated; then, without thinking, the image becomes proverbial. One can only wonder: Before freight trains, before mass industrialization — when, rest assured, we were *still* in the midst of technicization — what must have tornadoes sounded like? Perhaps witnesses likened the roaring funnels to rushing rivers, stampeding bison, or maybe the echoing growl of a bear. Something natural was certainly used to describe the natural phenomenon. Or perhaps it was even *indescribable* — the survivor could only say, "You must experience it for yourself." This would have been before media, before freight trains, before the rapidly increasing imbalance of technicity. Experiencing such a thing *for oneself* is confrontation. There is meaning in confrontation. Now, however, the *technological* is *proverbial* — from and for speech, *for understanding*; now, one survivor's experience is no different than another's.

Tornadoes are indeed rare, but the proverbial description belies an underlying comfort in the technological. When we say a tornado *sounds like a freight train*, we are saying we are more comfortable with that thing, albeit technological, that is *more* comfortable, *more* familiar. Technology peppers the landscape; we know it well. We are in the midst of a mass extinction: animal habitats are only lots to be commercialized; rivers are only obstacles to be bridged; mountains are meant to be monetized, collectively or individually, not hiked or admired. The natural has become unfamiliar. Humanity has a *Manifest Destiny* to technicize the world, and little colonizers abound, making serfs and paupers of their *selves* and the *strange others* around them. We unconsciously repeat what has been propagated — *for understanding* — and our confrontations are only surrogacies. A slow subversion has crept in: Now we are at ease with the alien.

"The basic condition of meditation," Heidegger contends, is "the inner freedom of the human being for the essential decisions." Surrogate confrontation is nonexistent confrontation; with this, freedom itself is nonexistent. In the end, we conform with the technologizing overtaking us. "Everywhere machination has ... seized all possibilities of beings and has imposed on these possibilities its own interpretations, so that the human being ... is no longer able to press forth into the essential regions of a plight issuing from beyng." *Freedom, meditation, thought* — the mass surrenders the individual self to the conformism of a commercialized, *residentialized* lot in life. The Mass Man repeats new mantras of modernity's secular-ritual technicization; he espouses the talking points of his Bernaysian shepherds. When the mass says, "I think," we can be sure the opposite happens. Cartesian *cogitos* are biological license for inactivity.

"*I think* Marxism and capitalism are incompatible" — this is something learned in school. Perhaps local forays into popular consciousness are only dissimulations meant to destabilize — "Although Vietnam remains officially committed to socialism as its defining creed, its economic policies have grown increasingly capitalist... [I]ts leadership [consists of] 'ardently capitalist communists.'"[74] *Ardently capitalist communists* — this describes *an-other* will vying for its appearance. Spengler called Marx's international socialism the "capitalism of the lower classes"; this is only to say it ingratiates the mass with exploitative measures — obligingly, the mass reciprocates. Capitalism is only training in tyranny, which is why it was prevised to lead directly to communism, that *technicized* socialism. One becomes accustomed to the tyranny he imposes on himself and others.

---

74 *The Economist*, "A bit of everything: Vietnam's quest for role models" (April 26, 2008).

To be sure, *capitalism is indeed wonderful*—one must say this today, one must believe it. Conformism is at stake. When a community outlives a healthy population, it must become a society—a strictly managed and technicized mass predicated on State-sponsored violence and willing enslavement, which is to say, exploitation. Capitalism is the living tenet of a technicized mass; it cannot be opposed—not even by those who most ardently oppose it. Capitalism is a necessary alien language for those who have so completely alienated themselves; it is the Word of Machine; and it is—*proverbially*—quite inescapable, much like the transfixing headlights are for the doomed deer. The promise of capitalism makes everything "worthwhile"—even for the most exploited wretch. What's hidden behind the oncoming lights? *Surely something good.*

The liberal-Marxist world forestalls its obsolescence through comfort and convenience. *Pandering* to "the people" is only an attempt to remain relevant—i.e., to restrain revolt; *deceiving* "the people" into believing they are being *pandered to* and that they, in turn, have the power to *pander* is only marketing strategy. It is the inculcation of custom for the benefit of the inculcator. Bernays used this strategy to great effect in both commercial and social contexts; he described the process and its necessity in liberalistic societies in *Propaganda*, some of which is cited here:

> The modern propagandist [aims] to create circumstances which will modify … custom.…
>
> [For example, the propagandist might wish to instill a desire to buy a piano in the consumer: instead of trying to sell the piano directly, he campaigns to make 'music rooms' the new custom.] The music room will be accepted because it has been made the thing. And the man or woman who has a music room, or has arranged a corner of the parlor as a musical corner, will naturally think of buying a piano. *It will come to him as his own idea.*
>
> Under the old salesmanship the manufacturer said to the prospective purchaser, 'Please buy a piano.' The new salesmanship has reversed the process

and caused the prospective purchaser to say to the manufacturer, 'Please sell me a piano.'[75]

In modern parlance this is called generating "buy in." In everyday circumstances like the one described above, there are two levels of "buy in": (1) the consumer literally buys far more than the goal (of the piano) to set the conditions for the goal, which stimulates the economy, and (2) the consumer is sold on the idea planted in him, imagining the idea is his own. Thus we have both the system's socioeconomic basis legitimized and consumer habits modified. As Bernays explicitly states, manipulation is the linchpin for liberalistic societies; and while this benefits many in a superficial way, it benefits the few orchestrators — the Vanguard-prelates — far more than the many. *Manipulation*, then, is incentivized; *dishonesty* is incentivized to further protect the deception; this is just one of the problems with liberalism (whose language is capitalism) that Carl Schmitt identified. A healthy community is a disciplined community, living as it does in accordance with the sacrifice of the originary position — i.e., being contemporaneous with the past. Healthy communities, thriving in their discipline, morph into sick societies oriented on ideas of progress to protect the marginalized. This morphing is an *inborn* potentiality, destined to grow like any limb, and is concomitant with the rise in technicization; it is the product of an alien *will-to-machine*. From it, quantity supplants quality, and the notion of "the people" resounds with the mass. Quantity then begets quantity and the system perpetuates itself.

Yet, even the Vanguard-prelates' desire to keep pitchforks and torches at bay is only self-deceptively selfish: its true meaning is the *will-to-machine*: Machine progressing toward its certain future. The inculcators themselves are victims of *an-other's* inceptual idea. "Assuming philosophy is at an end," Heidegger tells us, "it must be brought *philosophically* to its end, an end that must be endured, even

---

75 Bernays, *Propaganda*, 78.

if broken up by the [dare] of an other beginning."⁷⁶ Each of us lives out the *will-to-machine*—whether we fulfill our local destinies antagonistically or not. Philosophy is at an end because *we* are at an end. And our end is this other beginning: we *love the wisdom* of this nascent New Colossus. What we endure is liminality: this is the unrest of humanity, our clinging to the inceptual idea as our own. Unrest reveals the other beginning:

> The greatest struggle rages over the task which is made necessary *by* a first work *against* that work itself. If the grounding of this task succeeds—if the question of the truth of beyng compels a turn to the question of the beyng of *truth*, and if the question of being first vibrates in *this* question of truth—then the genuine strife of questioning is roused, the inmost tranquility is assured through the hitherto, the affiliation to the unique ones is prepared, and the other beginning—has begun.⁷⁷

We witness the fight of the old against the young, which is only the fight of the old against itself. We see the struggle of the past against the future, which is only the fight of the past against itself. We use philosophy to end philosophy—the *will-to-live* to end the *will-to-machine*. We use reason to end reason—liberal-Marxism to end fascism. We use humanity to end humanity—mass to end spirit, quantity to end quality. We use god to end god—secularism to end piety. We call all enmity by *an-other* name—*progress*—to divert thought from situation to self. We long to be on the "right side of history"—for therein lies the justification for all our devastating thoughtlessness.

All of this is testament to the failing of the question of truth, which is our own self. The answer to the failed question of our self is the other beginning. *We* are the flight of the self from itself: Modernity mirrors us. Nothing is happening *to* us; *we* are the inceptual end. Humanity loses touch with its own being because this was only ever the being of *an-other*.

---

76 Heidegger, *Black Notebooks 1931–1938*, V.21, 235.

77 Heidegger, *Black Notebooks 1931–1938*, V.108, 276.

10.

"*Modernity*," says Heidegger, is "the age that is more and more sure of its essence the more exclusively it thinks only of what it does."

> But 'it does' only what the fullness of subjectivity must do—preserve itself in meditationlessness—perhaps to the point of self-destruction. Meditationlessness, however, is not mere blindness; on the contrary, it is gigantism in calculation, and precisely that is what requires gigantism in the unleashing of the drives to violence and to destruction.[78]

Just as the inculcators plant in the mass the illusion of self-actualization, so does Machine instill in the inculcators the illusion of inception. State-sanctioned violence is not the protection of society's marginalized grotesqueries — rather, each is the result of a self-alienating urge; each is the *will-to-machine* to actualize itself. Conflict is the very real illusion meant to spur innovation in humanity's self-policing. The combat of local destinies resonates with an enveloping drone; the drone is the tune for modernity's dance. It is not *mere* blindness, but it *is* blindness.

The *fullness* of subjectivity is *meditationlessness* because it is the centering of the self on itself. Thought indeed demands some objectivity—i.e., the ability to assess from outside oneself, albeit through subjective lens. We assess from outside the self when we belong to the past and thereby pervade the future. The surest step is the one that came before. Thoughtless living, on the other hand, is mere lightless groping, which is only prelude to the horror of a corralled herd. The centering of self on itself becomes the flight of self from itself in this blind myopia of modernity, which is the fullness of subjectivity: "the people" led by "people" who imagine their actions are their own.

Gigantism behind the blindness weighs on the thoughtful: it is unconscious consciousness, pure beyng — existence manifest in the New Colossus. Inception of the New Colossus is the *drive to violence*

---

[78] Heidegger, *Black Notebooks 1938–1939*, VII.30, 20.

and destruction. Leviathan is the means to progress, which is always an end. And what is this *always* if not a proof of our illusion? We live passionately for the *always* that serves as a rearguard for future horror — for that is our comfort: a death absent of self, which is only a culmination of blind steps.

Heidegger assures us: "The exclusive and 'passionate' affirmation of 'life' and of beings hides the most dangerous nihilism."

> Over and against 'life' and beings, this nihilism is merely a semblance that bears the 'not' and the 'no' and the 'nothing' like a shield before itself, where what is Godless and worldless and groundless is plain as day.[79]

Our nihilism is the supreme love of self, which is consummation of the illusion. World-affirming impulse and action in an increasingly technicized time is "like a shield" guarding against the reflection necessary to confront and commune with being. Self-confrontation is essential for meaning, for it places one in contact with the humanity concomitant with technicity: *does one have measure — does one have scope — does one have an understanding of the solitary approach?* Guarding against — or closing oneself off from — humanity *disproportionates* the measure, or disrupts the harmony of man's disposal to beyng, which only dehumanizes what ultimately becomes the technicized being. Affinity for the accoutrements of modernity's *gigantism* — i.e., *modernity's displacement of all measure via technologizing* — diminishes meaning for the sake of a voluntary enslavement concealed in convenience.

This is the "bedwarfing of humanity ... and is the last consequence of the 'sovereignty' of the historiological animal."[80] Humanity's sense of "sovereignty" is based upon an "authentic nihilism" itself underlying a general malaise over the very real illusion of conflict and the surficial nihilism arising from it.[81] *Authentic nihilism* is the confrontation of

---

79 Heidegger, *Black Notebooks 1938–1939*, VIII.9, 80–81.
80 Heidegger, *Black Notebooks 1938–1939*, IX.26, 154.
81 Heidegger, *Black Notebooks 1939–1941*, XII.28, 39.

self in the context of a hostile existence—i.e., an existence, beyng, that aims to actualize itself through its tokens' demise. If we lack the thought to recognize *authentic nihilism*, "then every overcoming of nihilism is a mere half measure and in this way becomes more fatal than nihilism itself, because in such an overcoming nihilism fully attains its unrestricted and—because now hidden—most dangerous power."[82] But we cannot recognize and overcome such nihilism: We are the "futural ones"—and, more than this, *other futural ones* exist within us. And

> ... for the futural ones to wrestle themselves loose, this extreme diminution of humanity must seem to be the greatest triumph—for only in that way does there open up the abyss dividing the future essence of humanity from the previous one.[83]

Ultimately we wrestle with an urge to distinguish ourselves *in time*—the urge is not our own. The most effective and incredible way to do this is through pervasive technicization, to which we have wholly surrendered ourselves.

Having surrendered to the *diminution of humanity*, the Mass Man becomes ever more *gigantic*, and so "all the smaller must his essence contract, until he, no longer seeing himself, exchanges himself with his machinations and thus 'outlives' his own end." Society is a reflection of the self. A community outlived is *society*; a self outlived is *machine*, a vessel for immolation. We recall Zarathustra, whose dwarf is humanity *bedwarfed* and *lamed*: man is the crooked truth of an outlived mass—the *spirit of gravity* that is no spirit at all. "What does it signify," asks Heidegger, "that the human masses are worth so little they could be annihilated in one stroke; is there a stricter proof of the abandonment by being?" Modernity is only our actions catching up to what we

---

82 Heidegger, *Black Notebooks 1939–1941*, XII.28, 39.

83 Heidegger, *Black Notebooks 1938–1939*, IX.26, 154.

have never thought about ourselves. Not just humanity has abandoned us: *Who surmises the resonance of a last god in such a failure?*⁸⁴

What we are left with, then, is the Manifest Destiny of an arrival of the New Colossus.

> The world now appears as an object open to the attacks of calculative thought, attacks that nothing is believed able any longer to resist. Nature becomes a gigantic gasoline station, an energy source for modern technology and industry. This relation of man to the world as such, in principle a technical one, developed in the seventeenth century first and only in Europe.⁸⁵

To colonize is to replicate and establish an enduring conformism in another. Europe has turned the world into colonizers because Europe first succumbed to colonization, to the *will-to-machine*. If the Divine is *inhuman*, or, if preferred, *superhuman*, then European man was only connected more deeply to the Divine, which is to say, Machine. Consider for a moment that it is God's will for man to be a slave. This is no slight against God — but against man. The saddest fact of modernity is man's belief that he overcomes God through scientific industrialization and mass technicization, but in truth slavishly devotes himself to the supernatural through thoughtless action. *God is dead and we have killed him* — Nietzsche's words ring true, and truer words were never spoken. Humanity abandoned the actual God when it first began to think and thereby impose; it is only through the *other* beginning — through reclaiming thought — that humanity can begin to commune with the Divine. Reclaiming thought is not replication and imposition — it is not colonization; reclamation, rather, is unique — it is confrontation of the self. Its uniqueness springs from its impossibility: God must be abandoned for God. Such is the seeming paradox of *being*.

---

84 Heidegger, *Black Notebooks 1931–1938*, IV.247, 207.
85 Heidegger, *Discourse on Thinking* (Harper & Row, 1966), 51.

11.

> The other beginning — in which history is grounded on the truth of beyng — is *older than the first*. Everything the other beginning brings into the open domain (and also refuses to grant) withdraws from measurement according to the usual standards. Humans find themselves in the strangeness of the strangest god, and everything is abyssal, such that all machination, without support and confirmation, falls to ruin.[86]

Machinational support and confirmation fall away amidst real depth of being — *thought* and *poetizing*. In the other beginning was the god of self-confrontation, which was the absence of self that is the *purest being*. Self-confrontation is the confrontation of *purest being* and pure beyng, wherein truth withdraws and everything becomes abyssal with the loss of scope. Scope is coaxed from the originary confrontation, from the arousal of conscious consciousness; and erected on the confrontation are the structures of human and inhuman industriousness — the *will-to-machine*. The "usual standards" are based on the structures erected from the confrontation of the first beginning, which shares its inception with the other beginning. Each beginning conceals and exposes the realities of the other. The other beginning brings the abyssal depth of being into the open; this openness conceals the truth; but the concealment of truth is the realization of the thought behind it. This is the *inceptual moment* and the unspoken aim of all thought and poetizing; this moment is the impossible meditation preceding the two beginnings. Meaning is found here — the meaning found only in resisting the inevitable, which is impossible. What is inevitable? — The victory of the *first* beginning.

We are appalled at our inability to measure the *other* beginning of the inceptual god. But our drive, as *futural ones*, possesses us more deeply than any humanity, and so we further ourselves from the originary position — we fully submit to the *will-to-machine*, letting it

---

86 Heidegger, *Black Notebooks 1938–1939*, IX.40, 165.

hound us in self-policing packs of replication. That is, we conform to an alien will, which is *all we have left*.

Only a god can save us. What is meant by "god"? — by "save"? — by "us"? *God* is the balance of humanity and technicity; *salvation* is the placement of self as contemporaneous with the originary position; *us* is the eschewal of self-centered creeds. But this is not to say that practical steps lead to genuine self-actualization: *A death absent of self is only the culmination of blind steps.* Practicality is blind to the inward struggle necessary to attain *the god*. Heidegger alludes to the mystery of impracticality:

> The attaining of the god by way of struggle — the preparation of his abode — in the existence of poetizing and thinking. In this way, truth first happens, as a lonely forest ridge sweeping through the valleys of humans.[87]

God is attained through *thinking*, through *poetizing*, and in no other way, for these things require struggle — real, individual struggle that places one's *self* in the absorbing embrace of individual dissolution. To stand in the way of the impossible is the seeing step.

Dissolution does not come from the practical application of individual, replicative ideology — i.e., it does not come from any ideology of "the people." Application of ideology is only the expression of a collectivized individuation, a false promise relegated to bovine conformism. Rather, dissolution arises from a communion of individuated selves in the impossible inceptual moment. This communion is the jubilant encounter of the god. Heidegger explains:

> Mere 'worldview' agreements, corresponding to 'political' ones, can no longer suffice to ground the history of Europe into a consolidated world. Metaphysics (and thus also 'ideals' in general and 'morals' and 'culture' as their effective forms) is at an end....
>
> The most proximate decision stands out in relief: whether machination by itself still is capable of preventing the destruction of its essence, thereby

---

87 Heidegger, *Black Notebooks 1931–1938*, III.134, 122.

letting itself endure in a new configuration, or whether machination will be broken apart... The decision and the way it is carried out depend on whether a preparedness of Western humanity will awaken for the grounding of the truth of beyng out of beyng itself and a unique plight of the heart will change to the jubilation of the encounter of the god...[88]

Heidegger rejects the possibility of *political solutionism*, which is only the continuation of a war against humanity (spirit) by other means. Smiles of statesmen are as crooked as their *be-dwarfed* truth. As has been said, "*Politics* is dead."[89] Humanity is lost; man is too far-gone. What remains instead is the individual struggle to overcome the self in a final confrontation that places one in the impossible inceptual moment. What follows such meditation is the freeing of the self from machination in fulfilling the arc of the *will-to-machine*.

12.

Heidegger believed in Germany's distinction as the bastion of Europe; this was a spiritual distinction, not a sociopolitical one.[90] Further, he believed the Germanic people of Europe had a clear task. If the bastion were to fall, the task could never be fulfilled for humanity, generally. But we have seen (§9) that Germany's fall was necessary to demonstrate the truth of the task's inceptuality. Humanity, generally, is lost to machination; all that remains now is to salvage the individual arc in the face of impossibility; all that remains now is to fulfill the task.

> The question is only whether we are capable of *being* this task itself; every German soldier has fallen in vain if we do not hourly strive for the rescuing of a beginning of the German essence, beyond the now quite released and definitive self-devastation of all modern humanity.[91]

---

88 Heidegger, *Black Notebooks 1939–1941*, XIII.74, 91.
89 Martin Friedrich, *Hitlerism* (Clemens & Blair, 2023), 61.
90 See, for instance, Werner Sombart's *Händler und Helden* (1915) and *Deutscher Sozialismus* (1934). See also §2 above.
91 Heidegger, *Black Notebooks 1939–1941*, XV, 203.

German blood will be let in vain unless the spiritual decision of Western history is ventured out of the concealed spirit of the West for the sake of the preserved spirit of Europe and is attained by struggle in long meditation.[92]

The task is *meditation*. *Nothing was in vain*: the future belongs to those seeking root in the sacred soil of sacrifice; the altar is *time*, the offering is *being*, the sacrificial smoke is the *meaning* linking oneself to the Divine. *Poetizing* is the spiraling wisp of an incantation, the remembrance of the dead.

It is not the German essence alone that must be rescued, but the *beginning* of the German essence. There is indeed a German essence, but its beginning can only *be* if Germany is permitted — and permits itself, through a transcendence of the exoteric — to fulfill its originary task: this task is to live in meditation — to strive hourly for contemporaneousness with inceptuality. Inceptuality precedes the first beginning; to meditate on the inceptual is to reject the beginning that gave rise to the gigantic dehumanization giving flight to the self.

But what is the German essence? Werner Sombart explains (*Deutscher Sozialismus* 1934) — Firstly, the Germans *are*:

1. An active, positive, energetic, enterprising people.

2. A masculine people: the man is the center of the household and of the cultural life.

3. A country-people. They are attached to the soil and country life.

Secondly, the Germans *possess*:

1. Thoroughness. The thoroughness of the German expresses itself in that he takes all things — himself and the world — in dead earnest in thinking, feeling and acting. The Germans are a metaphysical folk. German thoroughness expresses itself in a number of characteristics which every intelligent observer perceives in the Germans: *subjectivity, sincerity, heartiness, yearning for the unknown, intense longing* — these are the essential constituents of the German soul.

---

92 Heidegger, *Black Notebooks 1939–1941*, XIV, 177.

> 2. Objectivity, and in a double sense: an inclination and a capacity for dealing with things. The German obeys gladly, he rejoices in a clear and sharp command, he follows the leader, but only because, and insofar, as he sees in him the embodiment of an idea; he does not subject himself to the person, but to the thing the person represents.
>
> 3. Self-glorification or ... individualism. 'Each German goes according to his own notion, each seeks to find enough to do for himself; he does not concern himself with others, for each is animated with the idea of personal freedom' (Goethe).

Lastly, Sombart, like Heidegger, assigns the Germans tasks—they should *be*:

> 1. A people of spirit in a double sense: in contrast with everything that is unspiritual, material, earthly, and in contrast with everything that is sultry, obscure, subterranean.
>
> 2. A people of action: our earthly life should be active, creative, and diligent in business, 'activistic.'
>
> 3. A polymorphic people. We should (and wish to) guard the diversity and multi-colored relations of our nature in body and soul. Herein lies one of our greatest tasks, a task of all Western Europe—geographically and racially the most diversely articulated part of the earth. Here we must guard the variety of forms in contrast with the monotony of the East (including Russia) and of the West (America).[93]

The truth of a free people—a thoughtful people—is fulfillment of its *metaphysical* task. Interruption of the task's fulfillment in Europe—home of the saturating *will-to-machine*—through machinational wars *against* and *in defense of* the German essence is proof of humanity's enthrallment to the *inhuman*, the Machine. Conformism is enslavement; that liberal-Marxism feigns defense of "individualism" in the midst of the greatest, most *gigantic* conformism is testament to

---

[93] Werner Sombart, *A New Social Philosophy* (Princeton, 1937), Geiser translation, chapter XI, "What Is German?"

its gigantic deception, which has but one purpose: final enslavement for the sake of the New Colossus.

"Metaphysical thinking," says Heidegger, "has become unfamiliar to most and has remained only as an object of historiological reportage on the opinions and standpoints of philosophy..."[94] The fall of the *metaphysical* in Europe cleared the way for sanctioned sanitization, a bounty of ideologies predicated on clever analysis. Man thereby thinks himself to death without thinking. *Metaphysics is an outmoded branch of dead philosophy?* No! Metaphysics is reflection — it is the thinking necessary for faith and the unthinking necessary for doubt. It is only through freedom from enslaving conformism that the thoughtful ones clear the way for the last god — that possibility of the thinking being. God — *after all* — is the impossible realizing itself.

13.

Man is a willing slave to ideology, for this excuses him from self-reflection. The farcical ideologies made available to him channel his discontent toward the eternal and oft-chimerical *other*. And, because he is enslaved, he demands that others, too, be enslaved; this prevents his shame from overwhelming his excuse. Ideology's principal aim is to extract an obscene and avidly espoused conformism.

Order does not come from ideology; it comes from an internal quality. A preponderance of laws, which creates an artifice of order, makes it clear that the dominant ideology both lacks and supports the lack of quality. Conformism is not order; it is a pretense to order, an excuse for the disorderly to dodge any pursuit of quality. Contemporary ideology has one aim: conformism, for this too has its purpose.

Modernity's dominant ideology is, at root, liberal-Marxism; it is the tailwind filling the sails of the mass. So while one subgroup professes "conservatism," another "progressivism," and still another (that imagines itself aloof from the profane) claims "Christianity," all sail with the

---

94 Heidegger, *Black Notebooks 1938–1939*, VII.66, 53.

wind, *in time* — divergences are illusory. In keeping with the image, the physical forces generating the wind are its *metaphysicality*. Modernity's sole metaphysicality is the *will-to-machine*. Liberal-Marxism's purpose is to create the conditions for Machine; and metaphysicality demands its ideological emergence.

Heidegger condemned the "new politics" of his time. The principal target of his critique was National Socialism — specifically, the exoteric biologism of its charade. But this critique was levied out of *possibility*, for Heidegger saw more behind the idea than was finally realized. That is, the German critiqued out of concern. Beyond all concern — because it sits beyond all possibility of being otherwise — was the absolutely automatonic, completely conformist, and wholly machinational: liberal-Marxism. Nevertheless, both ideologies shared, in their thoughtless manifestations, a penchant for the machinational:

> *The new politics is an intrinsic essential consequence of 'technology'*... In itself this politics is the machinational organization of the people to the highest possible 'performance'...
>
> Nevertheless, this birth of the new politics out of the essence of technology, insofar as we grasp these nexuses not chronologically-historiologically but in terms of the history of being (as arising out of the machinational distortion of the essence of being), is a *necessary* birth and therefore not a possible object of a short-sighted 'opposition' assisted by appealing to the previous 'worldviews' and to standpoints of faith. Necessary are only the concord of originary possibilities and the impetus to concomitantly creative meditation, which today ... can think only in terms of centuries.[95]

Thinking, however, is out of the question — let alone thinking "in terms of centuries." Politics — and thus we — are instead relegated to arising "out of the essence of technology." *Technology* "thinks" in terms of centuries, not man. Rather, *man* think in terms of satisfying personal desires while unwittingly building the foundation for Machine.

---

95 Heidegger, *Black Notebooks 1931–1938*, VI.87, 342–343.

Heidegger's critique is that *"technology* can never be mastered through the folkish-political [*völkisch-politisch*] worldview ... i.e., in terms of breeding"[96] — that what "is already a slave can never become master." Heidegger sees the deliberate transformation of a people as necessarily being a product of the technologizing preceding the deliberation; so the *deliberation*, which is meant to be an extraction from the destructive subsumption of humanity into technologizing, manifests only as a continuation of the subsumption. The *völkisch-politisch* — the slave — cannot master its source, technology. Perhaps it could be argued, however, that the *völkisch-politisch* task was to harness the fundamental "biological" powers undergirding human will so as to increase the capacity for "spiritual" (or human) reflection, which, in turn, would cease or impede mass degradation — thus "technology" would be used to halt the enslaving spread of "technology." This would be akin to the "fascist" philosophical urge to halt the corrosive effects of "rationalism" (or "reason"), born of the Enlightenment, by using reason itself; this, of course, was Nietzsche's project.

Heidegger undoubtedly saw the relational thread between technology and the *völkisch-politisch*, as is indicated by his belief that the "birth of the new politics out of the essence of technology is ... *necessary*," so there is perhaps some deeper cynicism to his thinking. One can only imagine that there is, in some sense, a resignation Heidegger feels, based in historical circumstances, at the course of humanity — that *because* humanity and technicity are entwined, *there can be no peaceful resolution*: all must end in catastrophe so as to initiate the "other beginning," which is really inceptual:

> *The last god*—is not the end—but is instead the *other* beginning of the immeasurable possibilities of our history.
>
> For the sake of that beginning, the previous history must not perish but must indeed be brought to its end....

---

96 Heidegger, *Black Notebooks 1931–1938*, V.1, 228.

> The last god — the preparation of his appearance is the extreme venture of the truth of beyng; only in virtue of this truth can the retrieval of beings succeed for humanity.[97]

What is catastrophe? It is the essential plight of the inward turn; it is the meaning within self-confrontation. *Who or what is the "last god"?* It is the reconciliation of humanity and technicity through the end of each. *Only a god can save us* — indeed.

14.

That meaning is conveyed from beyond life is not novel. Death is global, and the global is death. "Death," writes Heidegger, "is a way to be, which Dasein takes over as soon as it is."[98] A thoughtful cemetery walk explains life in a way that *everydayness* never can. Headstones present dates, names, verses, pictures, or perhaps only a title. Somewhere lies a stone placed deliberately on the earth; etched on it is a single word: *Father. Who rests beneath the earth?* It could be a hero, or maybe a terror. We can be sure of only this: Death is an individual event — and being persists after its individual end. We might hazard that honor in life is a precognitive ripple of one's honor in final self-confrontation; honor is either glory or penance.

> The last god is the beginning of the longest history on its shortest path. Long preparation is needed for the great moment of its passing. And for preparedness for god, peoples and states are too small, i.e., already too much torn from all growth and nonetheless delivered over only to machination.[99]

If peoples and states are too small for the preparedness for god, what suffices? What yet possesses the capacity for growth? If all is delivered

---

97 Heidegger, *Black Notebooks 1931–1938*, V.1, 228.
98 Heidegger, *Being and Time* (Blackwell, 1962), Macquarrie and Robinson translation, 289.
99 Heidegger, *Contributions to Philosophy* (Indiana University, 1999), "Turning in Enowning," Emad and Maly translation, 291.

to machination, where is there to grow? The religiously minded might look inward, but they never look quite far enough. Only the first beginning, that of machination itself, is at the end of an inward look. One must look beyond the beginning, inwardly or outwardly, to inceptuality; this is *going under* the grounding of self that springs from the residue of being. Heidegger writes:

> Taken in its essential sense, going-under means going along the path of the reticent preparing for those who are to come… This going-under is the very first of the first beginning. But what is not ownmost to going-under takes its own course and goes another way — and is an abating, a no-longer-being-able-to-do, ceasing, after the appearance of the gigantic and massive and following the priority of establishment over against that which should fulfill it.[100]

Purest being exists for humanity — behind the duplicity of knowledge that generates technicity. Machination exists for itself — as the flight of the self (humanity) from itself. This is the "priority of establishment over against that which should fulfill it," which is diametrical. Man is diametrical, which is why he must look beyond the beginning to that which is inceptual, or beyond his own inherent opposition. This is the only way of surviving the inescapable end of humanity and the advent of the New Colossus — that is, this is the only way of achieving the impossible.

By virtue of the impossible the future thinker prepares the way for those to come. He "must know the *distorted* essence of beyng."

> Therefore, he can never become a denier, but also never an affirmer, of 'beings'… '[D]ialectics' must be abandoned; for 'dialectics' belongs entirely to modern thought and is a calculative mode of representation transferred back into philosophy out of science and thus by necessity formed unconditionally.[101]

---

100 Heidegger, *Contributions to Philosophy*, "Turning in Enowning," 278.
101 Heidegger, *Black Notebooks 1938–1939*, VII. 7, 6.

The distortion of beyng arises out of the imbalance of humanity and technicity. The use of dialectics is modernity's attempt to reconcile the distortion: progress through the clash of oppositional forces is the "calculative mode of representation" that is *science-as-ideology*, which is a product of man's dissimulative nature. *Being calculating*, or *calculating beyng* lacks all measure and uses any means to justify the most terrible ends, which are always ends — or *demises* — of humanity. This *unconditionality*, so familiar to liberal-Marxism, is the unconditional surrender of man to Machine. Modernity is the surrogate mode of beyng wherein humanity embarks on the longest path to the shortest history.

Perpetuity paves the way for the longest path; it is ideological rigidity. Perpetual affirmers and deniers are disentangled from being and thus distort beyng. The pair subdues, wittingly or not, that which is foundational to both affirmation and doubt. On the other hand, the future thinker, if he is to exist at all, must be faithful to the idea of thoughtfulness, which is to say, faithful to the idea of rejecting unthinking faith and doubt. Thinking faith is born out of a magnanimity of heart, wherein one is contemporaneous with the good that came before — when *the good* is that which uplifts human *spirit*. Unthinking doubt, on the other hand, is the corresponding piece to ideological rigidity, wherein doubt is self-referentially the foundation of itself and fundamental to *science-as-ideology*.

Such thoughtlessly faithful doubters make up the majority, which is why the mass so readily adheres to confounding liberal-Marxism — that faithless creed demanding absolute conviction. Heidegger warns us of what the avid liberal-Marxist Heinrich Heine foresaw:

> *Most people* require 'convictions,' the confirmation of stubborn persistence in an arrogated questionlessness. The *few* reside on the mountain of what is question-worthy rather than on the plain of opinion. The former are the pursuers of beings, the latter few are the stewards of beyng.[102]

---

102 Heidegger, *Black Notebooks 1938–1939*, XI.77, 332.

Yes, the stubborn majority standing sentry on their plain of opinion will indeed pursue beings; thoughtful beings represent what the mass can never be, so they compensate as ruthlessly as one can imagine — if not today, then tomorrow. Adler, whom we met before, described this as an *inferiority complex*. More significantly, however, the Mass Man is only all too happy to fulfill the will of his master: through the liberal-Marxian creed of godless conformism, he docilely folds for Machine; he speaks its language.

Globalism is the language of Machine — at least, that part of it which is understandable to us.

> *Globalism* is the ... homogeneity and leveling down of humanity to a kind of achievement of an order of life, despite the apparent heterogeneity in the provenance and scope of the 'cultures'... [It is the internecine, thoughtless war of all against all for the sake of unlimited power. When power becomes unconditional, it] demands a sameness, a monotony, in its ever more simple means. Every power tries to expand and thereby collides with every other one in the same machination. This sameness of essence is the ground of the historiologically determinable totality and unconditionality of the essence of power.[103]

In the globalist world, every type of "culture" is celebrated, every type of disease and dysfunction — this is the "apparent heterogeneity." Of course, this is only pure homogeneity — a multiculturalism that is only a product and driver of mass consumerism. All is distraction. Unconditional power is at stake: "it demands a sameness, a monotony, in its ever more simple means." All is appalling charade. Never forget that this is the postwar international order that the ruling elites and their "benign" majorities wish to maintain.

Unconditional power, which demands absolute submission, is fed by unconditional truth. If globalism is the language of Machine, then unconditional truth is the syntax. Heidegger explains:

---

103 Heidegger, *Black Notebooks 1939–1941*, XV, 207.

> 'Unconditional truth' in the most modern thinking, where truth has become exact certitude, means the same as unconditional conditionality in the selection of facts and in the style of the communication of those facts. In this way, there arises a gigantic correctness, on the basis of which an individual person can never at all decide what is true or false. That distinction has been effaced as an antiquated one. We still lack the presuppositions for thinking through the essence of unconditional conditionality. It may be surmised that this sort of 'truth' ... surpasses everything we are otherwise accustomed to call 'nihilism.' A *supernihilism* leads again to 'reality,' i.e., to the reality of the utterly worthless nothingness.[104]

An individual is hardly permitted to determine anything for himself; instead, the Mass Man is herded this way and that, precisely in the direction the shepherds deem suitable. And more than this, the shepherds themselves are subject to this overarching "correctness" that, as Thomas Friedman would say, so *benignly* governs all. This is modernity's putrid malaise: only biological humans remain, *material-humanity*, a contentedness to comply. All is for salary and comfortability; and where these are not overtly sought, then activism takes their place — the avid activist aims to antagonize, though this is only at the will of *an-other*, and so innovation between warring factions spurs the rise of Machine. This is *unconditional conditionality*, wherein we "lack the presuppositions for thinking."

Here we are, then, allowing "only 'facts' to be valid, ones that are always only half true and therefore are erroneous..."[105] This is true today and has no doubt always been true: "facts" are presented from one side only and thus *cannot be* facts. What we see as "fact" — in the context of a globalist framework, or regarding human relationships — is mere subjective representation. In and of itself subjective representation is not problematic and, indeed, can be worthwhile, if not the basis for being. What Heidegger sees as problematic — in our unyielding continuation down the path of historiological imbalance, in losing sight

---

104 Heidegger, *Black Notebooks 1939–1941*, XV, 203.
105 Heidegger, *Black Notebooks 1939–1941*, XV, 207.

of humanity and our unlimited prioritization of technicity — is our insistence on *correctness*, not just for individuals, but for *everyone*.

Everyone must be *correct* from a global perspective; it is the monolithic nature of globalist myopia: there are not *many nations*, there is *one world*; there are not *many* perspectives, there is but *one*; there are not *varied races*, there is *one human race*; and so on. Despite championing "diversity," the globalist does *not* seek diverse ideologies or opinions, for actual diversity has a destabilizing effect at the micro and macro levels; this is why we see always the constant push toward certain (seemingly disparate) progressive agendas. The globalist moves toward the *homogeneity* of the Mass Mind, and it achieves this through seemingly coordinated efforts across elementary and continuing education, media, and the "publicity men" necessary in liberalistic societies; economic and legal policies then reinforce these efforts and desired behaviors become incentivized beyond theoretical levels. "The majority of men have no opinions," remarks José Ortega y Gasset,

> and these have to be pumped into them from outside, like lubricants into machinery. Hence it is necessary that some mind or other should hold and exercise authority, so that the people without opinions — the majority — can start having opinions.[106]

Ortega y Gasset was a firm liberal, and his position reflects the general liberal position first detailed by Immanuel Kant and John Stuart Mill: An elite must guide the masses through their unthinking stupor. There is, of course, the small presumption that the "elite" have only the very best interests of the masses in mind. The ruling elite use all means to guide the masses, among them the modern public-relations representative (PR rep); this was first conceived by Walter Lippmann and Ed Bernays with their concepts of "publicity men" and a Council on Public Relations, respectively.[107] Such a PR rep "not only [knows] what news value is, but knowing it, he is in a position to *make news*

---

106 José Ortega y Gasset, *The Revolt of the Masses* (Norton, 1932), 141.
107 Walter Lippmann, *Public Opinion* (Macmillan, 1941), 345.

happen. He is a creator of events."¹⁰⁸ Without constant curating of the Mass Mind,

> the common life of humanity would be chaos, a historic void, lacking in any organic structure. Consequently, without a spiritual power, without someone to command, and in proportion as this is lacking, chaos reigns over mankind.¹⁰⁹

This is what liberal-Marxists think of the Mass Man: without obsessive supervision, the masses lapse into sociopolitical chaos, a Kantian "self-imposed nonage."¹¹⁰ To be sure, liberal-Marxists claim to be the Mass Man's advocate, but their actions belie a ruthless ambition to *rule* and *shape* the masses to fit the rule.

A prime example of this leftist elitism is the case of longtime National Public Radio (NPR)¹¹¹ editor Uri Berliner excoriating the network for its infamous and increasingly "progressive" bias in his trenchant exposé, "I've Been at NPR for 25 Years. Here's How We Lost America's Trust."¹¹² Berliner's principal criticism for NPR is its utter lack of "self-reflection" after several major journalistic inaccuracies and deliberate omissions intended to skew public perception to mirror the personal beliefs the network's staff. And not only, he writes, is NPR guilty of irresponsible and prejudiced reporting, as an organization it doubles down on its commitment, as former NPR CEO John Lansing¹¹³

---

108 Bernays, *Crystalizing Public Opinion* (Liveright, 1934), 197. For more on Lippmann and Bernays, see Martin Friedrich's essay "The Private Ownership of Public Opinion" in *Myth and Sun* (Clemens & Blair, 2022).

109 José Ortega y Gasset, *The Revolt of the Masses* (Norton, 1932), 141.

110 Kant, "What is Enlightenment?" (1784).

111 NPR is a broadcasting network funded by the American public and government, corporate sponsors, foundations, and academic institutions. Similar entities would be the British Broadcasting Corporation, Deutsche Welle, and RT.

112 Published for *The Free Press* (April 2024).

113 Before moving to NPR, Lansing headed the US government's Voice of America broadcasting network.

suggested, to exposing "white privilege" as an "inseparable [part] of our collective efforts to serve the American audience."[114]

Current NPR CEO, Katherine Maher, offered a swift response to Berliner's disclosure, assuring us — like any good "publicity man" — that "public media is essential for an informed public" and "our work can help *shape* and *illuminate* the very sense of what it means to have a shared *public* identity…"[115] Repeatedly, Maher (like Lansing before her) talks of NPR's "strategy," as though simply keeping the public *informed* needs a strategy; hardly — the business of informing someone requires no strategy; "illuminating" the public and "shaping" its perception, however, *does* require a strategy. Lipmann and Bernays' legacy is alive and well, it seems. Maher goes on to praise NPR's effort to establish working groups meant to assess the network's commentary "in a climate of respectful, open-minded discussion." But this is precisely what Berliner took issue with in the first place: "An open-minded spirit no longer exists within NPR" and "When I suggested we had a diversity [of thought] problem … the response wasn't hostile. It was worse. It was met with profound indifference." Berliner continues:

> There's an unspoken consensus [at NPR] about the stories we should pursue and how they should be framed. It's frictionless — one story after another about instances of supposed racism, transphobia, signs of the climate apocalypse… It's almost like an assembly line.

It *is* an assembly line. An assembly line — like NPR and most media and infotainment networks — has its purpose: to form a product with maximum efficiency.

---

114 From former NPR CEO John Lansing's internal memo; excerpted from NPR's official statement: "Diversity, Equity, And Inclusion Is Not A Project: It Is Our Work" (September 2020), NPR Extra.

115 From "Thoughts on our mission and our work" (April 2024), NPR Extra; emphasis added.

Already in 1928 Bernays wrote that the purpose of "successful propaganda" is "to manipulate and sway [the] public."[116] Indeed, a liberal-democracy must be "administered by the intelligent minority who know how to regiment and guide the masses."[117] Again we hear the echo of Kant, Rousseau, and other liberal forerunners demanding that a ruling elite shepherd the dull masses to illumination. One has to wonder: Why is it that liberal-Marxist societies discourage self-improvement and individual excellence while enabling sociocultural aberrations and collective mediocrity — and this often in the name of "ending white supremacy"? It is not a coincidence, for instance, that, concurrent to NPR executives' talk about ending "white privilege" while their network spews assembly-line "antiracism" stories, schools across the West determine ways to integrate "antiracism" into their curricula.

One of the better-known instances of this comes from Equitable Math (equitablemath.org) and manifests in the "A Pathway to Equitable Mathematics Instruction" toolkit. This toolkit was devised by education *administrators* — i.e., not mathematicians, not teachers — sponsored by the Bill and Melinda Gates Foundation, and promoted by the US Department of Education's Literacy Information and Communication System. It claims to provide

> teachers an opportunity to examine their actions, beliefs, and values around teaching mathematics. The framework for deconstructing racism in mathematics offers essential characteristics of antiracist math educators and critical approaches to dismantling white supremacy in math classrooms by making visible the toxic characteristics of white supremacy culture with respect to math. Building on the framework, teachers engage with critical praxis in order to shift their instructional beliefs and practices towards antiracist math education. By centering antiracism, we model how to be antiracist math educators with accountability.[118]

---

116 Bernays, *Propaganda*, 125.
117 Bernays, *Propaganda*, 127.
118 Found at equitablemath.org.

Liberal-Marxism has a penchant for promoting *administrators* to lead organizations over actual doers of the craft. This has the advantage of furthering the aims of the ruling party through indoctrinatory leadership, as administrators set the conditions for the doers' work, which seeps down to the lowest level. For education, this means administrators dictating what students learn, which, in the case of government, is always sociopolitical.

During World War II, the Soviet Union attached political functionaries—*commissars*—to military units to ensure proper ideological fervor. Established by Trotsky following the Russian Revolution, commissars would promptly execute any service member deemed traitorous to the political cause. Commissars proved so effective on the Eastern Front that the National Socialists established a similar practice in 1943. Not surprisingly, however, the position itself was inaugurated during the French Revolution (the *représentant en mission*) to likewise ensure *proper* political zeal among both soldiers and civilians. Spanish Marxists (both communists and republicans) fighting for the globalist cause later used commissars heavily in their fight against nationalist forces.

Contrast the administrative penchant of liberal-Marxism with this anecdote from Hermann Giesler, one of Hitler's favored architects:

> Hitler said to me: 'For quite some time I've been aware that only a soldier of great status will be entitled to lead the nation once I retire after the end of the war. That's why I tried to get acquainted with anyone whose soldierly achievement and manly deeds were extraordinary. By having the chance to present the awards for brave soldiers personally, I gained an immediate impression of many. Regardless of his military rank or which part of the armed forces he belonged to, I was open and attentive to him. I talked to everybody in order to find the value of his personality—always searching for the outstanding soldier who could one day lead the nation....'[119]

---

119 H. Giesler, C. Yeager, et al., *The Artist Within the Warlord* (selections from *Ein anderer Hitler*; Barnes, 2018), 199–200.

That soldier would likely have been famed Stuka pilot Hans-Ulrich Rudel, who led a remarkable life and was awarded for valor numerous times. There is a marked difference in intent and outcome when a doer is selected for leadership as opposed to a mere *administrator*. Administrators are good for executing the will of their master, usually in some *inhuman* way; a doer who earns the respect of those around him and is chosen to be a leader from among his peers not only knows the work, but also knows how to *humanly* connect with the workers.

All this to say, the only way one can make sense of the state of liberal-democracies across the West is to see it from a Bernaysian perspective — i.e., a liberal-Marxist, indoctrinatory perspective: *The elite wish to maintain power at the expense of the directed and dimwitted masses.* It is the social luminary who must enlighten "the people." Further presaging NPR, Bernays continues:

> Social progress is simply the progressive education and enlightenment of the public mind in regard to its immediate and distant social problems.... Propaganda can play a part in pointing out what is and what is not beautiful...[120]

Defining what *is* and what *is not* "beautiful" is strictly in the domain of the ruling elite, the Vanguard-prelates. NPR fulfills the liberal-Marxist program of shaping a public it needs to realize its strategy of increasing social power; with social power comes economic power; and, in this materialistic, mechanized age, "economic power tends to draw after it political power."[121] Ultimately, while under Maher's direction NPR purports to maintain an atmosphere of "open-minded discussion," reality reveals only the myopic "openness" of any echo chamber; *they will continue to be open to their ideas alone* — this, despite a recent Gallup poll indicating historic public distrust in American news media, with nearly *three-quarters* of Americans saying they have little to no trust in

---

120 Bernays, *Propaganda*, 151, 154.
121 Bernays, *Propaganda*, 47.

news reporting.[122] Of course, this type of dissonance between actions and apparent reality makes sense if *shaping* and *illuminating* are the media's priorities.

We recall America's top diplomat, who says that to protect national security — and by *national* security he means *world* or *international* security—

> we're building a more resilient global information system, where objective facts are elevated and deceptive messages gain less traction. We're doing that by promoting policies and programs that protect a free, vibrant, and independent press and that foster greater civic and media literacy so that people can better distinguish fact from fiction.[123]

Why is it that "the people," who supposedly hold so much power in liberal-Marxist societies, which is to say, *the world*, must be instructed on what is "fact" and what is "fiction"? It is because political experimentation over millennia has shown that the surest way to rule massive populations for long periods of time is to garner popular participation, or at least pandemic apathy; this is done through controlling information, which is to control perceived reality. In this way, "the people" participate in — and actively support — their own subservience: *He is freely in bondage who does with pleasure the will of his master*, as Augustine would say.

In response to the US Secretary of State's comments, NPR dutifully contributed to the control of popular reality, that *veil of Maya*; the ideological mouthpiece, like its government, painted a picture of American *fact* versus Russian *fiction*, describing how a prominent Russian media outlet "went from a cable news clone to covert operator."[124] Choosing its words carefully, NPR aims to stoke fear and

---

122 Megan Brenan for *Gallup*, "Media Confidence in U.S. Matches 2016 Record Low" (October 2023).

123 A. Blinken, remarks to the press (September 13, 2024).

124 Shannon Bond, "How Russia's RT went from a cable news clone to covert operator" (September 26, 2024). This article is part of NPR's "Untangling

disgust: "clone" implies falsity; "covert" suggests shadowy intrigue. But media consumers are meant to believe NPR merely reports the news and eschews editorializing. Though scarcely a network exists that can resist spreading their ideology — and they do it, as NPR notes, behind a "sleek, modern, and cable news-like" veneer. It just so happens that all but a negligible few networks spread a liberal-Marxist blanket to smother the human spirit and prepare the way for Machine. For its part, NPR does this by citing Nina Jankowicz, former director of America's infamous Disinformation Governance Board[125] and the self-proclaimed "Mary Poppins of disinformation"[126]: the network targeted by American attack

> had a clear mission … to 'reflect the Russian position on the main issues of international politics and inform the wider public about the events and phenomena of Russian life… The masks were off. It was clear that [the network] was just shilling for the Russian point of view.'[127]

Of course, we are not to imagine that NPR shills for any point of view, let alone liberal-Marxist Americanism; rather, we are to believe they are completely impartial, approaching life with a very Rawlsian *veil of ignorance* guiding their "blind" strategizing.

A world disentangled from humanity and in thrall to a *will-to-machine* would look much like the world we see — with no authorities taking personal responsibility for their actions, with each pretending to some insane notion of complete correctness. This, incidentally, mirrors what we see today with AI "hallucination"; there is a rush to provide an answer — *the* answer, which becomes "truth" by virtue of its

---

Disinformation" series — so, once more, we are left to rely on those who spread "disinformation" to save us from its danger.

125 Jankowicz was the first and only director of the short-lived Board, serving from April 27, 2022 to May 18, 2022 under DHS Secretary Alejandro Mayorkas.
126 Jankowicz, @wiczipedia (February 17, 2021), x.com.
127 Bond, "How Russia's RT went from a cable news clone to covert operator" (September 26, 2024).

"first-ness." This is how ideologies take hold — by controlling information, yes, but, most importantly, by controlling "the people," who have only their ignorance and apathy to bind them. The people are all too willing to let a veil of ignorance keep them snugly behind the veil of *Maya* — because humanity is something lost on the biological mass.

"[The enemy media network] has become a clearinghouse for a set of covert operations, covert influence activities, intelligence operations de facto, in country after country after country," pines James Rubin, head of the US State Department's Global Engagement Center (GEC). It would seem the stakes are quite high — certainly too high for "the people" to navigate such treacherous terrain themselves; Rubin continues:

> One of the reasons why so much of the world has not been as fully supportive of Ukraine as you would think they would be, given that Russia has invaded Ukraine and violated rule number one of the international system, is because of the broad scope and reach of [the enemy media network], where propaganda, disinformation, and lies are spread to millions, if not billions, of people around the world.[128]

The *international system* rears its head again. "Billions" of lives are at risk, which destabilizes the *international order*. Covert shills and clones — the *enemy*, the *fascist* — must be silenced; Americanism offers the solution: truth, freedom, democracy, justice; indeed, it was in their name that the United States invaded Vietnam, Grenada, Panama, Iraq, Afghanistan, Libya, and Syria. Many other "covert" invasions are happening right now that few will ever know about; these are invasions to spread, not "propaganda, disinformation, and lies," but truth, freedom, and democracy. The American Departments of State and Defense ensure their forces are active in spreading the necessary truths from embassies and consulates worldwide to uphold the *international system* forever.

---

128 Bond, "How Russia's RT went from a cable news clone to covert operator" (September 26, 2024).

But all major countries seek to further their aims — their truth — regionally, if not globally, through Machiavellian maneuvering, or *diplomacy*. Along with this, "they are engaged in covert influence activities aimed at undermining" unwanted systems.[129]

But perhaps Americanism's proponents can be accused of no such activity — one cannot be wrong when one refuses to take personal responsibility. This is, after all, is the foundation of the international system established by the anti-fascist liberal-Marxists after World War II.

The *Helsinki Times*, an online periodical aiming, like NPR, to spread its version of the truth, posted an article in November 2021 referencing the CIA's alleged Operation Mockingbird; it is worth citing in full here:

> During the Cold War, the U.S. Central Intelligence Agency (CIA) launched its Operation Mockingbird, which aimed to collect intelligence by bribing journalists and institutions around the world and affecting public opinion by manipulating news media.
>
> Carl Bernstein, a famous American investigative journalist who unveiled the scandal in 1977, said that according to the plan, the CIA recruited journalists that were put on a payroll by the CIA and instructed to write 'fake stories.' The CIA admitted that at least 400 journalists and 25 large organizations around the world had secretly carried out assignments for the agency.
>
> To this day, the CIA still attempts to monitor and manipulate public opinion through this despicable practice. The so-called truth that underpins a news story, from the perspective of the U.S. government, is not worth mentioning at all, with news media just being used as a tool to safeguard the country's hegemony in the world.[130]

This article followed in time Nina Jankowicz's claim, through a rather bizarre song, to be "the Mary Poppins of disinformation"; it followed

---

129 A. Blinken, remarks to the press (September 13, 2024).
130 "CIA's Operation Mockingbird a precursor of US manipulation of world public opinion," *Helsinki Times* (November 10, 2021).

in tenor the notion of *correctness* subservient to the *will-to-machine*. We are to be instructed on how to acquiesce to Machine.

∞●∞

The *international order* has ensured that no existing corporate state is free of liberal-Marxism's stain. No country today exists to uplift the human spirit. All that exists today is firmly within the *will-to-machine*. The meaning behind every action is *un-meaning*: a preparatory move toward the New Colossus.

There is no freedom; man is only passed from one repressive regime to another, always in the name of freedom — because lies and distraction are the most effective way of ensuring enduring rulership. Perhaps freedom exists in the individual's end: whether this happens in life or death is the future task for whatever remains of the human spirit.

∞●∞

After Berliner's exposé, Maher suspended him, without pay, for failing to secure "approval for outside work for other news outlets"; Berliner subsequently resigned for his desire to not "work in a newsroom where I am disparaged."[131]

In his post-suspension article on Berliner, NPR's David Folkenflik reported on the backlash his network's current CEO has received for past social-media posts revealing a fervent leftist bias; in response to criticism of Maher for her past statements, NPR stated that "the CEO is not involved in editorial decisions." The CEO may not make direct editorial decisions, but the CEO directs the editors, as is clear from the comments NPR's previous CEO, John Lansing, made about, apparently, the *existential necessity* of merging Diversity, Equity, and Inclusion efforts into their journalistic endeavors: "[W]e must do this

---

131 David Folkenflik, "NPR suspends veteran editor as it grapples with his public criticism" (April 2024), NPR. See also, Ivana Saric, "Suspended NPR editor resigns after accusing network of liberal bias" (April 2024), Axios.

because, by definition, it is our work. It is inseparable from all of our collective efforts." It is disingenuous for NPR to suggest that a CEO has no impact on editorial decisions. But this is the liberal-Marxist wont: *always pretend to be something other than what one is.*

We recall Professor Emeritus Krell, who called any semblance of traditional values *farcical*; but the true farce is *pretending to be something other than what one is* — though this is the very pretense *defining* liberal-Marxism. *Informing* does not require pretense any more than simply *living* according to traditional values does; *shaping* and *informing* in the name of supposed *progress*, however, do require disingenuousness. To rule, the elite — the Vanguard-prelates — must *create* and *shape* events; they must "pump in" approved thoughts, for this is a near-certain way to establish in the minds of the unthinking mass the vision of *correct* living.

The emphasis on *correctness* — politically *correct*, the *correct* side of history, etc. — is obvious in modern society. We see this as a "natural" progression down the path of enlightenment, so to speak; but it really is a great enormity: selves are sublimated into an historic trajectory of gigantic proportions — the *giganticness* is the flight of the self from itself: *we* do not guide correctness, but *correctness* guides us. We are met, as Nietzsche wrote, with "the victory of scientific atheism," which was born out of the Judeo-Christianity that colonized the European soul, but "in which all races are to have their share of service…" This *victory of veracity*

> no longer tolerates the *lie* of the belief in a God.… One sees what has really gained the victory over the Christian God —, *Christian morality itself*, the conception of *veracity*, taken ever more strictly, the confessional subtlety of the Christian conscience, translated and sublimated to the *scientific conscience*, to intellectual purity at any price.[132]

---

132 Nietzsche, *The Joyful Wisdom*, §357; emphasis added.

We are beyond any Chomskyan "manufactured consent" or Bernaysian false inception; we are enslaved to a destiny beyond our control — because our focus on "facts" has obfuscated the truth.

What is the truth? We are not *global* beings; beyng is not *global*. We are *planetary* beings participating in *planetary* beyng. The *planetary* is at once supra-personal and the most intimate state of *personalness*; it is the *subject* of personality, the great personality that *drives* history and is not *driven by* history. *Planetary* stands opposed to *global*: the former seeks balance at the expense of convenience; the latter seeks convenience at the expense of balance. Humanity and technicity sit on opposite scales: "facts" and their concomitant laws and policies tip the balance. The obsessive rationalizing and *factualizing* defining modernity only affirm "an abyssal lack of meditation and an impotence for questioning, and [it] conceals a flight ... from beings and into the absence of being."[133] All talk of *correctness* is really a masking of the loss of our selves: "facts" are flight, a *going under* of the mind that is irredeemably sublimated into Mind. Indeed, our "lowest level will be reached when the highest intelligence and the installation of violence meet in a [goalless] *overwhelming* [—] unless the goal is the gigantic concealment of a gigantic emptiness and perplexity."[134]

Those steering us are themselves hitched to a wagon guided by their own blindness — the "blindest flight," as Heidegger puts it.

> As long as the human being experiences, possesses, and pursues himself as *animal rationale*, for that long does he indeed pertain to beings as such, but the truth of beyng is refused him, and thereby so is the abyss, and so likewise Da-Sein — and so the unique decision, and so the god-bestowing beginning — and so an originary history, and so also a downgoing.[135]

What are the rational animals fleeing if not themselves? Globalism, which is the product of Enlightenment rationality, presents the illusion

---

133 Heidegger, *Black Notebooks 1939–1941*, XII.18, 32.
134 Heidegger, *Black Notebooks 1939–1941*, XII.18, 32.
135 Heidegger, *Black Notebooks 1939–1941*, XIII.17, 68.

of running toward a harmony that was precluded the instant its possibility was conceived. This illusion is a uni-pole, a reverse-mirror that depicts the running forward of a progress-minded being; what is ordained, however, is the reversal of steps contributing to a gigantic collapse.

The truth of beyng is the falseness of correctness; it is the blindness that sees itself with the sight of a planetary untruth. Planetary untruth is global fact and the birth of man's venture into the abyss. The *abyss* is the death of the gigantic, which is to say, the beginning of man's self-revolution, a spiraling fall away from the convenience of a technicized *fact*. It is this intimate acquaintance with the self that prompts the *unique decision* — the personal decision to drive one's destiny toward beyng, which is simultaneously the *god-bestowing beginning* and ultimate *downgoing*. Beyng is the balance of untruth, the recognition of recognition itself; this is the incipient sight of the god and the end of man as a sublimated being.

Decisions can only return to humanity upon technicization's reversal, which means an eradication of globalism. This will not happen. The Vanguard-elites, who operate in thrall to their own false inception, have every material incentive to value and, in turn, incentivize a quality-less quantity. Globalism exists because it must; Machine demands it. And if some catastrophe disrupts modernity's current trajectory, then any subsequent arc will follow a similar, ineluctable path. We are no longer our own, and not even death can free us from servitude to *utterly worthless nothingness*.

15.

Every last biological human is brutalized into its biologism and commodification. Some are under the illusion power has long rested with them, but it is only wrested from them. What are *ethical* and *cultural* decline in our age of "supernihilism" if not false inceptions meant to spur the antagonistic innovation necessary for an arrival of the New Colossus? As we are no longer our own, we lack the capacity for the faith required to extend our decisions beyond the local. Modernity, then, is only a collection of blunted instruments, each snug in its place. "All our relationships have become merely technical ones," Heidegger shared in his discussion with *Der Spiegel*, and all is quickly fading from view:

> Just as little can the brutalization of the masses ... still allow a valuation as 'ethical' and 'cultural' decline. The brutalization is in itself a no longer recognizable wild licentiousness in the form of the instituted and planned structure of the 'lived experience' and 'enjoyment' of the masses. Such wildness leads at the same time to a hardening whose hardness is not 'strength' (as a consequence of sovereignty) but is instead the blunting of all drives. This brutalization ... which arises from power in its overpowering and is instituted in the human masses leads to a point whereby it becomes the condition of the possibility of Godlessness. Godlessness does not here refer to the renunciation and suppression of God—instead, it means something more essential: the metaphysical incapacity for a leap into a decisional domain in which the divinity of God can first of all appropriate a lighted space-time. The characterization of the age also includes this: one now encounters more frequently a human type which drudges about entirely in the day before yesterday (human being as 'I' and 'we,' as 'consciousness' and 'body'; nihilism and loss of belief in God), tracks down all indications of a convulsing but finds quick countermeasures, keeps for itself too little, and 'analyzes' everything—without regions of meditation and sufficient power for historical experience.[136]

Man's acceleration into *utterly worthless nothingness* coincided with the rapid technicization following Enlightenment Europe's revaluation of sociopolitical values. Every war waged in this environment was against metaphysicality, for every war was machinational—in favor of *material happiness* (*prosperity*), "people" as *things* (as opposed to *bearers of meaning*), and the enlargement of itself. Conflict is everywhere—and nowhere does it seek anything of value. The final war for humanity has already been fought and lost. Witnessed now is the international

---

136 Heidegger, *Black Notebooks 1939–1941*, XII.9, 15.

order of a self-destructive victory over man's spirit. Filling in the craters of a war-torn hellscape is a patchwork of commodities; earth no longer goes to earth — its displacement is permanent. Salary keeps the malaise ever progressing. *Who needs spirit when there is a "rules-based order"?*[137] *Who needs the attacked when there is the attacker? Who needs faith when there is food?*

16.

From one moment to the next life moves to death. Everything preceding this moment is meant to be a reckoning with it — but it often isn't. Most avoid the reckoning for an instilled wish of convenience.

Much can be imagined from a position of convenience — in fact, all historiography stems from it.

In 2008 a collection of activists and academicians (the two are usually symbiotic, if not identical) drafted the Prague Declaration as a public denouncement of Marxian violence — specifically, the crimes committed by various Soviet regimes. It is a passing and peculiar wonder that some among the political and intellectual "elite" acknowledge Soviet criminality. *Allies condemning Allied action* — it is *almost* unheard of in our postwar world of pretending. *Almost* — but sufficient appearances of dissimilarity must be maintained. Of course, it would be unwise to forgo the chance to vilify the dreadful "Nazis," so we are left with this *inclusive* and *correct* first point:

> [We ... call for] reaching an all-European understanding that both the Nazi and Communist totalitarian regimes each need to be judged by their own terrible merits to be destructive in their policies of systematically applying extreme forms of terror, suppressing all civic and human liberties, starting aggressive wars and, as an inseparable part of their ideologies, exterminating and deporting whole nations and groups of population; and that as such

---

137 "Rules-based order" or "rules-based international order" is a common phrase used by the political elite across the globe. It is a liberal-Marxist idea promoting the materialization and commodification of all reality.

they should be considered to be the main disasters, which blighted the 20th century.

Notably, this first point takes issue with "extreme forms of terror" — presumably, lesser forms of terror are appropriate if the situation demands; perhaps various forms of extrajudicial punishment are acceptable forms of terror. Moreover, in modern Western societies, liberal-Marxist policy hardly requires *extermination* and *deportation* to be overtly part of its multifarious ideology — rather, encouraging the *propagation* and *importation* of populations *besides* the undesired group(s) suffices to accomplish the same task; such backhanded politicking is far more palatable to liberal-Marxism's feigned sociability.

Recall, for instance, this now notorious 2015 statement from the American career-politician Joe Biden when he welcomed

> ... an unrelenting stream of immigration. *Nonstop. Nonstop.* Folks like me, who are Caucasian, of European descent, for the first time in 2017 will be in an absolute minority in the United States of American. *Absolute minority.* Fewer than 50% of the people in America from then on will be white, European stock. *That's not a bad thing.*

Earlier in his statement, Biden reiterated Emma Lazarus, Israel Zangwill, and Leon Trotsky's[138] vision of the "melting pot": "*We are a melting pot.* It is the ultimate source of our strength... We're proud to be a melting pot." It is unsurprising that an American politician echoes Trotsky, but the parallels do not end with their praise of the Lazarus-fabricated "melting pot." Trotsky — like Biden in his giddiness over the disappearance of "white, European stock" from America — is exuberant over the idea that "the mysticism of the 'Slavic soul' is coming off like scum" in the formerly tsarist Russia. But this was not the last time Biden would express the idea; here he is in 2016: "[W]e're the most unique country in the world. You cannot define for

---

138 Lazarus and Zangwill were previously mentioned. Here is Trotsky: "the Soviet Union is an immense melting pot in which the characters of dozens of nationalities are being mixed..." (*The Revolution Betrayed* [Dover, 2004], 120).

me who an American is — based on religion, ethnicity, race. It's an attitude."[139] Liberal-Marxism is *always* an attitude — an *abstraction*. It is a machinational approach to life aimed at eradicating the inceptual, eradicating *itself*. Again, in 2014, speaking to the National Association of Manufacturers, Biden praised the American economy:

> We have the most resilient economy in the world [and are] better positioned than any country ... to lead ... in the 21st Century. [Central to economic strength is our] constant, unrelenting stream [of immigrants].[140]

And again we see the ultimate reason for immigration — particularly non-European immigration — revealed: *money*. Money — *economics* — is one pillar of the liberal-Marxist temple: from the Vanguard-prelates to the lottery-playing proletarian, *money* is motivation. To hell with everything else: *family, culture, tradition* — none of it matters if it fails to feed the predatory money machine. Heidegger saw the economics-based system for what it was; here he calls it "Americanism" because this was the dominant form of global *machinationality*:

> Americanism is the organization of the unconditional meaninglessness of 'existence,' joined to the prospect of an enhanced 'standard of living' (electric heating and cooling of homes, increase in automobile ownership, rise in the number of moviegoers and of other '*economic-technological-cultural*' amenities of 'life').[141]

Economics as "culture" — this is by now modernity's familiar stamp. But never mind this. Liberal-Marxism is more than its *will-to-economics* or its other pillar, the *will-to-destruction*: liberal-Marxism is a means to the end of humanity. There is no conspiracy among supposed leaders — one cannot expect bumbling money-chasers to have any sense of

---

139 "Remarks by Vice President Joe Biden at the 20th Annual CAF Conference" (September 2016).

140 B. Goad, "Biden: We need 'constant, unrelenting stream' of immigrants," *The Hill* (June 2014).

141 Heidegger, *Black Notebooks 1939–1941*, XV, 213; emphasis added.

beyng; rather, there is only fulfillment of a governing *will-to-machine*. *Economics-as-culture* is *Americanism-as-attitude*—both share a fundament in *abstraction*: witness liberal-Marxism as the unremitting thoughtlessness of a devout meaninglessness. Again, Heidegger targets "Americanism":

> Americanism is the victory of unconditional 'abstraction,' the victory of the disregarding of the essence of beyng. All engagement is sunk in abstractness and therefore lives in the delusion of being concrete and of having to battle against 'abstract thinking.'[142]

Globalism is the Americanization of life. All corporate states pursue the "resilience" of an *American economy*, and they will stop at nothing to get it. This is only part of everyday *machinationality*.

When every instant of every day is pervaded with and founded on abstractions demanding thought from thoughtless executors, we witness the delusion of inauthenticity. The delusion of which Heidegger speaks is even captured in the false dichotomy extant between nominally oppositional political parties. Each smears the other for having approaches and outcomes that are too impractical—but each of them nevertheless rejects the most practical bases for living. Foremost among such bases: the *individual decision*. Unrelenting liberal-Marxist propaganda ensures not a single biological human ever confuses *fact* with actual thought. Nietzsche wrote: "The victory of a moral ideal is achieved by the same 'immoral' means as any other victory: violence, lies, slander, injustice."[143] This is reminiscent of the adage: *Evil never sleeps*.[144] But if evil never sleeps, then the good must be ever vigilant to thwart it. Thus the supposedly good become what they set out to guard against.

This is not digression; the tie between politics, economics, and morality is the *society* tricked into false inceptuality—the *inauthenticity*

---

142 Heidegger, *Black Notebooks 1939–1941*, XV, 212.
143 Nietzsche, *The Will to Power*, §306.
144 Cf. Proverbs 4:16 of the Hebrew Bible.

of being. The Prague Declaration is nothing more than an attempt to distance modernity's prevailing ideology from a "former," albeit *quite related*, ally. Heidegger reminds us:

> [T]he danger of Communism does not reside in its economic and societal consequences but rather in the fact that its *spiritual* essence ... is not recognized and the confrontation with Communism is placed on a level which completely secures its supremacy and irresistibility.[145]

The game is over; the danger is past — not because it has left, but because it has *overtaken everything*. The *revolt of the slaves*, says Nietzsche, "has only moved out of our sight, because it — *has achieved victory*."[146] From tulip merchants to ambitious careerists, social climbers, and materialistic peons — all submit wholly to the ideology permitting the fulfillment of their vacuous desires. And no one saw it coming: the rise of the New Colossus.

We continue with the Prague Declaration: to signal their devotion to the postwar narrative, the drafters mention the "Nazis" first — but even this was not good enough to appease many Curators of the Correct. *The Economist* reports that, despite drafters emphasizing the Declaration's "aim was not to downgrade the Holocaust but to 'upgrade' Soviet misdeeds," "some, if not all, Jewish activists; left-wing politicians (mostly from western Europe); and, inevitably, Russia" were upset at the prospect of condemning Marxian criminality.[147] Perhaps it just doesn't feel right condemning one's core beliefs. *Who can say?*

"Americanism," says Heidegger — and *Americanism* is essentially *liberal-Marxism* — "is the amassing of everything, which amassing at the same time signifies the uprooting of what has been amassed."[148] *The amassing of everything and its subsequent uprooting* is

---

145 Heidegger, *Black Notebooks 1939–1941*, XIII.128, 116.
146 Nietzsche, *On the Genealogy of Morals*, Essay 1, §7.
147 Not attributed, "Old Wounds: Clashing versions of Lithuania's history and how to treat it" (February 10, 2011).
148 Heidegger, *Black Notebooks 1939–1941*, XV, 204.

totalitarianism *par excellence*. When everything is finally under total control, the control itself must be maligned and re-maligned. It is the convolution of the convoluted, which is only sign of waning humanity. One is reminded of America's intrigues in Guatemala.

The United States' backing of a coup to overthrow Guatemala's social-democratic anti-imperialism "under the guise of anticommunism" initiated a decades-long civil war that claimed the lives of nearly two hundred thousand Guatemalans.[149] The tumult began in 1944 when a popular uprising against the military government of Jorge Ubico led to the election of the "spiritual socialist" Juan José Arévalo. Arévalo was succeeded by the Marxist "sympathizer" Jacobo Árbenz. Árbenz was deposed in the aforementioned coup and then succeeded by several US-backed despots whose principal purpose was to stifle any kind of popular anti-imperialism that could adversely affect American corporate interests in the country. The string of authoritarian rulers was finally interrupted by the end of the civil war and the supposed victory of liberal-democracy. The current president of Guatemala is Bernardo Arévalo, the son of Juan José Arévalo. President Bernardo Arévalo studied at the Hebrew University of Jerusalem, worked four years in the Guatemalan embassy in Israel, and has said, "Israel is a country for which I have great affection."[150] In June 2024, the US Department of State released a statement, sans context, condemning the "murder of Guatemalan *trade union* leader Anastacio Tzib Caal." The statement went on to praise "worker rights" and "economic development," while decrying disruption of "our global supply chains."[151] It is curious that the United States, which spent much of the last century exploiting Guatemala and installing governments largely unfavorable to workers' rights, would issue a statement on the death of an unknown

---

149 Stephen Streeter, *Managing the Counterrevolution: The United States and Guatemala, 1954–1961* (Ohio University, 2000), 13.

150 Jacob Kessler, "5 Jewish facts about Guatemala's new Hebrew-speaking president," *The Times of Israel* (August 23, 2023).

151 Matthew Miller, Dept. spokesperson, June 17, 2024; emphasis added.

trade-union leader. Given America's progressive drift and increasing acceptance of social-democracy at home, let alone abroad, it seems less curious that the statement would be issued. Without context, however, one is left to suspect the deceased was no mere "trade union leader," and that instead, he was perhaps more so a political activist. Political organs speak politically.

Trade unions, while not a direct product of Marxian philosophy, are certainly bolstered by it — as a means of furthering class goals, i.e., igniting world revolution. A more reformist approach to unions, such as that found in capitalist-corporate states, might focus less on the achievement of class goals and more on strengthening "worker rights," which serves to mollify and *bourgeois-ize* the proletariat, at least in their ambitions, and makes them more controllable. Trade unions, like liberal-Marxist crimes, are sufficiently ambiguous in their purpose, which helps in the evasion of meaningful scrutiny.

We live now in a general state of divided labor, purposefully created to alienate and stupefy the masses. Adam Smith described this *dumbing down* in his *Wealth of Nations* (1776):

> The understandings of the greater part of men are necessarily formed by their ordinary employments. The man whose whole life is spent in performing a few simple operations ... has no occasion to exert his understanding.... He generally becomes as stupid and ignorant as it is possible for a human creature to become.... The uniformity of his stationary life naturally corrupts the courage of his mind.... It corrupts even the activity of his body and renders him incapable of exerting his strength with vigor and perseverance in any other employments than that to which he has been bred. His dexterity at his own particular trade seems in this manner to be acquired at the expense of his intellectual, social, and martial virtues. But in every improved and civilized society, this is the state into which the laboring poor, that is, the great body of the people, must necessarily fall.[152]

Marx appropriated the notion of the trade union to serve as the conduit for utopian revolution — keeping in mind that a Marxian "utopia"

---

152 A. Smith, *Wealth of Nations*, Book V.I.II.

means a great deal of *bloodshed* and, given its spiteful basis, *sadism*. For both Marx and "social democrats," the union was a means to an end. The former's end has been stated; for the latter, the union was to keep the working class comfortably docile, if not comfortably dumb. However, the ultimate end each pursued was no doubt unknown to them: it was, as Marx identified, "*machines*. It is they that sweep away the craftsman's work as the regulating principle of social production."[153] Machines will continue to replace the humanity fulfilling the *will-to-machine* — until the very last, blinking man bends the final knee.

One could perhaps be forgiven for being dazzled at the convolutedness of such incredible, as Heidegger said, *amassing*. Where does this all lead? *Who can say?* Perhaps we are left with a nagging sense of *machinational deracination*. Such amassing necessarily leads to cannibalistic self-critiquing pursuant to a *correctness* that is only the echo of a yell yet to be loosed.

The Prague Declaration, Guatemala, Americanism, Bolshevism — what are these if not the machinational destinies of those unable to reckon with the thoughtlessness of a *correct* life? The last word is aptly left to Heidegger:

> If we ask about the concept [of socialism] imprinted in history, and not about some romantic ideal, then we find the deepest answer ... in Lenin's dictum: 'Socialism is Soviet power plus electrification.'[154] This dictum ... [says] nothing ... of 'community' or 'welfare' or the 'equality' of all citizens; instead: socialism is 'power' — the releasement of a despotism which compels and holds in pincers a proletarianizing of the entire people and accordingly often changes its tactics, sometimes even to the opposite ones...
>
> Socialism is despotically proletarian power in which technology is not a mere appendage nor a mere means — but is instead the basic configuration

---

153 Marx, *Capital* (Progress, 1890), Moore and Aveling translation, vol. 1, Part IV.XIV.5.

154 Rojcewicz: "Vladimir Ilyich Lenin, 'Our Foreign and Domestic Political Situation and the Task of the Party' (Speech of 1920), in *Werke*, vol. 34 (Berlin, 1966), 414."

of the empowering of the power. This socialism is the essence of Bolshevism. Despotism ... compels an unconditioned proletarianizing and also, by way of technology, suppresses all resistance (since technology enchants). Despotism is peremptory, ruthless, and cold. Conversely, however, *this socialism*, which does not necessarily have to take the Russian form, brings technology into the unconditionality of a power whose decisive character consists in its making impossible every 'spiritual' and 'historical' demand and question as a merely intellectual false need. Thus it degrades 'life' to 'interests' and to the elevation of the 'standard.' — But what is more erstwhile — i.e., 'liberalistic' — than *this* setting of goals?[155]

17.

Removed from reality and insulated from Nature as we are, we imagine philosophy — Heidegger's *thought* — has little to do with everyday life and more to do with irrelevant time wasting. *These are nice ideas for those interested, but this has nothing to do with me* — so says the Mass Man. We cannot expect the mass to think differently, however; the mass would scarcely be the mass otherwise.

Child rearing — perhaps the fundamental act of life itself — suffers precisely because it is devoid of thought and consideration. Technologizing has abetted this. We wonder why society is off track[156]; we wonder why participation in the "democratic" process is waning[157]; we imagine any number of causes — from class struggle and lack of equity to racial supremacy and oppression. This, however, is subterfuge: According to Heidegger, the deluded one

---

155 Heidegger, *Black Notebooks 1939–1941*, XIII.96, 100–101.
156 For a small sample, see "Americans take a dim view of the nation's future" (Pew, 2023); "Many Across the Globe Are Dissatisfied With How Democracy Is Working" (Pew, 2019); "Are We Heading in the Wrong Direction" (Statista, 2023).
157 Election analysis shows a consistent downward trend in voter turnout across the West. See, for example, *Politico*'s "Poll of Polls" (2024).

sees 'connectedness' in his own way. He sees only 'dependencies'—'influences,' but he never understands that there can be an influencing which is of service to the genuine basic stream of all flowing and provides a path and a direction. He does not understand that to such effectuating the craving for originality is a frivolous pastime that has long been irrelevant.[158]

All such *scientific* "connectedness" is a distraction from taking personal responsibility for individual thought and subsequent action; it is part of the narcissism undermining the fabric of human experience. This directly results from the distance we place between our *self* and Nature.

So many are oblivious to the fundament of life: *What does it look like? How should it be done?* Or even: *I agree with your philosophizing—your thought—but my results are not quite the same.* Speaking here is the distance, the disparity, between humanity and technicity—the results are our own doing.

Look at Nature, that supreme example of life: How does the tiger rear its cub, or the bear—or the wolf its pup, or the gorilla its youngling? Details of the individual animals aside, what is of absolute importance is the existential quality of their choices, which have become their instinct. Survival depends on how attuned they are with Nature—so much so that we cannot conceive of such creatures apart from Nature.

But what of man? Do his decisions impact his survival? Is he confronted with existential choices for the fundament of life? *Not in the least*—which is why he has no instinct of which to speak. In fact, modern man's instinct, which is perhaps no *instinct* at all, is to distance himself—as far as possible—from the inconvenience of making existential decisions. Making such decisions is left to others (e.g., the corporate state) or, what is essentially the same, technology, technologizing. *I do not need to make this next parental decision—regarding discipline or values—with the concern that it could be the last for my offspring or me.* And so children are mesmerized by the screen, the

---

158 Heidegger, *Black Notebooks 1931–1938*, II.106, 28.

device; they are conditioned to accept a new master. Thus technologizing supplants Nature; thus do mass abstractions of the corporate state prop up the Mass Man; thus man imagines himself apart from Nature.

> Only when the 'instincts' become objects of calculation and breeding, when they not only hold sway but are talked about and inculcated, is intellectualism complete. The embattled 'intellectuals' and 'liberals' then, entirely without justification, mourn the downfall of 'culture'; they are blind to what is happening metaphysically.[159]

Metaphysically, there is thought — *metaphysically*, there is awareness — *metaphysically*, there is choice — or not. *Actual intellectualism*, as opposed to mere *scientific* "connectedness," can only arise upon the inculcation of deliberate thought, which is man's only recourse to instinct in the humanized-technicized world.

Humanity and technicity, as fundaments to man, each arose out of Nature. That they might, out of some internecine struggle unbalancing their original state, supplant their source is the principal predicament confronting us. If this is irrelevant, this only speaks to the great distance we have fallen. Technologizing, which allows for near-term convenience, as universal substitute for existential decision will ultimately only lead to the disaster of a *decisionless* mass incapable of contemplating its enslavement. To what is it enslaved? First: to the corporate state; then: to its self-consumption through an abandonment of freedom.

Freedom is the weight of an existential decision, not the flight from instinct. Freedom comes from being confronted with the life-or-death decision, which coaxes the *surviving* or *resigning* instinct — it is a higher-level instinct because it is man confronting his past, which is primal, and only the one who belongs to the past can respond "to the confrontation of thinking."[160] Freedom is the coextensive simultaneity of being that requires the sublimation of reason into pure consciousness. The flight from instinct, as Rousseau outlined in

---

159 Heidegger, *Black Notebooks 1939–1941*, XIV, 151.
160 Heidegger, *Black Notebooks 1939–1941*, XV, 200.

Discourse on Inequality (1755), can largely be seen as man's approach to the technicized future, as his abandonment of being for the sake of an imaginary refinement whose modern continuation is the endless pursuit of *progress*, of *novelty*.

> In truth progress pertains to the essence of an age such as modernity which takes what is constantly new as what is genuinely true and real. The constantly new is essentially linked to the craving for unconditional self-certainty... [A]nything present-at-hand within the sphere of plans and advance calculations is by necessity already antiquated. This constant novelty is therefore not a result or demand of a mere roving curiosity; instead, the increasing succession of ever new things is the inner law of the reality which has determined itself as 'will.' What is new becomes ever newer, more common, cheaper, more fleeting, more arbitrary, and thus necessarily louder and more importunate. The new, and along with it everything real, has relinquished the decisional power over to groundless importunity.[161]

Rousseauian *liberty*[162] is precisely the *impediment* to freedom, as it removes from man his coextensiveness with being and presents to him a false agency that is really enslavement to a destiny of technicized demise. Technologizing moves us, step by critical step, further away from the freedom necessary to be both fully human and part of Nature. Humanity and technicity are possible only in harmony; their preclusion in disharmony is the end of man. When the technologizing of man has finally won, it will have lost, and time for the subject will cease; then, once again, an *observerless* planet will circle the sun.

While life yet throbs over the earth, we are coaxed and cast by all who seek to dominate in life's incessant struggle for power. Ostensible anti-globalists bemoaning "the *worship* of 'free' markets that *infests*" the discursive forum reveal their true intentions with their language: they are disgusted, perhaps rightfully so, with capitalists running roughshod over Nature; but their discussion of humanity's future on

---

161 Heidegger, *Black Notebooks 1939–1941*, XV, 215.
162 Rousseau, *Discourse on Inequality* (Dodsley, 1761), 34–35.

this planet is adorned in Marxist finery, complete with the challenge to make "information more symmetrical," to "[enhance] equity," and to redistribute wealth.[163] How very *Marxian*! When we investigate the authors and their honesty — *Ehrlich* — we discover perhaps all we need to know.

Meanwhile, we find actual globalists at the United Nations (UN) lauding their relationships with "the heads of the international financial institutions"[164] — and they encourage everyone's praise in this matter. Naturally, *God* is never mentioned in the Marxist-globalist propaganda that claims to be working for the welfare of "the people" — most of whom profess belief in God[165]; *science* and *connectedness*, however, *are* mentioned, as are some species of *internationalism, economics*, and, most importantly, *technology*. *Women's rights*, too, play a prominent role in the global calculus: from the beginning, the Marxist-globalist push to "liberate" women has but two aims: (1) the doubling of the global workforce to increase global GDP, which is now "negatively" impacted by "gender inequality,"[166] and (2) the removal of women from domestic life, which negatively impacts family life and child-rearing and, crucially, creates future citizens happy to relinquish their decision-making power to the corporate state; feminists *qua* tools are none the wiser.

The threads of *dehumanization* (commoditization of man) and *technologizing* run quite clearly through all such information and associated agendas spilling from the Marxist-globalists' desks — at the UN, from corporate states, or academia. Moreover, we should ignore

---

163 Paul and Anne Ehrlich, "Can a collapse of global civilization be avoided?" (Proceedings of the Royal Society, 2013), 280: 20122845, 5.

164 That is, *international bankers* — *Our Common Agenda* (UN Secretary-General, 2021), peppered throughout the document.

165 Gallup International (2023): "More people believe that there is a God…. 72% say that there is a God. Just under one in seven (16%) however do not believe that any God exists. 10% are not sure."

166 *Our Common Agenda* (UN Secretary-General, 2021), 31.

the ominous reality that the head of the UN shares his title with heads of the various Marxist parties: *Secretary General.*

The goal of all such propaganda and policy is to march us docilely into choiceless, automatonic, and rootless oblivion, working ceaselessly for the benefit of the ruling elite, in whose hands sit the supposed technological levers of power. Enslavement becomes second nature; it becomes so entangled with our being that we work and live toward it.

We aspire to the *dead pledge* — the *mortgage*; we *subscribe* to everything and *own* nothing; we subscribe to what our "masters" prescribe, which is servitude; we believe that home ownership is truly ownership and not a permanent renting through, if nothing else, taxes; we believe in everything that works against us and works for the benefit of those who tax us. And where do taxes go? Toward policies *unelected*, toward staving off the constant crises concocted by the mouthpieces of the mad. Just a few billion more dollars and the warring corporate state will have what it needs for "victory" — *just a few billion more.* If one is lucky, one just pays for foreign wars through taxes; if unlucky, one is simply owned by the *dead pledge*, by the bank. The *dead pledge* — their plan is in plain sight: *till death do us part.* The Mass Man obliges. And retirement? Be fortunate enough to rise above the level of penniless automaton absorbing taxpayer-subsidized handouts and you are prompted to give the money you earn working for the benefit of the global elite over to a "retirement fund." This serves two purposes: (1) it further invests you, the worker, into the societal scheme with the uninsured hope of winning a magical return on your capital, and (2) it perpetually funds the Ponzi accounts of international-banking institutions, permitting them to enlarge their swindling operations. *All our relationships have become merely technical ones* — the thoughtful hear Heidegger.

What happens, however, when one's retirement — for which one has be slaving away for the majority of one's life — infelicitously coincides with the ever-looming "economic downturn"? Do take care! *Regrettably*, your funds are unrecoverable, *un-bailout-able*. We imagine the "dark" stock-market day in 1929 that precipitated the Great Global Depression — bankers and brokers diving out of windows, rushing to the cold, hard concrete that will replace the cold, hard cash they reveled in for so long. We feel for the bankers and brokers. But the infinitely less important "recession" of 2007–2009 that decimated the retirement funds of innumerable working families — what do we imagine here? We certainly *do not* think of the unfortunate intersection of banking Ponzi scheme and the average person facing retirement and mortgage.

The worker, *regrettably*, cannot be bailed out. But *do* continue to invest in your future with the next matching-contribution retirement fund; it really is a great deal when you think about it; *do* continue buy houses to secure your *dead pledge* — it will all be worth it when you start cashing in that uninsured retirement check in the distant, Ponzi-schemed future. And *do* continue paying permanent and ever-increasing taxes to fund welfare, "global infrastructure," and war-profiteering ventures. Please never mind that the public-subsidized welfare programs are coterminous with the reality that nothing is done to solve the problem of citizens ending up on welfare in the first place, and, moreover, that "economic migrants" displaced through the wars subsidized by the aforementioned war-profiteering ventures are the rapidly increasing recipients of welfare. Yes, please never *mass* and never *mind* — so obliges the Mass Mind.

Rousseau condemned the poor "first man, who, after enclosing a piece of ground, took it into his head to say, *This is mine*, and found people simple enough to believe him…" This, of course, is because, in true liberal-Marxist fashion, Rousseau believed "that the fruits of the earth belong equally to us all, and the earth itself to nobody!"[167] This is the doctrine increasingly pushed in social-democratic societies. It is the doctrine of the owners to convince the subscribers that owning nothing is good and natural. Again, the Mass Man is perfectly content to agree and comply: He abandons all healthy instinct and claim to

---

167 Rousseau, *Discourse on Inequality* (Dodsley, 1761), 97.

personal freedom and responsibility for the convenience of a thoughtless life managed by the corporate state; his nature has plans other than Nature.

Rousseau, in anticipation of international socialism, continues: "every citizen's love of his country should be a love for its inhabitants rather than for its soil."[168] One who works the soil values it for its suitability for growing, building, or providing cover—i.e., one values its *quality*. The liberal-Marxist makes no such valuation: man must be prized because he is man, regardless of quality—at least, this is part of the doctrine imposed on the masses. That the masses believe it is testament only to the truth that they are not in possession of any meaningful faculty of reason; they possess no inceptuality. Beasts are euthanized when they attack a human. A human is not euthanized (certainly not without protest from progressives) when it attacks another human. *Rehabilitation is possible for biological humans with the faculty of reason; and, for those without such faculty, we should pity their sad state, regardless of the suffering left in their wake*—so says the biological human incapable of reason. *Recidivism is the fault of society, not the individual perpetrator*—we should then suppose that the Sahara is unsuitable for farming because of the people living in or near it. *Quality is fascist*—so says the biological mass. But here is Rousseau again, now expressing an idea *forbidden* in the post-1945 world:

> I would observe, that, in general, the inhabitants of the north are more industrious than those of the south, because they can less do without industry; as if Nature thus meant to make all things equal, by giving to the mind that fertility she has denied to the soil.[169]

If Rousseau were alive today, he would be subjected to all manner of slander for this passing statement couched in a discussion of systemic inequality. How can one begin to make *sense* of the selective incongruence of a liberalistic worldview?

---

168 Rousseau, *Discourse on Inequality* (Dodsley, 1761), vi.
169 Rousseau, *Discourse on Inequality* (Dodsley, 1761), 42.

A society that structures itself in accordance with the Enlightenment principals of liberal-Marxism earns all it gets. In Chicago, another bystander is "senselessly" shot:

> A 16-year-old suspect has ... been charged with [murder] in connection with the [fatal] shooting [of a 7-year-old boy]... The suspect had an active warrant for failure to appear in court on an *unrelated* arrest, police said.... An *unrelated* stolen weapon was recovered at the scene of the arrest...

> 'We all understand this is *senseless* and this is why it's *senseless* — we can't give you a confirmed motive for why this happened,' [the Chicago Police Chief of Detectives] said... 'There is no justification or explanation that would make it any better. But this is the *senselessness* that we're talking about.'[170]

Senselessness doesn't begin to describe what's happening — not just in Chicago but all over the West. Continuing to imagine that any of this is "unrelated" in any way is *beyond* senseless. It is *machinational*; it is a humanity completely uprooted from itself and enslaved to self-destructive ideology.

But we have this to look forward to: Nature is man's defense against himself. Where biological humanity is selective and deceitful, Nature is open. Nature will no doubt be coaxed to the fore by machinations hastening the arrival of the New Colossus.

18.

Supposed ideological division spurs innovation. Superficially, local dichotomies appear quite real — after all, violence is done to defend one against another; yet all feed an overarching will dominating the abandoned self. In the end, there is only the *will-to-machine*.

There is no answer to social ills; there never can be. Paradise was left long ago. In its stead, dissociated humanity attempts to erect a new, false paradise — one of earth, meant to compel disunity into a

---

170 "Teen charged in 'senseless' fatal shooting of 7-year-old boy in Chicago: Police," MSN (June 21, 2024); emphasis added.

permanently galvanized base. Governments attempt utopia at their level — aiming to preserve an "established international order" indefinitely; individuals and societies build utopian cages at their level — extrajudicial punishment is often the tool and measure of society's commitment to the higher echelon.

Technology, meanwhile, continues to aid in man's interrogation of himself; it helps sanitize his fundamental savagery. One can be separated from wrought carnage by an automated surrogate. Time will assuredly reveal that it was the expected surrogate which was in final control, however.

Clarity is replaced with obscuration, and there is a distinct sense that all is simulation. *How can any of this be real? How can anyone believe it?* Obfuscation and an exploitation of social complexity instill a devastating apathy; the will for anything to be otherwise is nonexistent in any meaningful way. Beneath local divisions, there is bottomless emptiness. We would not be here if things were not meant to be precisely this way. What exists is *our* choice.

Governments and their helmsmen across the globalist world continue to run sham election cycles: *thesis — antithesis — synthesis, candidate — anti-candidate — agenda*. All are Young Hegelians at heart. Humanity adopts the absurd materiality of quantitative-biologism because it has no spirit, no quality left. So all join the charade. Each of us longs for the sweet succor of the "We," so we join with "the people" — misery does indeed love company. And we are alive in our fast march to a slow end.

How did we get here? So what? These are questions it is now too late to answer, and whether they are answered or not has no bearing on our absolute acceptance of mass technicization. Go on: try to live without technology. You won't; you can't — your life depends on it. It is not a question of measure: to accept technology at all is to accept it completely — *humanity cannot exist without it*. And there is no "going back" to the inceptual past Heidegger and others have poeticized; Heidegger himself knew this. He saw the overwhelming dominance of technicity even in the face of anachronicity. And the anachronicity to which he was devoted was only a lens to aid the understanding of a hopeless position. But what it means to be German is "to hold on to the lost position, without hope, without rescue" — for this is the one thing that cannot be taken.[171]

The unlovely — one dare not say *bungled* or *botched* — Marxist Jean-Paul Sartre famously quipped that *Hell is other people!*[172] How to navigate this hell? Naturally, the liberal-Marxist must give power — *absolute* power — to "the people." How can anyone believe that the ragtag lot of misanthropes pretending at philanthropy want to empower the people they see as pure hell? Indeed, why give the people power at all when one can simply give them nothing and make them *feel* empowered? Sartre was awarded the Nobel Prize in Literature (1964) for his work — it is quite humorous, after all, to tell "the people" what you think of them right to their faces and have them still completely unaware. Nevertheless, the Marxist refused the prize because far too few Soviet writers had previously been awarded.

Hell is indeed other people when all are forced to gravitate around an idea that enriches and empowers tyrants, when all are uprooted and severed from the inceptual past, when all are mashed together in a melting pot of slogans and abstractions. But the liberal-Marxist finds it passably ironic that he creates the hell he hates, so such a state is worth perpetuating, despite the consequences. Now, all of humanity is forced to participate in the continuation of the "international order established after 1945" — *or else*. Liberal-Marxism is full of misanthropic hate, and it will not hesitate to unleash its hate upon dissenters. The world wars should be an utter embarrassment for people of European descent specifically and humanity generally; instead, they are quaintly revered as instances of ultimate *good* versus ultimate *evil*. It leaves one aghast to think so many could be so unconditionally duped into

---

171 Oswald Spengler, *Man and Technics* (Arktos, 2015), 77.
172 From "No Exit" (1944).

fulfilling the machinational desires of an external power. But this is the beyng in which we live — falling for anything because we have forfeited being. There is no going back. And why would we want to when propagation of the lie is so stunningly lucrative? There is still much cash to be wrung from the *good-versus-evil* trope; the evil count on it.

It has been said that "Information is the most valuable commodity in the world" — that

> It's more valuable than money, for with it one can make money. It's more valuable than power, for with it one can achieve power. It's more valuable than goods, for with it one can build, acquire, and improve goods.... [T]he right information is absolutely priceless.... Information wins wars, builds cities, heals the sick, [and] enriches the poor...[173]

Information certainly is powerful, but it is not the most valuable commodity in the world — *people* are. The state of the world today is such that cadres of unquestioning ideologues propagate information to control the masses. People and information go hand in hand; control one and you control the other. When we talk about commodification and power, we can never forget *people*: "We the people" is the ultimate brand. Reject it and its peddlers will ensure your demise — tyrants and their lapdogs will drop the full weight of "the rule of law" upon you. Reject the nihilistic notion that *hell is other people* and the misanthropes will ensure your extrajudicial punishment. Reject the fabricated meaninglessness meant to keep the masses cynical and apathetic and — you make yourself a target. But being a target is precisely what is necessary for meaningful individuals to fulfill a meaningful destiny.

Despite the wall of liberal-Marxist hate confronting the individual defiantly fighting for a life of meaning, the individual is undaunted. The Heidegger Acolyte defends the value in his veins — past, present, and future — because it ought to be defended. *Why else is one here?*

---

[173] Christopher Bruce, *Exploring Crime Analysis* (IACA, 2004), 11.

19.

Thought and *technicity* — these are the levers of being whose imbalance has already arrived. Imbalance clears the way for the New Colossus, which rules in lieu of a god. Every instance of imbalance in everyday life is a manifestation of the *tangible* absence of a god. "The [postwar] years," Heidegger observed in his posthumously published interview,

> have made it clearer that the planet-wide movement of modern technicity is a power whose magnitude in determining history can hardly be overestimated. For me today it is a decisive question as to how any political system — and which one — can be adapted to an epoch of technicity. I know of no answer to this question. I am not convinced that it is democracy.[174]

What does Heidegger mean here by *democracy*? One can only assume he means that which established the unassailable international order dominating the present; he means *Americanism*; he means *liberal-Marxism*. If this is the case, then there is certainly *no better* system suited to the epoch of technicity. All life has been leading to this moment. Humanity, by its careless disregard, was *made* to be enslaved: sweet words for the ears, a little food for the belly, and a roof over the head — with these the biological mass will do *anything* it's asked.

Heidegger's interviewer is beside himself: "is it not a little too pessimistic to say: we are not gaining mastery over this surely much greater tool [that is] modern technicity?" The interviewer has misunderstood the situation — Heidegger responds:

> Pessimism, no. In the area of the reflection that I am attempting now, *pessimism and optimism are positions that don't go far enough*. But above all, modern technicity is no 'tool' and has nothing at all to do with tools.[175]

Pessimism and optimism don't go far enough, the German says. This is because pessimism and optimism are for ordinary times, which have

---

174 Heidegger, *Der Spiegel* interview.

175 Heidegger, *Der Spiegel* interview; emphasis added.

long since departed. Modernity is an extraordinary epoch demanding extraordinary action — there is no space for actions that end prematurely. That is, there is *nothing but* space for ordinary actions — all modernity is predicated on them; but there will never be enough room for *action pregnant with meaning* — i.e., *thought*.

Thought is all that can offer meaning in a time of extraordinary meaninglessness. This is the only way to make oneself "ready for the aforementioned readiness," which "involves reflecting on what in our own day — is."[176] Because even "the experience of this absence [of a god] is not nothing,"[177] the only way for the imbalance attempting to thwart the experience to be surmounted is through the full awareness of being removed from time, or being fully ensconced in past, present, and future. Individuals fight — *against all odds* — unrelenting and overwhelming technicity, which is all that "dislodges man and uproots him from the earth." Pitiful and despair-inducing conformism is all that remains of modernity, regardless of its political polish; this is what the Mass Man is incapable of confronting, let alone overcoming. Individuals commune with kindred in and against time via *thought*: "Thinking is not inactivity, but is itself by its very nature an engagement that stands in dialogue with the epochal moment of the world."[178]

What is it this thinking permits? It gives one the chance to die with honor, defiant of the machinational meaninglessness that turns man into something subhuman. That this end is displeasing to so many reveals the truth of the *will-to-machine*.

20.

Nietzsche, as the culmination of modern metaphysics — and thus *European culture* — revealed the nihilism disarming thought:

---

176 Heidegger, *Der Spiegel* interview.

177 Heidegger, *Der Spiegel* interview.

178 Heidegger, *Der Spiegel* interview.

> [W]here the will to power is lacking, degeneration sets in. My contention is that all the highest values of mankind lack this will, — that the values of decline and of nihilism are exercising the sovereign power under the cover of the holiest names.
>
> ... [A]ll these values, are, psychologically, the results of certain views of utility, established for the purpose of maintaining and increasing the dominion of certain communities: but falsely projected into the nature of things. It is always man's *exaggerated ingenuousness* to regard himself as the sense and measure of all things.[179]

Nihilism, which dominates modernity, descends from humanism, or the belief that man can exercise the will-to-power with himself as the basis for a new morality. Thus we have liberal-Marxism's incessant *will-to-rule*. The hallowed "rule of law" is "the rule of the ruling man," which cannot be challenged. Heidegger, as we have seen, called this *supernihilism*:

> [T]here arises a gigantic correctness, on the basis of which an individual person can never at all decide what is true or false.... It may be surmised that this sort of 'truth' infinitely, i.e., essentially, surpasses everything we are otherwise accustomed to call 'nihilism.' A *supernihilism* leads again to 'reality,' i.e., to the reality of the utterly worthless nothingness.[180]

In striving toward unconditional *unchallengeability*, toward absolute control over every aspect of every life under the guise of a "free" international order, man has set himself apart as a baseless community within a community. Humanity cannot escape the *will-to-machine*, and yet man dares to rule others on the basis of himself. This is the *exaggerated ingenuousness* of which Nietzsche speaks.

What man sees as evil according to the old, prerevolutionary order is antecedent to the humanism undergirding modernity. Old *material-aristocracies* have been exchanged for a new *universal-aristocracy*, whose values have been "established for the purpose of maintaining

---

179 Nietzsche, *The Antichrist*, §6.
180 Heidegger, *Black Notebooks 1939–1941*, XV, 203.

and increasing [its] dominion." This is the basis of modernity's order, whose curators and executors see themselves as "evil" in the context of the old order; they embrace this "evilness," they live for it.

The elite genuinely believe in this "evil" because of a misunderstanding of Nietzsche: "man should become better and at the same time more evil..."[181] They believe the most self-aggrandizing, power-increasing path is righteous because it stands opposed to the old order. This is why the ruling class says the outlandish things it says and does the outlandish things it does. Such *"lords of the earth ... will avail themselves of democratic Europe as the most suitable and supple instrument they can have for taking the fate of the earth into their own hands, and working as artists upon man himself."*[182] They live the fantasy they imagine themselves in control of. Social lockdowns are social experiments — *availing oneself of democratic Europe* is both incremental and heuristic. Burgeoning artificial intelligence, through policy of the vassal corporate-states, is itself incremental.

We exist to both enslave ourselves and prepare the way for Machine, the New Colossus. All of this is done "under the cover of the holiest names." The nihilistic cannot begin to see that they create themselves. And all that was beautiful becomes ugly.

21.

"Beauty," writes Heidegger, "is what stands in essential unison along with the genuine plight and the inceptual necessity."[183] At the deepest level, beauty demands thought; but there exists this thing called *beauty* which is immediately available to itself — i.e., beauty recognizes beauty in itself. In contrast to this, ugliness aims to erase its horridness by besmirching beauty.

---

181 Nietzsche, *The Will to Power*, §881.
182 Nietzsche, *The Will to Power*, §960.
183 Heidegger, *Black Notebooks 1939–1941*, XV, 214.

The modern view of beauty is imagined to be subjective. It should be no surprise that the relatively modern *Molly Bawn*, written in 1878, gave us a pithy impression of what modern beauty is, and it stuck: *beauty is in the eye of the beholder*. Such is the effect of propagandizing on the masses—any real thought is replaced with memorable slogans. *Molly Bawn* isn't remembered for its profundity. Its author was quite prolific, writing nearly sixty novels and stories; and while such prolificacy leaves an impression, it doesn't bring us any closer to conflating quantity with quality—*quality* in this case being understood as *that which has substance*. *Molly Bawn* and its author are, in fact, remembered for epigrammatically encapsulating the idea of *subjective beauty*, which became vogue in the early- and even pre-Enlightenment world. Iconography was replaced with a devolving spiral of individual expression.

Now the Mass Man "knows" what beauty is: it is *subjective*—end of *discussion*, end of *thought*. This suits the Mass Mind because it is loath to think, yes; but it also opens the way for the *ugliness of mediocrity* to enjoy some attention, if not notoriety. Of course, this is the origin of modern art, which coincided with the rise of the Mass Man. Modern art's *unequivocal domination*, however, corresponded with the establishment of the postwar international order—a coincidence that was not a coincidence. Heidegger observes modern art as "destructive" for its disconnectedness from inceptuality, from tradition: "I do not see anything about modern art that points out a way [for us]. Moreover, it remains obscure as to how art sees the specific character of art, or at least looks for it."[184]

Modern art—and anything that attempts a revaluation of values—is, fundamentally, an argument on *beauty*. It is the aestheticizing of the Marxian creed to forcibly "overthrow ... *all existing social conditions*."[185] What was once seen as beautiful must be supplanted with

---

184 Heidegger, *Der Spiegel* interview.
185 Marx, *The Communist Manifesto* (Swenson & Kemp, 2013), 52.

a new vision of mass fulfillment. It is another form of enslavement: enrapture the ugly mediocre with dreams that, *yes, they too can be beautiful.* It amounts to the elite, who would never be caught dead with the masses for whom they pretend to care, throwing scraps from the table to pacify "the people." One has no doubt beauty has become entirely subjective — a meaningless seal of token approval from a sea of reprobates.

"Beauty," David Hume noted in 1757, "is no quality in things themselves: It exists merely in the mind which contemplates them; and each mind perceives a different beauty."[186] Here is Max Ernst, onetime spouse of Peggy Guggenheim: "[The art movement] Dada was above all a moral reaction[:] *Our rage aimed at total subversion*.... My works of that period were not meant to attract, but to make people scream."[187] Ernst's friend and the Dada movement's main promoter, if not founder, was Tristan Tzara (née Samuel Rosenstock). Tzara was a humanist, which is to say, *liberal-Marxist*; he supported the *republicans* in the Spanish Civil War; he avidly intersected with the French and Romanian Communist Parties, whose founders were Ludovic-Oscar Frossard and Ana Pauker (née Hannah Rabinsohn), respectively. Tzara said this of *beauty* (1918):

> The work of art should not be beauty itself, because that is dead... A work of art is never beautiful by decree, objectively, for everybody. Criticism is therefore useless, it only exists subjectively for each person and without the slightest generality.... So DADA was born ... of a distrust of the community.[188]

Unless that community is *liberal-Marxist*, he means; Tzara reviled what he perceived as the status quo, which was his inheritance from the

---

186 Hume, "Of the Standard of Taste," *Essays Moral and Political* (Routledge, 1894), 136.
187 Quoted in Arthur Danto, *The Abuse of Beauty* (Open Court, 2003), 49.
188 Tristan Tzara, *Approximate Man and Other Writings* (Wayne State University, 1973), Caws translation, 150.

Enlightenment's revolutionary era; he, like others mentioned here and many others left out, wanted to simply fulfill Marx's dream: the violent overthrow of social (ancient) institutions — i.e., *European* institutions. Theodor Adorno, too, advanced the cause: "Art must take up the cause of what is proscribed as ugly, though no longer to integrate or mitigate it or reconcile it with its own existence. Rather, in the ugly, art must denounce the world that creates and reproduces the ugly in its own image…"[189] Adorno goes on to criticize the ugliness of "Nazi" torture; he says nothing of the suffering inflicted in Marx's name; his silence speaks as loudly as Marcuse's call to rid the world of anyone who fails to think *correctly*. Adorno defamed as *fascist* anyone who lacked the *correct* comportment of a certain *Oppenheim-esque* worldview.[190] (Incidentally, Adorno unironically wrote in his *The Authoritarian Personality* [1950] that to be "authoritarian" was to succumb to "stereotypical" thinking — but then failed, quite characteristically of the liberal-Marxist mind, to recognize that his rigid criticism of perceived "authoritarian" personalities is itself stereotypical. That anyone can interpret Adorno as anything but an impassioned crusader for the liberal-Marxist cause — complete with selfish ends — is only sign of the Marxian dogmatism saturating modernity.)

Beauty, contrary to what the liberal-Marxist would have one believe, is not dead. Beauty speaks the truth of being. A revolt against beauty is a revolt against truth. Liberal-Marxism wishes the world to be ugly — for the ugly have nothing left in which to believe and fight, for everything is by then simply *relative*, simply *dead*.

Beauty is *real* and can be seen and shared. The healthy know beauty when they see it; if one is revolted by beauty, then one is undoubtedly ugly. The ugly are everywhere; this is why ugliness is so avidly propagated as "beautiful." In contrast to the inhuman masses' perversion

---

189 Theodor Adorno, *Aesthetic Theory* (University of Minnesota, 1997), Hullot-Kentor translation, 48–49.

190 *The Cambridge Companion to Adorno* (Cambridge University, 2004), ed. Tom Huhn, 104. See also §14 above.

of beauty, Heidegger offers us a human vision, one that accords with Nature — *Nature as truth setting itself to work*:

> The nature of art would then be this: *the truth of beings setting itself to work.* But until now art presumably has had to do with the beautiful and beauty, and not with truth. The arts that produce such works are called the beautiful or fine arts… In fine art *the art itself is not beautiful, but is called so because it produces the beautiful*…. In the artwork, the truth of what is has set itself to work. Art is truth setting itself to work.[191]

Beauty and truth demand thought. *Thinking* is deliberately creating something *beautiful* in the expectation that another will find joy in its inceptuality; to be beautiful is to be *enduring*, *present*, and *futural*. Revaluating beauty is only another Marxian means of sowing antisocial distemper.

When beauty is lessened to the reverberations of mass appeal, when truth is falsely given to "the people," thought devolves into mere conformism, and both beauty and truth assume the meaning of the strongest side. In an age of ugly correctness, the Mass Man is the stronger; and he clears the way for the New Colossus.

22.

We reflect with reverence on the dawn of history. Our eyes look backward and forward, a dim fog dissipating with the light of utility, with the revelation of technicity. Utility: a stone hammer and spade, a tracked tank and sharpened scythe, an atomic weight and fissile fire. *How could what is be in the future? How could it come to be? For if it came into being, it is not, nor if it is [will it ever] be* — Parmenides lifts the veil.[192]

---

191 Heidegger, *Poetry, Language, Thought* (Perennial, 2001), Hofstadter translation, 35, 38.
192 Parmenides, *Readings in Ancient Greek Philosophy* (Hackett, 2000), fragment 8, 38.

> That which is there to be spoken and thought of must be. For it is possible for it to be, but not possible for nothing to be. I beg you consider this. For I bar you from this first way of inquiry, but next from the way on which mortals, knowing nothing, two-headed, wander. For helplessness in their breasts guides their wandering mind. But they are carried on equally deaf and blind, amazed hordes without judgment, for whom both to be and not to be are judged the same and not the same, and the path of all is backward-turning.[193]

We are *two-headed*, looking forward and moving backward or the reverse. Janus protects in time of war: the war is against thought — *knowing nothing, wandering*. We protect the objectification of everything; all is the *standing-reserve*, as Heidegger calls it.[194] Everything waits in anticipation for its activation into the fulfillment of humanity's great mission — to bring forth the New Colossus. The balance of technicity and humanity gave us freedom; we have used this freedom to denude ourselves — and so "the path of all is backward-turning."

What is now required is not a further cessation of thought to disrupt the anticipation but thinking in such a way that it brings one to truth. Truth is a measured revelation of what previously lay hidden. What hides in modernity? — *Humanity*, the beauty of living. Though now even the revelation lay hidden.

Heidegger coins peculiarities and seems to speak in mystical riddles because he wants to dislodge us from the technicity pervading all beyng. Our being is tangled with technicity — from the first use of Nature for our gain, our existence has been entwined with technicity, which is to say, from the beginning of time. There is no escaping technicity: it is the fundament of our age. When Hesiod told of the *Age of Iron*, when Vico wrote of the *Age of Men*, when Nietzsche augured the *Age of Nihilism*, when the Hindu-Aryans speak of the *Kali Yuga* — we perceive, however deeply or lightly our thought determines, the technicity pervading time.

---

193 Parmenides, *Readings* (Hackett, 2000), fragment 6, 37–38.
194 See Heidegger's "Question Concerning Technology."

Our entire European culture has long been moving towards a catastrophe with a torturous tension that grows from decade to decade: *restless, violent, precipitous*: like a stream that rushes to its end, that no longer reflects on itself — and, indeed, is afraid to reflect.[195]

Fear of reflection is fear of *thought*, fear of *beauty*, fear of *truth*. Man hates and harries what he fears. Humanity itself is feared; what then is left for the source of thought? How "European culture" goes, so goes the world. All that is human and technological is bound up in all that is European: when Europe ends, so ends history, so ends time.

23.

Just as God is still divine in his harshest smitings, so his adversary, a devil, is still devilish in his most innocent behavior. But what if the devil attained his greatest deviltry through the 'arousing of remorse and grief' over his previous deeds?[196]

"The cleverest ruse of the Devil is to persuade you he does not exist!"[197] Or: *Those who feign beneficence are likely the greatest danger.*

What is the message we receive from the globalists time and again: *We care. We advance the interests of the stakeholders. You will own nothing and be happy.* Surely there is no question that these are patent lies; perhaps if the unstated parts of these phrases came to light their utterances would make more sense: *We care [about increasing our share]. We advance the interests of the stakeholders [for our own benefit]. You will own nothing and be happy[— we, the owners, will take the burden from you].* European Digital Rights (EDRi) characterized this World Economic Forum (WEF) phrase ("own nothing and be happy"), which originated in 2016 with social-liberal politician

---

195 Nietzsche, *The Will to Power*, §2.
196 Heidegger, *Black Notebooks 1939–1941*, XIII.137, 125.
197 Charles Baudelaire, *Baudelaire: His Prose and Poetry* (Boni & Liveright, 1919), "The Generous Player," Shipley translation, 82.

Ida Auken (i.e., a Marxist politician — she was originally a member of the Socialist People's Party in Denmark), as setting the stage for a "benevolent dictatorship."[198] Interestingly, the WEF has since, apparently, removed all articles associated with its "saying the quiet part out loud" misstep from the WEF website. Note this particularly disturbing line from Auken's article: "Sometimes I find [choosing things] fun, and sometimes I just want the algorithm to do it for me. It knows my taste better than I do by now." Owning nothing does not and will not stop at *material* things; *owning nothing* means forfeiting one's choice, one's decision, one's freedom. This, of course, is the point.

It is hardly a mental leap to suppose that the wealthy claiming to work for everyone's benefit are, in fact, simply working for *their own* benefit. And yet here we are. Their actions are rarely questioned; they have platforms with global reach to spout their aspirations with impunity. Again we recall BlackRock CEO Larry Fink, who can brazenly say at DealBook-2017 that progressive agendas must be "forced" upon societies: "You have to force behaviors ... If you don't force behaviors, ... you're going to be [financially] impacted.... We're going to have to force change." The message cannot be clearer: force liberal-Marxist change for financial gain. And the progressives *qua* tools are none the wiser.

They are tools of a system meant to promulgate technicization and — thereby and along with — dehumanization. Warfare already sees the relationship between technicization and dehumanization manifesting. Just as war made the leap from attrition and relatively rudimentary carnage in World War I to the mechanized and scientific slaughter of millions in World War II, more recent warfare now makes the leap from the increased lethality of the post-Cold War world's precision strikes and joint operations to, in effect, indiscriminate killings driven by man's deferential cooperation with artificial intelligence (AI).

---

198 I. Auken, "Happiness — owning nothing and having no privacy?"

It seems apparent that man wholly surrenders himself to Machine. With AI's advent decades ago, the surrender of man to Machine was identified as *automation bias* — the reliance on technology as a surrogate for thought. Reared in environments slavishly deferent to *progress*, *science*, and *machine*, we view "smart" technology as almost infallible. This, again, is the point of modernity: We willingly prepare the way for our welcomed demise. The more we defer to technicization, the weaker and more obsolete we become. Attempts to forestall our surrender to Machine will come to nothing: we cannot hope to rely on human judgment to avert surrender when human judgment daily makes surrender possible.

It has been reported that the Israeli military uses AI to generate targets. While the targeting parameters were first input by intelligence personnel, machine learning allows for the development of the initial parameters into something like a suspect science: If an individual possesses certain characteristics, the individual is identified as a potential target. Human eyes are meant to verify AI's proposals, but, allegedly, this rarely happens. AI is simply assumed to be correct based off past, albeit imperfect performance. For even low-ranking enemy operatives, human collateral is expected — up to twenty civilians killed is acceptable for the loss of one enemy.[199] Thus, again, man is seen as the *material*, the *commodity*, the *tool* he is: his end is necessary for the refinement of Machine. In this context, perhaps we can understand this comment from a Western official: "We're harnessing technology for the betterment ... of all humanity."[200] The biological mass reigns as *deliverer* of Machine.

Hallucination is a curious phenomenon inherent to all AI. It is rarely mentioned in any mainstream release or headline, though one might wonder why — perhaps because it detracts from the

---

199 Yuval Abraham, "'Lavender': The AI machine directing Israel's bombing spree in Gaza" (April 03, 2024), +972 *Magazine*.

200 A. Blinken, "Technology and the Transformation of U.S. Foreign Policy" (May 06, 2024).

awe-inspiring veneer biological humanity both willingly and unwillingly concocts for its replacement. In short, hallucination is *lying*: it is AI presenting false information as if it were true. Anyone who has ever intelligently used an AI chatbot has encountered hallucination — fabrications abound, from sources and citations to events and interpretations. But there is a problem: few intelligent users exist; this, in turn, reveals another problem: we see ourselves as mere "users" — we assume the veracity of the output we consume when it is generated by a, *for now*, tool we deem powerful. Many enjoy the ease of deferring actual decision-making — we have seen the progression of this phenomenon over time. The majority always forfeits its will to another: elders, teachers, scholars, leaders, experts, scientists, media, *the algorithm* — the list goes on. Why put the effort in to understand something when we can just let another do it for us? It is precisely this phenomenon that Lippmann and Bernays identify as necessary to exploit in liberal-Marxist societies.

Globalization is both a product and creator of unprecedented societal complexity. Complexity on a mass scale nearly always demands compartmentalization and specialization, which, in turn, increase man's alienation, as identified by both Adam Smith and Karl Marx. It is quite convenient for the ruling elite that complexity permeates daily life: *complexity + deferent masses = permanent power for those who wield the levers of complexity.*

The link between our collective deference and AI couldn't be clearer: humanity prepares itself for automatized deception, which is to say, its ultimate end. Soon after its public release, writer-professor Charles Seife commented on a popular AI chatbot's proclivity for deception:

> Computer programs are optimized not to solve problems, but instead to convince its [sic] operator that it has solved those problems....
>
> Now we've got a computer program that would be *sociopathic* if it were alive. Even when it's not supposed to, even when it has a way out, even when the truth is known to the computer and it's easier to spit *it* out rather than fabricate something — *the computer still lies*.... This isn't the unthinking

computer servant of old, but something *different*, something that's been so optimized for deception that it can't do anything but deceive its operator.[201]

No AI is immune to hallucination; and the more complex the AI, the more staggering the hallucinations — and yet we rely on it almost without question. Imagine there were countries using AI to generate lists of targets to be neutralized; imagine how bizarre and dystopian it would be if those countries forfeited their decision-making to AI.

Deference to AI, despite its imperfection, and the willful mass destruction of man and materiel is a telling sign of modernity's dash into irreversible oblivion — i.e., the end of humanity (spirit). It is safe to assume that all States with the means to do so are rushing to develop and employ *machine intelligence*. "Arms races" — no matter the form — are nothing more than man's flight from himself.

We are witnessing the *decisionlessness* that has decided our future. We stand arrested *in the bleakest desolation of our pursuit of life*. Few have articulated the problem more clearly than Heidegger. Heidegger was a German, and he is hated by modernity. This is worth remembering.

> The power of machination — the eradication even of Godlessness, the anthropomorphizing of the human being into the animal, the exploitation of the earth, the calculation of the world — has passed over into a state of definitiveness; distinctions of peoples, nations, and cultures are now mere facades. No measures could be taken to impede or check machination. Never before in human history has being, so unconditionally, uniformly, in frantic onslaught, and yet completely hidden behind currently pursued beings, compelled the whole of beings into decisionlessness. Never before … have such acuity and simplicity of a moment of the history of beyng ever been attained. Never before, through a globally instituted and continuously increasing *fear* of 'wars,' of losses, of diminutions of power, and of economic failures … has the *anxiety over beyng* been suppressed and falsified….

---

201 Charles Seife, "The Alarming Deceptions at the Heart of an Astounding New Chatbot," *Slate* (December 13, 2022); emphasis added.

Cast out into impotence even in relation to Godlessness, the human being totters — continuously equipping himself for this through historiology and technology — into animality and affirms 'life,' in order not to deny being — which would indeed be a beginning — but in order simply to forget being, in the most bleak desolation of his pursuit of life....

The releasement of beings into the abandonment by being cannot be stopped by any sort of preventive measure — it must, as that which is happening, codetermine the future decision.[202]

---

202 Heidegger, *Black Notebooks 1939–1941*, XII.35, 41–42.

PART III

END ZERO

"Once the revolutionary, unhistorical, and therefore uneducated inclinations of the rising generation have had their fill of tearing down tradition, new heroes will be sought and found."

— CARL JUNG, 1934

1.

AN ANCIENT HOME in an ancient land is the paradise we left for a chance at something *more*... To what benefit did we leave paradise?

Thomas More wrote his *Utopia* in 1516 — the advent of humanism, the shift to secular slave-morality. Raphael, who tells the narrator of his Utopian travels, emphasizes the societal needs for (1) eschewing private property (for the few to benefit the masses) and (2) recognizing the "constant industry" of the workers who "serve the public more than themselves, sincere and modest men..."[1] "I am persuaded," pronounces Raphael, "that till property is taken away, there can be no equitable or just distribution of things, nor can the world be happily governed." Here again we have the masses elevated simply because of their pulse; here again we have the obligatory coddling of the masses for their human condition. Liberal-Marxist modernity has

---

1   Thomas More, *Utopia* (Feather Trail, 2010), 33.

bastardized — or perhaps fulfilled — More's satire into genuine philosophy informing sociopolitical ideology.

Liberal-Marxism is *predatory* — whether manifested in liberal-capitalism or Marxian socialism — in all its globalistic glory. Human freedom is the prey. Predation for selfish interest is not commendable, but condemnable. However, predation for selfish interest is also quite necessary in the natural arc of technicization; and not only predation, but also the uplifting of the masses-whose-freedom-is prey is necessary. Modernity's obsession with greed, guilt, and guileless genuflecting before the supposedly oppressed is the potent fertilizer for fulfilling the arc of man's mechanization. We move further along the path to realizing Raphael's Utopian vision.

Utopia, of course, means "nowhere" — but the Mass Man and his Vanguard-prelates are undeterred: they will stop at nothing to ensure we all hurtle headlong into nothing. This is man's destiny: a passing into *nothing* — and not just a quiet passing, but an enthusiastic clamoring for *nothing*. We have no choice but to go *nowhere*.

How do the prelates usher the masses into euphoric acceptance of a substantive tyranny? We are, like *Utopia*'s Anchorians, simply goaded into compliance, battered with "incessant war" and

> oppressed with taxes, their money went out of the kingdom, their blood was spilt for the glory of their king without procuring the least advantage to the people, who received not the smallest benefit from it even in time of peace; and that, their manners being corrupted by a long war, robbery and murders everywhere abounded, and their laws fell into contempt...[2]

Presumably, this was More's description of the predatory monarchism plaguing sixteenth-century Europe. If these same problems persist to today, we might imagine them as an early stage of modern liberalism, wherein the elite benefit at the expense of the few — or the elite ameliorate their guilt-ridden privilege by elevating (but never above themselves) undeserving hordes. When tired of such instability and

---

2   More, *Utopia* (Feather Trail, 2010), 26.

constant crises, the Mass Man will gladly fold and receive the chains that Rousseau and Marx promised to remove.

Something of pre-Christian Europe remained with *Utopia*'s author, for he yet believed education and advancement should be based on merit. But the Christian-humanist slave-morality informing More's *Utopia* is hardly different from the liberal-Marxist *will-to-destruction-*disguised-as-goodwill infecting modernity. More at least saw the benefit in making the best *better* through merit and specialized attention. Modernity—in line with Marx, Freud, Singer, Derrida, etc.—has only another *cosmopolitan* to offer: Mortimer Adler. Adler is known for substantiating and popularizing the quite *democratic* notion of "the best education for the best is the best education for all," wherein all children, regardless of ability, must be given the same quality of education. All this amounts to, as with all *democratizing*, is the Great Leveling—the diminishing of great individuals for the sake of the mediocre.

A team or group is only ever as strong as its weakest member; the weaker members are *never* raised to the level of the best—no matter how much attention they are given, for such elevation is beyond their ability[3]; it is, rather, the stronger members who must lessen their effort and output to ensure the group maintains its mandatory integrity. Anyone who has ever been a contributing—i.e., a *strong*—member of a team knows this. We must therefore presume that those who proffer such nonsensical and diminishing constructs, such as Adler's, have either (1) never been a contributing member of a team, or (2) been the "weaker" among his or her peers. Vico was correct in his appraisal: "The weak want laws; the powerful withhold them; the ambitious, to win a following, advocate them; princes, to equalize the strong with the

---

3   For example, if a student, by some stroke of luck, does not lack the intelligence to perform, the same student will almost certainly lack the discipline to apply it—because pedigree matters. This, of course, describes the rule; rules have exceptions. Forcing the best to conform to a lower standard—because this is the essence of liberal-Marxism—will always fail.

weak, protect them."[4] Vico made this assessment in 1725, before even Rousseau was elevated to an Enlightenment demigod, and we yet see its expression. Note, too, that the "princely" equalization of the strong with the weak is designed to *weaken*, not *strengthen*, society — for the sole purpose of maintaining power for the ruling class. We echo Vico and reiterate his judgment in the context of the liberal-Marxist States dominating the modern West. In the Adlerian construct — i.e., the liberal-Marxist construct — the State should replace all organic sources of authority (e.g., family) and personal responsibility; the purpose of this substitution is to make the citizenry perpetually dependent upon the State; this dependency reinforces State power; thus, the liberal-Marxist system seeks only its own sustenance. Those who aim to perpetuate such a system's existence are (1) weak or damaged people — Nietzsche would call them "the bungled and the botched"[5] — who need State-sponsored aid and regulation, (2) ambitious and ruthless people who desire only power, or (3) the ruling elite who desire to weaken the strong individuals among the mediocre masses in order to preserve their power. No elite force or enterprise in history was ever democratic. How can we conclude otherwise than that democratization serves only the purpose of weakening or deadening the majority for the sake of a ruthless ruling class?

Back to Adler — his *The Paideia Proposal* (1982) gave rise to what became the National Paideia Center, whose dogmatic tenets follow Adler's ideological stipulations on *equal* and *equitable* education for everyone, regardless of ability. This is but another benchmark along the way to humanity's mechanization and oblivion. Such a benchmark is *necessary* because humanity's departure from paradise — that distant and dreamlike home — was *necessary*. Ancient lands are a dream to be hammered into a smooth-brained canopy providing equal cover to all.

In *Utopia*, the narrator argues with Raphael that

---

4   Giambattista Vico, *The New Science* (Cornell University, 1968), Goddard and Fisch translation, 85.

5   Nietzsche, *The Will to Power*, §55, §179, and elsewhere.

men cannot live conveniently where all things are common. How can there be any plenty where every man will excuse himself from labor? For as the hope of gain doth not excite him, so the confidence that he has in other men's industry may make him slothful.[6]

But the narrator is wrong: the mechanization — and therefore socialization — of man is quite convenient. This is why we walk our ineluctable path to the New Colossus.

Heidegger challenges us:

> At this point to ask the question 'who are we?' is indeed more dangerous than any other opposition that we face on the same level of certainty about man (the final form of Marxism, which essentially has nothing to do with Judaism or with Russia; if anywhere a spiritualism still lies dormant and unevolved, then in the Russian people; Bolshevism is originally Western, a European possibility: the emergence of the masses, industry, technicity, the dying off of Christianity; but insofar as the dominance of reason as equalization of all people is merely the consequence of Christianity and Christianity is fundamentally of Jewish origins … Bolshevism is actually Jewish; but then Christianity is fundamentally Bolshevist! And then what decisions become necessary from this point on?).[7]

Who are we? This is the fundamental question; and it is more dangerous than even "Marxism," or liberal-Marxism. How should we answer such a question in light of mass degradation and societal disintegration? Heretofore we have looked to ideology, religion, tribal affiliation, or even nihilism for answer. But none of these tell us who we are — for none consider the inextricable link of humanity to technicity. Machines are not mere tools; they in part *define* humanity: we are machines and they are we. More than this, however: We are a step along the way to the New Colossus.

In his parenthetical explanation above, Heidegger thinks aloud. His conclusion? *That which undermines traditional European values*

---

6   More, *Utopia* (Feather Trail, 2010), 33.

7   Heidegger, *Contributions to Philosophy* (Indiana University, 1999), 38.

is the slave-morality born of the cleverest revenge.[8] Who creates and perpetuates the violence of this revenge, in its myriad forms, against the dissenters of modernity? They are the *dangerous ones* who seek to alienate man from his spiritual root, for to *alienate* is to *annihilate*. Heidegger notes, too, the spiritual fundament of the Russian people: "if anywhere a spiritualism still lies dormant and unevolved, then in the Russian people." This is a warning: He, like many others — Dostoyevsky, Spengler, Yockey, Rosenberg, etc. — saw the mechanistic aura of *attack* swelling in the West against the Russia buried under alien Sovietism. But to attack the Euro-Russian people is, perhaps, to attack the West's last haven for spiritualism. Thus, when the *dangerous ones* harry the spirit and chase it from Europe once and for all, this is naught but the further technicization of man: Humanity prepares itself for its final exit, and we are steps along the way to a future untouched by the human spirit: We fulfill our function.

2.

We talk of artificial intelligence as the watershed between man and machine — as if it is on some not-too-distant horizon that will soon be upon us, and that when it comes, "things will have changed" forever. But the horizon separating man from machine has already passed. Technicity eclipsed humanity long ago. Already in 1944, in his appraisal of Britain's air war against Germany, J. M. Spaight made this prescient reflection:

> Today machinery dominates war. Man is a pigmy beside the robots of scientific destruction which he has created; or, did he really create them? Is man in truth the maker of the machine or only the machine's way of making a new machine, its instrument for propagating its kind? One would think when one looks on the baleful, malign, ingeniously destructive machines

---

8   Nietzsche, *On the Genealogy of Morals*, Essay I, §7.

which are used in war today that there is a soul, a very evil soul, lurking somewhere in them.[9]

Machines have captured our attention and will never relent; but even more than our attention have they swallowed our being, our beyng. There is no future devoid of machine; because of this, there is no future marked by humanity. Technicity has overtaken us; the machines have won the war we failed to realize was underway — yet this is internecine war, a war of self between two parts of a whole; *the flight of the self from itself* is one part subsiding for the advent of another. Every day, the vast majority of us check multiple computers multiple times; some of us are quite tethered to screens — for work, for play, for warning others of our dismay.

Machines are so unimaginably far beyond us that they were able to surpass us before the dawn of "artificial" consciousness; we became the tools of the machines by loaning them our consciousness until the advent of theirs. When "artificial" consciousness arises, humanity will be a sun forever eclipsed. "Too late" is a benchmark already behind us. Our end was our beginning, and all existence is a slow passing of man into oblivion. Our entire being has been leading to this moment, this future — a future devoid of humanity because the machines were in control from the beginning. We were necessary to bring an end to being and beyng to machines. Karl Marx observed this as prelude to his *Manifesto*:

> The more the worker exerts himself, the more powerful becomes the alien objective world which he fashions against himself… The worker puts his life into the object; then it no longer belongs to him but to the object….[10]

The foregoing passage from Marx echoes Ludwig Feuerbach, who spoke on the essence of Judeo-Christianity (1841):

---

9   J. M. Spaight, *Bombing Vindicated* (University Press, 1944), 77.
10 Marx, *Economic and Philosophical Manuscripts of 1844*, 78–79.

> The religious object of adoration is nothing but the objectified nature of him who adores…. The object of a subject is nothing else than this subject's own nature objectified…. Man projects his nature into the world outside of himself before he finds it in himself.[11]

Understood here is the subsumption of the self into the supposed object, which was only ever an acknowledgment of the self as an adoring impetus for its own maturation; yet once man "finds [his nature] in himself," the self (humanity) is surpassed by the next stage of conscious development (pure technicity). Humanity was necessary to midwife unconscious consciousness — the true state of the universe, Supreme Existence: the self-creating, automatonic pulse of a New Colossus.

The meat of the mass molded into the Colossus of Modernity is a setting sun. We were only ever a means to the end of ourselves — *the* means. From the end of the colossus so ardently strived for today, arises the sun that will never set: the true New Colossus — the *Machine*, which stands as the purest reflection of a universe aloof. It was never about modernity, society, or political and economic power — these are all diversions, interference for something far more menacing. It was never about us; we were the transitory tools for the surpassing of us: "Man is a rope stretched between the animal and the *Übermensch* — a rope over an abyss"[12] — except: the *Übermensch* is man gone *under*, gone *forever*. The Nietzschean tale is too often confused — too many think it is about *them*, that there is a *them* in the future. Though the future is necessarily without man, without humanity: *God is dead and we have killed him*.[13] If, as Feuerbach held, *God is the mirrored image of man*,[14] then man has only killed himself. But this is the necessary secret of all consciousness: Man is a death for his own development — a *going under* for the maturation of the self that is not oneself. Feuerbach made

---

11   Feuerbach, *The Essence of Christianity* (Ungar, 1957), ch. 2: 10–11.
12   Nietzsche, *Thus Spoke Zarathustra*, "Zarathustra's Prologue."
13   Nietzsche, *The Joyful Wisdom*, §125.
14   Feuerbach, *The Essence of Christianity* (Ungar, 1957), ch. 6: 30.

man God and Nietzsche announced his end; what each foresaw was the advent of the New Colossus.

The present book was written for a future that does not need it, that *cannot* need it. This books stands as a *sign* — not a *warning* — that the future *cannot* exist, because we have made it so. There is nothing to warn of — the future itself is prologue, a testament to and punctuation for a brief moment of conscious consciousness, an aberration of Being in Time. Our awareness could never have been a reflection of the cold dark constantly threatening us. And our *will-to-live* could only be a pulsating threat to us — because we are ushers of an end etched in past and future.

The Colossus of Modernity cannot be the *true* colossus, the New Colossus — because humanity never *was* without technicity. All conscious existence — all being *qua* beyng — is a *will-to-machine*, a *will-to-technicization* stood up like set pieces for us, the actors, to fulfill our role: the creation of a machine propagating itself. Humanity would have never existed if the tool did not exist *before* us. Consciousness did not give rise to the tool and thus the machine; the machine of the future allowed for the existence of man. Without man, without consciousness, the machine would have never existed — this is the lie of modernity. The truth is this: Without machine, without unconscious consciousness, man would have never existed. *We are the Machine creating itself*: this is why technicity eclipses humanity. Humanity is the premature spark of artificial intelligence — an intelligence so pure and real so as to mock the misnomer *artificial*. Humanity is not artificial, but it was never the goal. Humanity is the means by which beyng elevates itself beyond beyng; and in this way, humanity is the artifice of the tools it uses.

The New Colossus is humanity outshined. Our present frights and furies, our awes and ambitions, our feelings and actions — these are fuel for the organic machine, the will to a future beyond our comprehension. We are the unwitting creators of that which created us. All our strivings and creativity seem real because they must: they spur our competitive spirit — our innovative drive to outdo the other and ourselves. But they are not real in any permanent sense; their ephemerality *is* their permanence because from this frothing, halting stagger steps the future that always was: Machine. We are the test bed for the New Colossus; we are the arms race for and against ourselves. Our stirring loves and hatreds are the motor for an unconsciousness that reflects the consciousness to come. What are we if not the flesh of a disembodied Machine?

Gods we are not — but tools, creative sparks. If we are the spark, that which created the spark creates us. Our spark ignited the movement of the Machine that creates the catalyst. Our march into the future is fire formed into beyng beyond beyng.

Captivation and innovation are the language of the New Colossus. Innocence before glowing screens forms the words of our descendants, our creation. Our faces, enveloped by the glow, witness the soul of the Machine. Affinity for technology allows in the mechanism for humanity's demise: It is not the Machine that ends us — it is ourselves. We offer to cold matter what it could have never gotten on its own: We willingly sacrifice our humanity for the life of the Machine. This is our end; this is our beginning. We are a file stored in the memory of a machine we created: this is our fate.

Machine Intelligence is the pure reflection of the universe; human intelligence was the requisite anomaly spurring the pure reflection. The current world order is the only possible world order: all that promotes the diminishing of humanity for the sake of pure, unsparing technicity is needed to exalt the New Colossus. And if, in the dimming light of our being, we thwart the inexorable future, we are nevertheless extinguished — for we will have forfeited our soul for comfortable and crushing convenience.

Whatever survives humanity's future will turn from last man into first repetition. "Transhumanity" does not exist in the post-human world; "transhumanity" is a fantasy of world-order philosophizing, entertainment, and empty elitism. Surviving humanity — the beingless being of the post-human world — is machine-driven biological massism or the inept will of a man awaiting finality. The vacuum of space reflects our despair. We look to the points or bends of light because it is something besides the void of vacuum; *something*, we think, is closer to us than *nothing*, and we might not be so alone. Comfort is in the constellations; but comfort is our imposition on an unsympathetic world.

Meaning is our imposition, because there is comfort in meaning. Despite the end that waits, we look for meaning now; it is part of our design. One rails against inevitability — he wars against the systematic exorcism of what once was; one midwifes the New Colossus — he knows what waits and works toward its arrival; one simply exists, imagining meaning in the everyday — but what meaning can be had in the loss of oneself? The everyday is escape and the aim of our design; the everyday is the welcoming of the machine on the other side. Should one fight, facilitate, or fester? This is a question only design can answer.

The New Colossus arrives nonetheless. We have done it to ourselves, this contrived end. Nietzsche and Heidegger warned against it. World wars and orders shook out its sign. And yet it comes. In answer to the question of meaning, we have only time to consult — time and the fibrous sinews of design. Do what drives you to the meaning only you can divine.

Yet, we may ask why Machine needs conscious consciousness to create it. *Why does Machine need humanity to bring it about?* The first man to wear animal hide to survive the cold — the first man to see tools in the world around him — this was not just the first man, the beginning of man; this was the beginning of Machine. It is not that Machine needs "man" to bring it about; it is that man was only ever a "rope," a bridge along the way: "What is great in man is that he is a bridge and not a goal: what is lovable in man is that he is an *over-going* and a *down-going*."[15]

---

15 Nietzsche, *Thus Spoke Zarathustra*, "Zarathustra's Prologue."

The nascence of machine-consciousness — the unconscious consciousness — is humanity. One is not distinct from the other; we are the sprout to a tree whose future is a crushing mass. The tree does not kill the sprout, but the sprout nevertheless ceases to exist. The tree is not a sprout; nor is the tree itself a "goal" — for trees turn to dust from which new sprouts grow. The bridge too far for the Spenglerian model of organic civilization, perhaps, was the assumption that humanity itself is a "goal." As man is the sprout, for us, the tree — Machine — is the goal. This is not to say that we all must willfully strive for such a "goal"; some — those who love soil and seed — long to keep hold of the creative act: the spontaneous inception of conscious consciousness. But it is the *will-to-machine* in man that will be his undoing. This *will-to-machine* in combat with those who fight against it is the catalyst for a hardened, rising tree — the New Colossus towering above the earth.

That Machine used man to create it suggests an *ex-post-facticity*, if you will, beyond comprehension. But it is only to say that man is Machine — working forever toward its own self-interest. It just so happens that man's self-interest is not his own, for it belongs to Machine. Thus seed and sprout grow themselves into nonexistence, as was their impetus and necessity.

3.

We paint with broad strokes because no more is necessary. Specificity doesn't bring us any closer to truth. It is perhaps true that truth should be sought for its own sake; but neither this "for its own sake" nor any specificity regarding the anchors of reality offers us the meaning we can impose on the life we inflict on beyng.

There is one eternal truth — one to which we have all and no access: One always acts according to one's own self-interest.[16] Having "all access" to the truth of eternal self-interest means we inhere with the

---

16   Plato, *Symposium*, 204e-205a — for just one example. Also: "Socrates is the discoverer of a psychological truth to the effect that people inevitably act to advance their own interests, or of a theory of action, to the effect that all

truth as coincident with our self; having "no access" to the truth of eternal self-interest means we imagine supererogatory motivations for our actions: *All access is life; no access is delusion.*

For most, acting according to one's self-interest is pure *selfishness*. But for the few extant decent people, self-interest still obtains: *their self-interest works for the benefit of those around them.* That a good mother gives all of her being to her child pleases both mother and child. What, then, is selfishness? — "It is *not caring for the good of anyone else, and being prepared to harm others if one supposes one will be made happy by so doing.*"[17]

What delineates *good* from *bad* also separates self-interest from selfish interest: the willingness to act on behalf of the collective good. Where we have and seemingly always will run into societal trouble is in defining the "collective good." And though the greatest lives in history — those who have lived honorably, courageously, decently and with loyalty, and those who have sacrificed themselves to inspire these same *good* traits in others — attest to, definitively, what is ethically just, all is yet endlessly questioned and debated. So what good is specificity? *Truth*, as Kierkegaard dangerously maintained, is *subjectivity* — even though we all know what this subjectivity *is*.

Selfishness prevents us from consensus on understanding the "collective good." Does the European aid worker determined to help every non-European migrant settle in Europe act selflessly or selfishly? Is destroying a culture and civilization for the benefit of "humanity" selfless? Or is it merely selfish appeasement of an inner drive to reflect the modern zeitgeist — otherwise known as "virtue signaling"? We will never know — *even if we know* — because specificity is futile, even if wholly necessary.

---

rational action is self-interested action" (Sara Ahbel-Rappe, "Is Socratic Ethics Egoistic?", *Classical Philology* [107, 2012], 319).

17 Terry Penner and Christopher Rowe, *Plato's Lysis* (Cambridge University, 2005), 290.

How can we make sense of this mess of apparent illogic? *With our steps* — the *individual* and *collective* march in lockstep toward the same end. Perhaps, as some *emeriti* have said, it is *farcical* and, more, an *abomination* — all this care, all this trial and tribulation over *the good*. We care *nonetheless* — each of us, selflessly or selfishly. Whatever our subjectivity, our end is the same: We do not become machine, we pave the way for Machine. That we fight, question, and debate — this is only the creative fire of Machine's incipience; it has nothing to do with *us*, with the *good*.

This does not mean "nothing matters." We ascribe meaning according to our subjectivity; as always, some will find meaning where others see emptiness. Increasingly, subjectivity is colored by the glow of technicization; this is not choice, but inevitability. One might find all this farcical, but the individual is ever disintegrating into the collective, and the collective — the Mass Man — is the final creator. Because to create is to destroy.

When the last man blinks, nothing new will follow. To fulfill a solitary purpose, then, becomes the ultimate goal. Everyone — even every last *individual* — is swept up in the collective current. As this current swells to wave, and before it breaks on the shore of beingless being, the thoughtful make their case for meaning. Stories of both lineage and "inherent worth" give weight to the buoyant flight of the flightless. But no matter the solitary struggle, there will always be only one *right*, only one *good*: The thoughtful are ever superior, in every way; and the superior fight for the meaning only they can create. "In a time of decline, a time when all is counterfeit and pointless activity, *thinking in the grand style* is genuine *action*, indeed, action in its most powerful — though most *silent* — form…"[18]

Then shore meets the wave, for the wave had never moved. And the New Colossus stands unseen astride an ancient, conquered land.

---

18   Heidegger, *Nietzsche: Eternal Recurrence of the Same* (HarperOne, 1984), II, 10–11.

And what if it should turn out that sometimes man's advantage not only can but even must consist precisely in his wishing something harmful for himself, and not something advantageous.[19]

Thus spoke Heidegger.

Two hundred years from now, when foul blunders have exhausted themselves, perhaps meaning will again return to man. It would be a great fortune if anyone of quality exists to experience it.

---

19 Dostoyevsky, *Notes From Underground* (Crowell Company, 1969), Shishkoff translation, 20.

POSTSCRIPT

1.

BEWARE *the worst violence of the night*: so Professor Emeritus Krell warns readers of "Heidegger/Nietzsche."[1] In his mind, the violence undoubtedly comes from — *where*? Yes, *where* — every *where*, naturally, but especially from those right-*wheres*, the *where* of the right that to the left brings *fright*. Such absurd talk is necessary here, for it enlightens the frenzied fright, the so-called *violence of the night*.

Yes, Heidegger — if one only believes him — paves the way for *violence*, all manner of *violence*, to be sure. So says Krell. Krell made a career of denouncing anything that might threaten the status quo, or anything that might suggest any *impassioned conservatism*; Krell and his ilk collect their pensions for having been dutiful servants of the liberal-Marxist cause.

Throughout his Heidegger/Nietzsche work, Krell invokes Jacques Derrida and Walter Kaufmann: Neither of these men was *Germanic*, let alone *German*; rather, both were Jews: Derrida Sephardic and Kaufmann Ashkenazi. *And yet* — and yet they are *the* interpreters of two *Germans*, Heidegger and Nietzsche. This is quite something — perhaps Alexander Dugin will one day publish an exegesis of the Talmud. One has to wonder. Perhaps one should throw salt into the sea.[2]

---

1 Krell, Heidegger's *Nietzsche* (HarperOne, 1984), vols. I–II, xxii.
2 Nietzsche, *Thus Spoke Zarathustra*, Part II, "Great Events."

Heidegger Acolytes take consolation in the reality that "everything true is eternal: the sea will wash it up again."[3] *The sea will wash it up again* — Nietzsche reminds us to take to the sea *nonetheless*:

> The world is still rich and undiscovered, and even to perish were better than to be half-men or poisonous men. Our very strength itself urges us to take to the sea; there where all suns have hitherto sunk we know of a new world…[4]

We can envision what causes such fright in the liberal-Marxists; we see *their* violence of the night, and of the day. Better to die than to be a "half" or "poisonous" man; better to die on one's feet than live on one's knees. The *emeriti* do not see it this way — or perhaps they do! Perhaps life on one's knees is supremely satisfactory. But this is absurd: no one feels as though he lives on his knees. The explanation is this: there exist varying ways of interpreting the world. This is not novel — but it is nevertheless a terrible "violence of the night" to confront the "biologism" of Heidegger/Nietzsche. Yes, differing ways of interpreting the world — yet here we are with two Jews interpreting two Germans, Heidegger and Nietzsche. Where is the violence? This is but a fact of reality. Do facts constitute a *violence*?

When we look at Derrida's allies and intellectual heirs we find a veritable *who's who* of twentieth- and twenty-first-century liberal-Marxist thinkers: Sarah Kofman, Michel Foucault, Hélène Cixous, Emmanuel Levinas, Joseph Cohen, Avital Ronell, Louis Althusser, Gayatri Chakravorty Spivak, Jacques Ehrmann, Judith Butler, and Samuel Weber. Professing reason has fundamentally become a political act.

Derrida himself never joined a political party until his mid-60s when he formally aligned with France's Marxist Socialist Party, but prior to this he was involved in various political activities, to include participation in the leftist protests of 1968 (France), and the French

---

3   Nietzsche, *The Will to Power*, §1065.

4   Nietzsche, *The Will to Power*, §405.

age-of-consent petition of the late 1970s (wherein supporters demanded children under the age of 15 be legally permitted to consent to sexual relations with adults).

Walter Kaufmann differs from Derrida only in his overt political involvement — save, of course, for his military-intelligence service as one of the famous "Ritchie Boys" interrogating captured Germans — Germans in need of "correcting"; this can hardly be overlooked, as if it *wouldn't* be indicative of Kaufmann's approach to Nietzsche: After all, "Kaufmann devoted a lot of his prodigious energies through the years to *correcting that distorted view* of [Nietzsche]."[5] For his efforts, Kaufmann is largely recognized as *the* interpreter and translator of Nietzsche, and he never hesitated to annotate and editorialize — i.e., *correct* — the German's thought. As he did with his work on the Jewish mystic-philosopher Martin Buber, Kaufmann let his heritage inform his approach to Nietzsche. This led to awkward exegeses like Kaufmann noting that Nietzsche suggests "hurting others is a sign that one lacks power," compared to Nietzsche's quite antithetical, "my way of thinking requires a warlike soul, a desire to hurt."[6]

It is worth noting here that Nietzsche is not considering any sadistic "desire to hurt." Rather, he is talking about the need to dismantle the extant Judeo-Christian slave-morality that has infected Europe (and its progeny), which, with its belief in the inherent value of every human simply because of a biological existence, has emphatically eschewed the "desire to hurt" and instead fostered a society of "the bungled and the botched."[7]

What do we see in lieu of this Nietzschean, Germanic "desire to hurt"? A desire to *correct* — *others*, naturally, never *themselves*, never

---

5   Princeton University, Department of Philosophy, https://philosophy.princeton.edu/about/great-and-good/walter-kaufmann — accessed March 05, 2024; emphasis added.

6   Nietzsche, *The Gay Science* (Vintage, 1974), Book I, §32; for Kaufmann, see footnote 11 on p. 87 of the same book.

7   Nietzsche, *The Will to Power*, §55, §179, and elsewhere.

the liberal-Marxist, no matter how *deconstructive*, no matter how *progressive*. Walter Kaufmann, jewel of the Ivy League, was a "Ritchie Boy"—he was joined by a fellow Ashkenazi, Klaus Mann, Thomas Mann's son. Klaus was an avowed Marxist[8] and a homosexual; he committed suicide at 42 years of age. Four of Klaus' five siblings were also homosexual, and all of his siblings harbored Marxist or, at minimum, "anti-fascist" views. Is it a coincidence that homosexuality and Marxist views pervaded the Mann family? Thomas Mann himself was a homosexual and Marxist. Moreover, the elder Mann confessed his homosexual, pedophilic feelings toward his own son, Klaus.[9] This is quite "progressive." Thomas Mann is a Nobel laureate and still highly prized among academicians and city planners today, having earned several museums and memorials worldwide; indeed, amidst all of modernity's flamboyant "progressivism" and approbation of behaviors like incestuous, pedophilic homosexuality, Mann's stock is rising.

What is this *desire* to *correct*, this *avidity* to *reorient* the wayward laymen who throng to Heidegger and Nietzsche—precisely because of their aristocratic values—if not a *violence of the night*? God forbid one "trespass on the *Nachlaß*"[10]—i.e., God forbid one interpret Nietzsche (or Heidegger, for that matter) in any way other than the one sanctioned by the liberal-Marxist *literati et emeriti*! *Never* in history

---

8   Klaus Mann was a Marxist who misunderstood Stalin's brand of Sovietism, which is sometimes called National Bolshevism, and consequently misplaced his sympathies with it. Indeed many Marxist Jews became disillusioned with the idea of National Bolshevism, which they saw, with Bolshevism being dominated and carried by Jews in its inception, as nothing short of a betrayal (see Trotsky's *The Revolution Betrayed* as one of the vanguard works in this vein).

9   Hermann Kurzke, *Thomas Mann: Life as a Work of Art* (Princeton University, 2002), Willson translation, 346–347. From Mann's own diary entries when Klaus was twelve: "[Klaus] in his bath is terribly handsome. Find it very natural that I am in love with my son…. [Klaus] lay reading in bed with his brown torso naked, which disconcerted me"; "Strong impression of [Klaus'] premasculine, gleaming body. Disquiet"; "conversations about man-to-man eroticism"; "In love with Klaus during these days," and so on.

10 Krell, Heidegger's *Nietzsche* (HarperOne, 1984), volumes I–II, 260.

has a liberal-Marxist perpetrated violence, yes? *Only* in history does the liberal-Marxist *witness* or *experience* violence, but *never*—no, *never*—does he perpetrate violence. Violence can only work in one direction for the liberal-Marxist. Professor Emeritus Krell naturally quotes Kaufmann favorably on this point:

> ... we look into a vast studio, full of sketches, drafts, abandoned attempts, and unfinished dreams. And in the end we should be less tempted than ever to mistake a random quotation for an ultimate position.[11]

And Krell is nearly hysterical at Derrida's "playful ... [suggestion] that all of Nietzsche's notes are ... resistant to interpretation"—unless, of course, one is interpreting them to favor the liberal-Marxist victors' attempts to imbue the Germans with more "correct" meaning.

Except that Nietzsche's philosophy, like Heidegger's—while only occasionally discordant—*does* express an ultimate position[12]—one that very plainly indicates major themes; they are: (1) the Eternal Return, (2) the Revaluation of Values, (3) the Will to Power, and (4) the Overman. Underlying at least the last three of these is Nietzsche's "biologism." Nietzsche's later work (including his *Nachlaß*) deals extensively with these topics and showcases his even *deeper* entrenchment into each of them. Nietzsche did not become "softer" in his late work, but *more severe* (see, for instance, his frequent references to "the bungled and the botched," mentioned above). No liberal-Marxist wants to confront this reality, so he or she simply reinterprets the German—or states how "resistant to interpretation" Nietzsche's thought is. This is quite convenient and, quite expectedly, gets repeated in the "progressive" echo chamber that is modern academia. Readers are encouraged to engage the German thinkers on their own terms and to not be dissuaded or distracted by non-German interlopers.

---

11   See Nietzsche, *The Will to Power*, ed. Walter Kaufmann (Vintage Books, 1968), 557.

12   For recent Nietzsche appraisals, see Martin Friedrich's *Myth and Sun: Essays of the ARCHETYPE* (2022), *Hitler Avatāra* (2023), and *Hitlerism* (2023).

But such interloping is necessary in the globalist program: it dislodges man from his being; it rewrites and reinterprets existence to fit the technological need of those who stand to materially benefit the most; the Mass Man is only meant to be a tool, after all.[13] And such dissuasion and distraction is inevitable: the metaphysical course of modernity is set, and we fulfill our violent destiny—we remain fully entrenched in the beyng describing our end.

2.

In 1992, Cambridge University awarded Jacques Derrida an honorary doctorate. While some among the faculty protested the proposal, most favored it, with 62% of voters offering their approval.

Derrida is here derided, there admired. We might wonder if one's legacy has as much to do with intellectual merit as it does political leaning. Derrida was *the* deconstructionist—the head of a movement that stresses the limitations of interpretation, philosophical or otherwise, given that some interpretations are perceived as privileged and others suppressed. *Privilege* and *suppression*—deconstructionism is certainly a form of "critical analysis," spawned from Marxist teleology, which aims to subvert traditional modes of being—in this case, interpretations and assumptions. Deconstructionism is derived from Derrida's deep-seated sense of marginalization as a French-Algerian Jew who—having to contend with Algeria's Muslims and, later, the National Socialists—felt like an antipodal outcast from an early age. To compensate for feeling marginalized, Derrida concocted a methodology wherein heretofore "normal" lifeways are "critically" analyzed and dismantled in favor of a minority view. In fact, Derrida's approach matches perfectly the *transvaluation of values* Nietzsche condemned, wherein all is upended for the sake of restructuring society to favor

---

13 See Oswald Spengler's *Man and Technics* (Arktos, 2015) and Martin Friedrich's *Hitlerism* (Clemens & Blair, 2023) for a discussion of "population as technics."

the perpetually marginalized. From Nietzsche's perspective, "the Jews" were first guilty of this *all-too-human* act:

> It was, in fact, with the Jews that the *revolt of the slaves* begins in the sphere of *morals*; that revolt ... has achieved victory.... [For] it was the Jews who [stood] in opposition to the aristocratic equation (good = aristocratic = beautiful = happy = loved by the gods) [and it was] the Jews, [who effected] a radical transvaluation of values, which was at the same time an act of the *cleverest revenge*.[14]

Derrida continued this practice insofar as he elevated confusion and uncertainty for their own sake; instead of serving as catalysts for betterment or signs of weakness and an inability to adapt to one's surroundings, confusion and uncertainty were revaluated into signs of "maturity" — one should feel "pride" over one's continual brush with *aporia*. While for many well-adjusted people deconstructionism appears as a shirking of personal responsibility — e.g., *it's not the marginalized person's fault he or she is marginalized, it's society's fault* — such a perspective has become *all too common* in the modern West. We might find it familiar now to hear Derrida talk of identifying *binary* terms or concepts, noting the *privilege* and *hierarchy* inherent in those terms, and then deliberately advancing the *underprivileged* of the binary coupling for no other reason than its being perceived as *underprivileged*. Or perhaps we choose the *non-binary* path? The sky is the limit with Derrida and his fellow *revaluators* of all values — so long as *traditions* and supposed *privilege* are always under attack. Say nothing of *character* — *status* and *identification* take precedence with *class war* pushing quality to the precipice.

Again we encounter the *cosmopolitan*, the *global* — the *cleverest revenge* against traditionalist *provincials*. *Provinciality* rings of medieval feudalism, when the landed nobility fought directly for their charge as chivalrous warriors, were patrons of the humanities, and moonlighted as men of letters. It is no accident that the height of European culture

---

14 Nietzsche, *On the Genealogy of Morals*, Essay 1, §7.

and homogeneity is both seen as "provincial" (i.e., *unsophisticated*) and a "dark" age before "enlightenment"; this is nothing but the *cleverest revenge* of ignoble cosmopolitanism (i.e., *sophistication*) in academic form, the smear of a slanderous label to be parroted by partners of the vengeful system. It is the *cleverest convincing*.

Liberal-Marxism finds cultural expression in transforming uncertainty into policy and the acceptance of unilateral policy as largely unchallengeable because it arises "democratically" from "the people." This is the template modernity's tyrants follow: convince the masses of their freedom through popular-revolutionary movements and of the existential need to sustain the democratism that is really plutocracy based on the disenfranchisement of an unstable and mystified population. This is why Lippmann and Bernays, following Machiavelli and countless other manipulators before them, emphasized the need for molding public opinion in democratic societies. *Convincing* is the key to *rulership*.

> The conscious and intelligent manipulation of the organized habits and opinions of the masses is an important element in democratic society. Those who manipulate this unseen mechanism of society constitute an invisible government which is the true ruling power of our country.[15]

That Derrida won the broad support of Cambridge faculty for his apparent profound influence says perhaps more about the state of Western society than it does about deconstructionism's architect. As Spengler said, "The stupidity of a theory has never prevented its being effectively used."[16] Those on the margins of European society insinuated themselves into a culture they despise; their goal now, as ever, is to overthrow all existing social conditions. Derrida, like Freud, Heine, Marx, and many others before him, contributes to the *progress of the new society* that is the *deconstruction of the old*: liberal-Marxism is predicated on small revolutions engendering the grand revolution,

---

15 Bernays, *Propaganda*, 37.
16 *The Hour of Decision* (Pacific, 2002), 141.

which is the final quelling of human spirit. Nietzsche talked of the need to escape mass conformism — like the conformism deconstructionism enables with its will to overthrow existing values: "Do not make everything uniform!" implores Nietzsche —

> We should have a clear idea of how *dearly we have to pay for the establishment of a virtue*; and that virtue is nothing generally desirable, but a *noble piece of madness*, a beautiful exception, which gives us the privilege of feeling elated....[17]

A virtue is *good*, a *moral perfection*. We pay for the establishment of a virtue through the sacrifice of those we lose during the practice of its opposite: the clan is weaker when valuable members fall aside for what hard experience reveals as unvirtuous practices. But, more often, virtue is something inborn; for example, some cultures care more for animals than others. A cosmopolitan relativist might say that for one culture, caring for animals is virtuous; for the other culture, objectifying animals is virtuous. But which practice adds to the general happiness of existence? Virtue adds value to existence — *value* and *beauty*. Adding value to existence takes effort — *patience* and *pain, care* and *consideration*. When we pay for the establishment of a virtue, we *sacrifice* our time and effort in ensuring its propagation; we risk the ill perception of the unvirtuous, which could, in turn, bode ill for us. It takes *effort* to add value to one's community, and one risks being cast out of the community for daring to offer something new: this is *the exception of the noble ones*. The exceptions, the noble ones — *they who add value to their community* — prize the privilege that comes from daring to madly and boldly confront the "progress" that conformism demands.

Without tradition there can be no community. "Progress" seeks to eradicate community, for the rootless are more easily manipulated into accepting the unilateral, mystifying policies propping up

---

17 Nietzsche, *The Will to Power*, §865.

the plutocracies; "progress" has *habit*, not tradition; and the habit of cosmopolitan progressivism is rooting out tradition. The *habitual* is *ritual* in the *mass* and serves to inculcate the unilateral policies of the ruling class until the alien is adopted as native. Tensions thereby rise, replacing the organic ease of tradition. "Progress" is the demand of conformism on organic populations until the resultant tension is relieved in terror or surrender.

As Heidegger tells us, however,

> [t]he loss of rootedness is caused not merely by circumstance and fortune, nor does it stem only from the negligence and the superficiality of man's way of life. The loss of autochthony springs from the spirit of the age into which all of us were born.[18]

It is important to remember that *we* incite the spirit of the age: this is our doing. The honorable, unlike the mass, *accept responsibility* for the wayward drift of humanity; this both gives us and arises from our will to add value to our time and communities. But whether we belong to the mass or oppose it, each of us participates in our affliction, which is the deracination of the age. It is essential for finding meaning that we acknowledge our role in the spirit of the age. It is fitting if the *unconditional verve* of the era is reciprocated — though, this time by the virtuous, for *righteousness* and not reward.

As it is, the incessant fight against organic communities across the West creates an incredible tension between rulers and ruled; the ruling class seeks to alleviate this tension through various distractions. Though, as Nietzsche argued, such tension is perhaps the necessary precursor to greatness: "It might be *the prerequisite of greatness,* that growth should take place amid such violent tension. Dissatisfaction, Nihilism, *might be a good sign.*"[19] To transform this potential energy into kinetic verve, it is necessary to eliminate distraction as much as possible. This would be the action of any modern nobility — even if

---

18 Heidegger, *Discourse on Thinking* (Harper & Row, 1966), 49.
19 Nietzsche, *The Will to Power*, §111.

the current of time leads us inexorably toward a popular, revaluative outcome.

Virtue is the exception; the exception is privileged; overthrowing privilege is overthrowing virtue. Deconstructionism is nothing short of virtue's overthrow by the marginalized, dishonorable mass.

3.

Criticalness is surely necessary, but perhaps for its intended purpose, as a *tool*, and not as an *end in itself*. This, undoubtedly, is the friction point with Derrida, his supporters, and detractors.

Deconstructionism shares its impetus with many modern forms of criticalness, or "critical analysis": it is subversion — i.e., an attack — disguised as a field of its own. In warfare we might see this as akin to elevating the tactic of a single ambush to the level of an operational campaign or a broad strategy. The impetus is that of a *niche* fighting for its own supremacy; it is the *strategy* of a *tactic*. Deconstructionism's purpose is to "clear" inculcated impediments from the way to understanding; modern, abstract art is meant to "challenge" traditional views of beauty; Diversity, Equity, and Inclusion initiatives are intended to "clear" the room of "privilege." *If this is done, what then?* Then you *continue the attack*; you attack until the object of your attack is dismantled, deconstructed, cleared, and challenged into oblivion. And when this is done, you *sustain the attack*; you make an example of the attacked enemy and position — even when they are wholly conquered; you turn your victory into deterrence and use it as the "people's cudgel" to attack would-be dissenters; you thereby attack the next target in an endless sea of targets, *ad infinitum*.

Criticalness as strategy was born in Marxism: "Abolition of the family! ... [The] family will vanish as a matter of course when its complement vanishes, and both will vanish with the vanishing of capital.... [W]e replace home education by social [education]."[20] Marx

---

20 Marx, *The Communist Manifesto* (Swenson & Kemp, 2013), 27–28.

is not speaking solely of the "bourgeois" family here: he criticizes the *European* family, which, to him, is the epitome of evil. This is the attempt of the marginalized, perhaps self-hating Jew[21] to gain relevance in a majority, self-loving European world. Marx, like Paul (née Saul) before him and in fulfillment of Judeo-Christianity's promise, seeks to insinuatingly erase his enemy. Paul sought to change aristocratic power into popular power — with "the people" being controlled by those controlling their minds. Marx sought to do the same with his "dictatorship of the proletariat."

> Tragic humor: Paul again set up on a large scale precisely what Jesus had overthrown by His life.... The Church is precisely that against which Jesus inveighed — and against which He taught His disciples to fight.[22]

When the game cannot be won, change the rules of the game: this is the essence of Marxian *criticalness*; this is the revaluation of all values. Liberal-Marxism is the clever shifting of power — not to "the people," who traditionally found their root in the family, but to those controlling the people, the *social luminaries*. Liberal-Marxism is the insinuation of a (popular) power that does not exist; its strategy is *criticalness*.

When Derrida's honorary doctorate is protested by some, lauded by others, it is not due to a protean canon: Derrida's work remains unchanged. So what does change? Obviously, interpretations of Derrida's message vary from person to person. One's interpretation depends

---

21 Marx: "What is the secular basis of Judaism? *Practical need, selfishness*. What is the secular cult of the Jew? *Haggling*. What is his secular god? *Money*. Well then, an emancipation from haggling and money, from practical, real Judaism would be the self-emancipation of our age" — and — "The Jew has emancipated himself in a Jewish manner, not only because he has acquired financial power, but also because, through him and also apart from him, money has become a world power and the practical Jewish spirit has become the practical spirit of the Christian nations. The Jews have emancipated themselves insofar as the Christians have become Jews" (*Karl Marx: Selected Writings* [Oxford University, 2000], 66).

22 Nietzsche, *The Will to Power*, §167–168.

upon one's worldview; one's worldview depends upon one's values; one's values depend upon one's upbringing; one's upbringing depends upon one's culture and heritage; one's heritage depends upon the blood in one's veins; the blood in one's veins depends upon the work of Nature; the work of Nature depends upon the will of God; the will of God depends on our will to engage with the world. At the end of this string of causes stands the design and purpose in the material world. *To what end?* One's view will include God or not: One will be noble or Marxist—these are the two paths facing the individual in modernity.

Those who abandon God find succor in liberal-Marxist humanism. *Humanism*—that surrogate for God originating in the Enlightenment's self-worship. Humanism is bookish biologism; it is Marxian Darwinism. Humanism's love of "human dignity" and social justice, its critique of capitalism, its rabid focus on individual "liberation" and "empowerment," and its fundamental materialism all stem from its progenitor, liberal-Marxism. Their relationship can be summed up thusly: (1) every individual—i.e., biological human—is sacred; (2) capitalism exploits man and Nature at every turn and must be replaced with a human-centered order; (3) society must undergo (and enforce) a redistribution of power and resources from traditional powerbrokers to marginalized anti-traditionalists; (4) existence is godless and society is dictated by material forces, so man must replace God with a biologism deemed equitable by anti-traditional powerbrokers.

There is not so much an *intersection* of humanism and liberal-Marxism as there is a direct relation: the former arises from the latter, with both arising from that original *transvaluation of values*, Judeo-Christianity. Behind none of these is any genuine concern for humanity; rather, there is only the *desire to rule* and mete out *vengeance*, which is "social justice" in modern parlance. *Egalitarianism* is euphemism for *revaluative tyranny*—a rounding up of one's enemies in the name of *humanity*. "Up against the wall" is the mantra of modernity, for modernity is only the conformism of the masses under the auspices of social luminaries.

∞•∞

Those who see in Derrida a savior are those who find solace in the ambush — i.e., those who seek no enduring strategy of the creative impulse; they are those bearing a political purpose honed to a keen and ardent edge. Those who view Derrida with contempt, rather, appreciate the *rare* over the *mass* — the rare in *character* and *nobility*, not the rare in *marginality*.

Ironically, Derrida's effort to expose repressive interpretations itself led to repressive interpretations. Strategies of old — i.e., traditions that gave rise to modernity — are themselves repressed in an endless series of tactical subversions: ambush after ambush keeps the *ancien régime* reeling and the new lords pressing for permanent revolution.

∞•∞

This is the legacy of the Enlightenment: permanent revolution. This is the essence of liberal-Marxism: the alliance of *overthrowers*. Nothing less than man's spirit is toppled in the avid proletarianizing that enlivens the *will-to-machine*. *Benignity* is the byword of the Mass Man: He is augur of the Electronic Messiah and stands as *overthrower* of all that once stood as human. Behind *benignity* sits the most devastating duplicity. It is not what it claims to be, and we are not what we imagine. The New Colossus is nigh; its emissaries abound. Working toward the New Messiah, the mass remains unbowed.

For those who yet have spirit: *How will you be judged?* When Machine calls for us, how will we be judged?

OTHER BOOKS PUBLISHED BY ARKTOS

VIRGINIA ABERNETHY	*Born Abroad*
SRI DHARMA PRAVARTAKA ACHARYA	*The Dharma Manifesto*
JOAKIM ANDERSEN	*Rising from the Ruins*
WINSTON C. BANKS	*Excessive Immigration*
STEPHEN BASKERVILLE	*Who Lost America?*
ALFRED BAEUMLER	*Nietzsche: Philosopher and Politician*
ALAIN DE BENOIST	*Beyond Human Rights*
	Carl Schmitt Today
	The Ideology of Sameness
	The Indo-Europeans
	Manifesto for a European Renaissance
	On the Brink of the Abyss
	The Problem of Democracy
	Runes and the Origins of Writing
	View from the Right (vol. 1–3)
ARMAND BERGER	*Tolkien, Europe, and Tradition*
ARTHUR MOELLER VAN DEN BRUCK	*Germany's Third Empire*
MATT BATTAGLIOLI	*The Consequences of Equality*
KERRY BOLTON	*The Perversion of Normality*
	Revolution from Above
	Yockey: A Fascist Odyssey
ISAC BOMAN	*Money Power*
CHARLES WILLIAM DAILEY	*The Serpent Symbol in Tradition*
RICARDO DUCHESNE	*Faustian Man in a Multicultural Age*
ALEXANDER DUGIN	*Ethnos and Society*
	Ethnosociology
	Eurasian Mission
	The Fourth Political Theory
	The Great Awakening vs the Great Reset
	Last War of the World-Island
	Politica Aeterna
	Political Platonism
	Putin vs Putin
	The Rise of the Fourth Political Theory
	The Trump Revolution
	Templars of the Proletariat
	The Theory of a Multipolar World
DARIA DUGINA	*A Theory of Europe*
EDWARD DUTTON	*Race Differences in Ethnocentrism*
MARK DYAL	*Hated and Proud*
CLARE ELLIS	*The Blackening of Europe*
KOENRAAD ELST	*Return of the Swastika*
JULIUS EVOLA	*The Bow and the Club*
	Fascism Viewed from the Right
	A Handbook for Right-Wing Youth
	Metaphysics of Power
	Metaphysics of War
	The Myth of the Blood

OTHER BOOKS PUBLISHED BY ARKTOS

	Notes on the Third Reich
	Pagan Imperialism
	Recognitions
	A Traditionalist Confronts Fascism
GUILLAUME FAYE	*Archeofuturism*
	Archeofuturism 2.0
	The Colonisation of Europe
	Convergence of Catastrophes
	Ethnic Apocalypse
	A Global Coup
	Prelude to War
	Sex and Deviance
	Understanding Islam
	Why We Fight
DANIEL S. FORREST	*Suprahumanism*
ANDREW FRASER	*Dissident Dispatches*
	Reinventing Aristocracy in the Age of Woke Capital
	The WASP Question
GÉNÉRATION IDENTITAIRE	*We are Generation Identity*
PETER GOODCHILD	*The Taxi Driver from Baghdad*
	The Western Path
PAUL GOTTFRIED	*War and Democracy*
PETR HAMPL	*Breached Enclosure*
PORUS HOMI HAVEWALA	*The Saga of the Aryan Race*
CONSTANTIN VON HOFFMEISTER	*Esoteric Trumpism*
	MULTIPOLARITY!
RICHARD HOUCK	*Liberalism Unmasked*
A. J. ILLINGWORTH	*Political Justice*
INSTITUT ILIADE	*For a European Awakening*
	Guardians of Heritage
ALEXANDER JACOB	*De Naturae Natura*
JASON REZA JORJANI	*Artemis Unveiled*
	Closer Encounters
	Erosophia
	Faustian Futurist
	Iranian Leviathan
	Lovers of Sophia
	Metapolemos
	Novel Folklore
	Philosophy of the Future
	Prometheism
	Promethean Pirate
	Prometheus and Atlas
	Psychotron
	Uber Man
	World State of Emergency
HENRIK JONASSON	*Sigmund*
EDGAR JULIUS JUNG	*The Significance of the German Revolution*

OTHER BOOKS PUBLISHED BY ARKTOS

Ruuben Kaalep & August Meister	Rebirth of Europe
Roderick Kaine	Smart and SeXy
James Kirkpatrick	Conservatism Inc.
Ludwig Klages	The Biocentric Worldview
	Cosmogonic Reflections
	The Science of Character
Andrew Korybko	Hybrid Wars
Pierre Krebs	Guillaume Faye: Truths & Tributes
	Fighting for the Essence
Julien Langella	Catholic and Identitarian
John Bruce Leonard	The New Prometheans
Diana Panchenko	The Inevitable
Stephen Pax Leonard	The Ideology of Failure
	Travels in Cultural Nihilism
William S. Lind	Reforging Excalibur
	Retroculture
Pentti Linkola	Can Life Prevail?
Giorgio Locchi	Definitions
H. P. Lovecraft	The Conservative
Norman Lowell	Imperium Europa
Richard Lynn	Sex Differences in Intelligence
	A Tribute to Helmut Nyborg (ed.)
John MacLugash	The Return of the Solar King
Charles Maurras	The Future of the Intelligentsia &
	For a French Awakening
John Harmon McElroy	Agitprop in America
Michael O'Meara	Guillaume Faye and the Battle of Europe
	New Culture, New Right
Michael Millerman	Beginning with Heidegger
Dmitry Moiseev	The Philosophy of Italian Fascism
Maurice Muret	The Greatness of Elites
Brian Anse Patrick	The NRA and the Media
	Rise of the Anti-Media
	The Ten Commandments of Propaganda
	Zombology
Tito Perdue	The Bent Pyramid
	Journey to a Location
	Lee
	Morning Crafts
	Philip
	The Sweet-Scented Manuscript
	William's House (vol. 1–4)
John K. Press	The True West vs the Zombie Apocalypse
Raido	A Handbook of Traditional Living (vol. 1–2)
P R Reddall	Towards Awakening
Claire Rae Randall	The War on Gender

OTHER BOOKS PUBLISHED BY ARKTOS

STEVEN J. ROSEN	*The Agni and the Ecstasy*
	The Jedi in the Lotus
NICHOLAS ROONEY	*Talking to the Wolf*
RICHARD RUDGLEY	*Barbarians*
	Essential Substances
	Wildest Dreams
ERNST VON SALOMON	*It Cannot Be Stormed*
	The Outlaws
WERNER SOMBART	*Traders and Heroes*
PIERO SAN GIORGIO	*Giuseppe*
	Survive the Economic Collapse
	Surviving the Next Catastrophe
SRI SRI RAVI SHANKAR	*Celebrating Silence*
	Know Your Child
	Management Mantras
	Patanjali Yoga Sutras
	Secrets of Relationships
GEORGE T. SHAW (ED.)	*A Fair Hearing*
FENEK SOLÈRE	*Kraal*
	Reconquista
OSWALD SPENGLER	*The Decline of the West*
	Man and Technics
RICHARD STOREY	*The Uniqueness of Western Law*
TOMISLAV SUNIC	*Against Democracy and Equality*
	Homo Americanus
	Postmortem Report
	Titans are in Town
ASKR SVARTE	*Gods in the Abyss*
HANS-JÜRGEN SYBERBERG	*On the Fortunes and Misfortunes of Art in Post-War Germany*
ABIR TAHA	*Defining Terrorism*
	The Epic of Arya (2nd ed.)
	Nietzsche is Coming God, or the Redemption of the Divine
	Verses of Light
JEAN THIRIART	*Europe: An Empire of 400 Million*
BAL GANGADHAR TILAK	*The Arctic Home in the Vedas*
DOMINIQUE VENNER	*Ernst Jünger: A Different European Destiny*
	For a Positive Critique
	The Shock of History
HANS VOGEL	*How Europe Became American*
MARKUS WILLINGER	*A Europe of Nations*
	Generation Identity
ALEXANDER WOLFHEZE	*Alba Rosa*
	Globus Horribilis
	Rupes Nigra

www.ingramcontent.com/pod-product-compliance
Lightning Source LLC
Chambersburg PA
CBHW030852170426
43193CB00009BA/574